EXPLOITING
AFRICA

EXPLOITING AFRICA

THE INFLUENCE OF MAOIST CHINA
IN ALGERIA, GHANA, AND TANZANIA

DONOVAN C. CHAU

NAVAL INSTITUTE PRESS
Annapolis, Maryland

Naval Institute Press
291 Wood Road
Annapolis, MD 21402

© 2014 by Donovan C. Chau
All rights reserved. No part of this book may be reproduced or utilized in any form or by any means, electronic or mechanical, including photocopying and recording, or by any information storage and retrieval system, without permission in writing from the publisher.

Library of Congress Cataloging-in-Publication Data
Chau, Donovan C.
  Exploiting Africa : the influence of Maoist China in Algeria, Ghana, and Tanzania / Donovan C. Chau.
    pages cm
  Includes bibliographical references and index.
  ISBN 978-1-61251-250-1 (hardback) — ISBN 978-1-61251-251-8 (ebook) (print) 1. China—Foreign relations—Africa. 2. Africa—Foreign relations—China. 3. China—Foreign relations—1949–1976. 4. China—Foreign relations—Algeria. 5. Algeria—Foreign relations—China. 6. China—Foreign relations—Ghana. 7. Ghana—Foreign relations—China. 8. China—Foreign relations—Tanzania. 9. Tanzania—Foreign relations—China. I. Title.
  DT38.9.C5C474 2014
  327.5106—dc23
                                                              2013038913

♾ Print editions meet the requirements of ANSI/NISO z39.48-1992 (Permanence of Paper).
Printed in the United States of America.

22 21 20 19 18 17 16 15 14   9 8 7 6 5 4 3 2 1
First printing

Maps created by Charles Grear.

Whatever the proximate cause, China is an authoritarian regime, and its foreign as well as its domestic policies emanate from that immutable fact.

—Robert I. Rotberg
China into Africa: Trade, Aid, and Influence

Thus it is noteworthy that the Chinese themselves have traditionally conceptualized the Middle Kingdom not as one bounded state in the company of others, but as a civilization so uniquely superior that it cannot be presumed to have frontiers.

—Adda B. Bozeman
Strategic Intelligence and Statecraft: Selected Essays

CONTENTS

List of Maps viii
Acknowledgments ix

Introduction: The Chinese Arrive 1

I — WHY AFRICA?

1. Objectives 9
2. Organizations 22

II — NORTHERN EXPOSURE

3. Initial Entry 35
4. Supporting Independence 42
5. Close and Militant 54

III — NO GOLD

6. Ripe for Revolution? 73
7. Toward Revolutionary Friendship 80
8. Revolution Derailed 94

IV — EASTERN JEWEL

9. Independence and Revolution 103
10. Open Door 111
11. Railway to Friendship 129

Conclusion: The Chinese Remain 143
Notes 149
Bibliography 185
Index 205

MAPS

1 Algeria 34
2 Ghana 72
3 Tanzania 102

ACKNOWLEDGMENTS

Writing a book is more aptly phrased doing a book *project*. So many people are involved in the process; it is not an individual but a collective effort. Though all errors or omissions are my own, I would like to recognize individuals who were critical along this path to the book's completion.

Thanks, first and foremost, to the amazing team at the Naval Institute Press (NIP). Good organizations are comprised of good people. Such is the case with NIP. In particular, I would like to recognize Adam Kane and Emily Bakely, who have done magnificent jobs managing the entire effort. Thanks also to Matt Simmons who helped create a fine cover based on my list of "I do not want's." Many individuals outside of NIP assisted in the project, two of whom deserve special mention. I recognize Alison Hope for her tremendous effort editing my words, crafting better sentences and paragraphs, and, ultimately, making a better book. On a short timeline, Charles Grear worked his map-making magic, catering to a map-lover's needs, for which I give many thanks.

The origins of this project are over a decade old. The project began while I was a doctoral student in Reading, United Kingdom, endured trying years in Washington, DC, and culminated in my new life as an academic. Special thanks go to my PhD supervisor, Colin S. Gray, who took a chance on the ideas of a young Californian in England. Thanks, also, to my *viva voce* committee, Tom Kane and David Lonsdale, who elevated my research—and me. Though none are Africanists or Sinologists, all know international politics, particularly war and strategy, well. Very special thanks go to my intellectual forefathers, Bill Rood and Bill Van Cleave, while I was in Claremont and Springfield, Missouri. Sadly, both have now passed. Yet their influences persist: I encourage my students and shape my research to reflect the world as it is, not as we would like it to be.

I would not be who I am without the love and support of my parents, James and Esther. My brother, Derrick, has the knack of steering me in the right direction at the right time, as only an older brother can do. Finally, I thank my wife, Sarah, for her abiding love. Our adventure has just begun; and her love and God's love are all I truly desire in life.

22 October 2013
Redlands, CA
DC

INTRODUCTION
The Chinese Arrive

The African continent has been on Chinese horizons for centuries.[1] Rather than colonizing the continent piecemeal in European fashion, early Chinese interest focused on commerce and interaction with the African people, particularly in greater Eastern Africa.[2] Internal politics and war led the Chinese to turn inward, leaving the continent for several centuries until the establishment of the People's Republic of China (also known as the PRC, Communist China, modern China, or China) in 1949. During the Cold War, Western scholars paid modest attention to China's relations with fledgling African nations and independence movements.[3] In contrast, Communist China devoted considerable amounts of its attention to the African continent. Over time, the Chinese came to understand Africa as a continent comprising multifarious people, cultures, societies, and nations. Within this expansive and resource-laden environment, China perceived the distinct possibility for political, economic, and, ultimately, strategic exploitation. China chose to engage the African continent to gain influence and to achieve its strategic objectives.

The purpose of this book is to provide a historical examination of China's activities in Africa, which is an important yet overlooked aspect of the general topic of China in Africa today. The book is suitable to a general audience, but particularly to students and analysts, as well as to policymakers interested in understanding the policy of China in Africa in the heart of the twentieth century. One must analytically scrutinize modern China's historical presence in Africa in order to understand the context of its current and future actions on the continent.

China in the past meddled in the affairs of Africa. It did so for self-interest, for the benefit of the Communist Party of China (Communist Party, or CPC), specifically for its leaders' strategic objective, which was to demonstrate influence in the world, that is, power in international politics. Though its material resources were scant in the 1950s, 1960s, and 1970s, China nevertheless used them, in addition to devoting time and attention to Africa. It was exploiting Africa to serve Chinese interests.

China was not required to devote time, attention, and resources to Africa. But it did. China skillfully used its limited diplomatic, intelligence, and economic means to gain traction on the continent. It sought influence with a combination of tools—through shaping perceptions (for example, regular public statements), developing personal relationships (key and senior leadership influence through frequent exchange visits), and providing tangible assistance (immediate, human-needs, and symbolic projects—development and security oriented).

Since early 2004 Western observers have paid attention to China's involvement in Africa. While some analysts have focused narrowly on Chinese interests in raw materials, others have recognized China's broader interests on the continent.[4] As in the past, China has continued to emphasize its historical ties and shared common experiences with African nations, voicing the position that China too is part of the developing world (also called the Third World or Global South).[5] Also as in the past, however, Western assessments of China's operations in Africa have been flawed. Western policymakers, diplomats, and academics have cited China's recent increased or rising interest and engagement in the region and identified its objective of attaining status as a major player on the world stage.[6] However, their commentaries have demonstrated a general lack of understanding of or concern for China's historical presence on the continent.

Works on China in Africa have been in abundance, even overabundance, since the mid-2000s. While African authors have written about the presence of the Chinese in their own lands, much of the literature has been from a Western perspective, American and European. Most, if not all, tend to view China's presence as new or singularly focused on gaining access to natural resources. Notable contemporary single-author works on China in Africa include those by Chris Alden, Deborah Brautigam, and Ian Taylor.[7] Significant contributions of edited works include those by Robert Rotberg; Arthur Waldron; and Alden, Daniel Large, and Ricardo Soares de Oliveira.[8] The only recent book to attempt to capture China's role across the entire African continent, including some historical content, is by David Shinn and Joshua Eisenman.[9]

All of these works add to the debate about China's current presence in Africa, with potential ramifications for the future. What these works tend to overlook, however, is the great import of China's early entrance into and presence on the African continent.[10] This oversight is cause for alarm, for the origins of China's presence in Africa reveal much about its approach to the continent today. Thus, the main aim of this book is to fill the void in contemporary literature on China in Africa, focusing from the very beginning on Chinese meddling on the continent.

There was a rhyme and reason to China's early approach to the continent, and that rhyme and reason remains much the same today. Viewed in the broader historical and strategic context, China's current presence in Africa demonstrates continuity with the past rather than a renewed focus in the present or altered direction for the future. This book contributes a vital message to the discourse on Sino-African history and adds to the contemporary strategic understanding of and debate about China in Africa.

While the Chinese for the past century have been interested in Africa—from the Strait of Gibraltar to the Cape of Good Hope—three regions in particular have garnered Chinese attention. North, West, and East Africa are all strategically significant to the PRC because of their positions on major bodies of water: the Mediterranean Sea, the Atlantic Ocean, and the Indian Ocean. In addition, like much of the African continent, North, West, and East Africa are blessed with vital natural resources such as minerals, petroleum, and natural gas. Since the African continent is large and diverse, it is prudent to isolate and examine specific historical cases to study China in Africa. Geographically, therefore, the book focuses on China's presence in three specific African countries—Algeria, Ghana, and Tanzania.

This book will analyze China's operations in Africa from 1955 to 1976, during the era of Mao Zedong's rule.[11] An argument could be made to examine Communist China's operations through 1976 and perhaps to the present. However, it is more logical to examine the latter period in a different study altogether.[12] In addition, the period under Mao was marked by an active foreign policy. No other Chinese leader, in all likelihood, will ever gain as much power and influence on the state apparatus in Communist China as Mao did. Comprehending China in Africa during the Maoist era reveals the nature and character of its operations in Africa, providing conclusive evidence that China's approach—pragmatic and long term—remains the same today as it was in the past.

From the African perspective, Chinese operations in Africa and interaction with Africans were readily apparent from the mid-1950s onward. One African, who spent time as an exchange student in China, wrote in 1967, "Africa figures prominently in the scheme of Chinese political designs."[13] While not as noticeable as white Europeans who dominated the African landscape for centuries, the Chinese were immediately recognizable in any African country or colony. But their presence was not a clear indication of Chinese strategic interest. "Red China [had] multi-facet [sic] dealings with Africa, which [made] it complicated for Africans to discern the Chinese communist policy and get a clear picture."[14]

For non-Africans, the Chinese presence in Africa was both puzzling and fascinating, much as it is today. European nations that had an interest on the continent made note of the Chinese, and some went so far as to monitor Communist Chinese activity.[15] For the rest of disinterested Europe and the remainder of the world, China's active participation in Africa and interaction with Africans throughout the continent came as a surprise. Why would an Asian nation, fresh from a civil war and from establishing itself as a nation-state in October 1949, concern itself with events in Africa? Moreover, in the aftermath of the Korean War (1950–1953) and the First Indochina War (1946–1954), as well as continual tension over the renegade Republic of China on Taiwan (also known as ROC or Taiwan), why would China devote any effort, time, or resources to distant Africa? The answer lies not so much in the words of Communist Chinese leaders as it does in the simple fact that China—taking into account its central geographic position, its size and population, and its enduring history—was and continues to be determined to become a great world power.

Before examining specific case studies of China in Africa, therefore, one must understand China's central objectives to comprehend its main purpose for being in Africa. The book begins with a discussion of the strategic objectives of China, explaining the country's international motivations and intentions and describing the organizations used to influence events in Africa. Each region involved different geographic, political, and economic realities between 1955 and 1976. Thus, China used differing tools to obtain its objectives. At the same time, while each context was unique, China's main purpose for being on the continent remained steadfast, through both successes and failures.

This book examines China's objectives and organizations by in-depth case studies of China's activities in Algeria, Ghana, and Tanzania. In each case, China used a mix of international political support, tangible development aid, and economic and security assistance, both covert and overt. In order to place Chinese activities into context, it is necessary also to have a cursory understanding of each country, historically and politically, so each case study begins with local background histories leading up to relations with China. China's tangible support for

Algerian independence from France is often overlooked, as is the intimacy of relations between China and Ghana's first leader, Kwame Nkrumah.[16] By the time it extended its activities into East Africa, China had learned from experiences in North and West Africa. Along the Indian Ocean, Tanzania became one of China's closest yet most unnoticed allies on the continent, and remains so today. Taken together, the three case studies provide a realistic, historical picture of China in Africa.

The Chinese arrived on the African continent without fanfare, yet maintained an active and influential presence, a presence that ultimately was more pragmatic than revolutionary. Though often couched in ideological rhetoric, China's behavior in Africa in the 1950s, 1960s, and 1970s demonstrated goals and actions of an aspiring great power in the world. Contemporary China receives much more attention in Africa, as it does everywhere else around the world. Nevertheless, it is crucial to understand the nature and character of China's historical actions on the African continent in order to properly grasp its policies, today and tomorrow. Rather than merely looking forward, one must look backward to comprehend the true nature of China in Africa.

PART I

WHY AFRICA?

One

OBJECTIVES

The desire for great power status motivated China to gain a foothold and, later, influence on the African continent, and to maintain a strategic, political, and economic presence there. The words and statements of China's leaders, if examined carefully, reveal the objectives of the Communist nation. To identify, as precisely as possible, and analyze Chinese objectives, I will make a distinction between China's central and secondary objectives. But identifying and ascertaining Communist Chinese objectives is an exceedingly difficult task. Very little scholarship has been devoted to this specific endeavor. Chapter 1 uses an "educated skepticism" to determine China's objectives.[1] Moreover, as with any nation with global interests, China's objectives may have changed over time according to international and domestic political contexts; this adds to the complexity of determining its objectives. This book analyzes China in Africa from 1955 to 1976. It is necessary and, indeed, essential, however, to delve into the words and statements prior to 1955 to determine long-term strategic Chinese objectives: China's historical words, ideas, and objectives may continue to influence China's actions today.

China's central objectives were global, strategic, and long term. Its secondary objectives were, for the most part, regional and short term. Although in reality there might not have been such a clear or neat distinction between the two, this book separates central from secondary objectives to clarify the motives and intentions behind China's actions in Africa. It is convenient—and easy—to note China's actions in the narrow context of each domestic and international political situation. For example, one might conclude, inaccurately, that China pursued relations in Africa solely to gain representation in the United Nations (UN). But examining China's policy in such a vacuum belies the strategic outlook throughout Chinese history. Therefore, this book first and foremost considers China's central objectives. Emmanuel John Hevi leans toward hyperbole in his statement, but it is worth noting nonetheless: "Few subjects are as complicated as China's African policy and the motives behind it."[2] This chapter clarifies China's intentions in Africa.

China's central, strategic objectives may be derived from its desire to become a great power, which requires the attainment of substantial military, political, and economic power. This simple assertion may be deduced from China's geographic size and historic self-perception of superiority, as well as from the policy statements of its leaders. In a Communist dictatorship, few leaders exerted as much power over the entire population of a country as did Mao Zedong. Chairman Mao, Premier Zhou Enlai (who was also foreign minister), and a select group of high-ranking Communist Party of China officials determined and dictated the objectives of the People's Republic. Chairman Mao, more than any other Chinese official, influenced the fate of the PRC. Therefore, one must carefully analyze his words and statements for their implications for Chinese policy and objectives.

On 15 June 1949 Mao delivered a speech at the Preparatory Committee meeting of the Chinese People's Political Consultative Conference. He stated in plain terms the central objective of the forthcoming People's Republic: "We will build up an entirely new, strong, and prosperous People's Democratic Republic of China, not only in name but in fact."[3] Although this simple statement of intent may be viewed as an obvious desire of any new nation, one cannot overlook its importance in the context of Chinese political culture.[4] The emphasis on creating a strong and prosperous China was the clear, central objective of the Communist government. Howard L. Boorman made an accurate assessment of China's central objective in 1960: "Internationally, revitalized Chinese national power, under Communist control, has signaled Peking's primary foreign-policy goal: recognized status as a major world power on its own terms." Boorman added a significant and useful caveat, namely by identifying Communist China's self-perception of a major world power with the words "on its own terms."[5] With his speech, therefore, Mao set the tone for later policy statements.

A little over two weeks later, commemorating twenty-eight years of the Communist Party, Mao's *On People's Democratic Dictatorship* was released. In this seminal policy pronouncement, Mao laid out the direction for China—politically, economically, and socially. Most relevant to this historical analysis of China in Africa, Mao espoused a clear line for China's foreign relations: "Externally, we must unite in a common struggle with the peoples of all countries and with those nations which treat us as equals. This means allying ourselves with the Soviet Union, with every New Democratic country, and with the proletariat and the broad masses in all other countries. This means fostering an international united front."[6] For a new nation such as China, it was vital to identify nations and peoples who might have been friendly; this was part of China's central objectives.

Mao expanded on China's strategic direction by reiterating who China's allies were. He stated, "Internationally we belong to the side of the anti-imperialist front, headed by the Soviet Union. We can only turn to this side for genuine and friendly assistance, not to the side of the imperialist front."[7] It is important to recognize here that Mao, in one of his earliest policy statements, envisioned the Chinese on the side of the anti-imperialists rather than in the Communist or Socialist bloc.[8] Although later viewed as a radical ideologue, Mao was principally a pragmatist in international politics. He used Communism as a vehicle to unify the Chinese people within the PRC; thus, Mao intentionally created an authoritarian government to rule China. That China continues to be dominated by a select group of CPC members today supports this assertion. During his lifetime, Mao's statements and China's foreign relations supported the essential pragmatism of the nation.

A second important objective derived from *On People's Democratic Dictatorship* was the international united front objective. Similar to the Soviet Union and "every New Democratic country," a central objective was to gain the support of the "proletariat" and "the broad masses" around the world.[9] China aimed to obtain as much support from peoples and nations around the world as possible—to become a global power. This international united front objective was part and parcel of Communist China's desire to be strong and prosperous. By gaining the support of foreign nations and peoples, the PRC would profit from the exchange of peoples, goods, and services, and would thereby be capable of building China's economic, political, and military power—all of which are essential for a great world power. Moreover, an international united front would naturally place China in a superior position because of its geographic size and population. Thus, *On People's Democratic Dictatorship* laid down clear objectives for China.

On 29 September 1949, shortly before the inauguration of the People's Republic, the Chinese People's Political Consultative Conference, led by the Communist Party, released its Common Program.[10] The Common Program was the first strategic document for the Chinese government, acting in the same way that an interim constitution would for a developing democracy.[11] Article 54 of the

Common Program stated clearly China's foreign policy objectives: "The principle of the foreign policy of the People's Republic of China is the safeguarding of the independence, freedom and integrity of territory and sovereignty of the country, supporting of international lasting peace and friendly cooperation between the people of all countries, and the opposing of the imperialist policy of aggression and war."[12] Although not citing this important document, two scholars echo the Common Program's foreign policy objectives. According to journalist Alan Hutchison, the central PRC objectives were "to ensure the security of the state of China and to ensure the continued authority of the Communist party within that state."[13] Professor Bruce Larkin asserted something similar: "The central end is that the Chinese state endure, and endure with continued CCP [CPC] authority throughout China." The critical aspect of China's objectives, then, was to maintain the security of the PRC and the authority of the CPC. Another aspect was to create an international environment conducive to the economic, political, and social development of the People's Republic. The emphasis on cooperation with the peoples of all countries and the identification of imperialism as the only enemy are noteworthy. Although not citing the Common Program directly, Larkin noted strategically, "The CCP [CPC] strives to establish and maintain Chinese freedom of choice. To attain that end fully it attempts nothing less than to restructure and to transform the world."[14] Larkin made a significant point, associating China's international sovereignty and its desire to create, in effect, a new international order. This pragmatic and realist analysis reveals China's central objective.

The Common Program clarified two issues associated with China's central objective: diplomatic and economic relations. With regard to diplomatic relations, the Common Program was explicit in requiring the severance of relations with the ROC government prior to the establishment of relations with the PRC. "The Central People's Government of the People's Republic of China may negotiate and establish diplomatic relations on the basis of equality, mutual respect for territory and sovereignty with foreign governments which sever relations with the Kuomintang reactionaries and adopt a friendly attitude towards the People's Republic of China." On the other hand, the Common Program was more flexible in economic relations. "The People's Republic of China may restore and develop trading and commercial relations with foreign governments and people on the basis of equality and mutual benefit." The Common Program envisioned restoring and developing economic relations with foreign governments and peoples. Rather than focusing exclusively on governmental institutions, the Common Program was congruent with Mao's united front objective of gaining the support of all peoples around the world, by political and economic means. Moreover, the Common Program was prescient in its advocacy of developing a scientific and technological base for Communist China. "Efforts shall be made to develop the natural sciences to place them at the service of industrial, agricultural and national defense construction. Scientific discoveries and inventions shall be encouraged and rewarded and scientific knowledge shall be popularized."[15] Clearly, the Communist Party–led CPPCC understood the strategic implications of science and technology for national power. Therefore, a robust scientific and technological base forms part of the basis of national power, regardless of a nation's political ideology. In 1962 the U.S. Central Intelligence Agency (CIA) noted, "[T]he country is ruled by a strong regime which is determined to make China a modern industrial power."[16] China wanted to become militarily powerful and, thus, a strong and prosperous nation—and a global power—and moved toward that goal by developing diplomatically, economically, and scientifically.

The Common Program, released shortly before the establishment of the PRC, was explicit in identifying China's central, strategic objectives. Maintaining the security of the nation-state of Communist China and the authority of the CPC government were two clear long-term objectives. Also apparent were Chinese aims to create an international united front and to develop China's economic, scientific, and technological bases. Thus, PRC security, CPC authority, international unity, and economic and scientific development were the central objectives of the People's Republic. These objectives remain central to China today. For example, China's important 1998 National Defense white paper stated, "Mankind is about to enter the 21st century of its history. It is the aspiration of the Chinese government and people to lead a peaceful, stable and prosperous world into the new century."[17] China's central objectives all contributed directly to its paramount aim of becoming a world power.[18]

Another Chinese official of considerable influence was Liu Shaoqi. Although Liu was speaking as Beijing's labor representative at an international unionist conference, he also held the following governmental positions: vice chair of the Central People's Government of the People's Republic of China (since 1949), vice chair of the Chinese People's Revolutionary Military Council (since 1943), member of the secretariat of the Central Committee of the CPC (since 1943), and member of the political bureau of the Central Committee of the Chinese Communist Party (since 1932). Liu thus was a high-ranking official speaking with authority for the PRC government.[19] His World Federation of Trade Unions (WFTU) speech in Beijing on 16 November 1949 was a significant Chinese policy pronouncement, particularly because it was delivered immediately after the establishment of Communist China. This speech indicated China's desire to become a leader in the world Communist movement and, by implication, a global power. In Marxist-Leninist terms, Liu Shaoqi enunciated this objective: "To fight for national independence and people's democracy is therefore the supreme task of the working class in the colonial and semicolonial countries." To achieve this supreme task, Liu echoed Mao's call for a united front. "It is therefore necessary for the colonial and semicolonial people and the working people in the imperialist countries to unite together to fight against their common enemy—imperialism."[20] Liu's policy statement was not novel in nature but it was novel in character.[21] Earlier, Mao noted the importance of uniting with the proletariat and the broad masses; in his WFTU speech in Beijing, Liu specified uniting with the working class (or proletariat) in colonial and semicolonial countries. This was one of the earliest references in Communist China to what was then called the Third World, and now is known as the developing world or Global South. Professor George T. Yu later asserted, "Like the interaction with select Third World states, China's identification with and support of issues of common interest has been directed at establishing a united front with the Third World. China has consistently supported the Third World's demand for a restructuring of the international order, one not dominated by the superpowers. China's Third World policy has sought a new international order."[22] The CIA noted, somewhat more mildly, "[T]he Chinese Communists will probably be increasingly active in encouraging and supporting indigenous left-wing revolutionary movements throughout the underdeveloped world."[23] This perspective, like Larkin's, integrated China's central objectives and placed them in a strategic context. Furthermore, Yu noted, "Peking's campaign to impose its leadership upon Africa represents a long-term goal."[24] By restructuring the international order, China aspired over the long term to become a world power.

Nearly a decade prior to the publication of *On People's Democratic Dictatorship*, Mao hinted at China's objective of becoming a global power. In 1940 Mao's *On New Democracy* was released. In it, Mao wrote, "[W]e want to change a politically oppressed and economically exploited China into a politically free and economically prosperous China." Moreover, Mao indicated his desire for the new China to have freedom of action to ally with whomever it chose. "All the imperialist powers in the world are our enemies; so if China wants independence she can never attain it without the aid of the socialist state and the international proletariat."[25] Although Mao differentiated a Socialist and a non-Socialist state here, the differentiation was not in a strict ideological context. Rather, as Mao put it, "We must draw a clear distinction between ourselves and the enemy."[26] But Mao was not averse to working with the enemy, either.

Bearing in mind his objective of international unity, Mao viewed it expedient at times to compromise with imperialists. According to the Spring 1964 issue of *Orbis*, the *Peking Review* of 20 December 1963 quoted him as stating, "Sometimes it is necessary for the socialist countries to reach compromises with the imperialists."[27] Although perhaps novel to uninformed Western scholars at the time, his statement of compromise was not new. Returning to Mao's *On New Democracy*, the paramount leader of the PRC wrote, "China should assimilate from foreign progressive cultures in large quantities what she needs for her own culture and we did not sufficiently do so in the past. We must assimilate whatever we find useful today, not only from contemporary foreign socialist or new-democratic cultures, but also from the older cultures of foreign countries, such as those of the capitalist countries in their age of enlightenment."[28] Mao's words here were written in 1940. Clearly, he wrote from a pragmatic and realistic point of view, and China's central objectives reflected this perspective.

Mao's *On the Ten Major Relationships* is perhaps the most neglected policy document of China today. Although published globally in 1977, this work was originally released in 1956. *On the Ten Major Relationships* provided a realist point of view of power and explained the importance of economic development to a strong national defense. It stated from the onset Mao's conception of the central objective for Communist China. "In short, we should mobilize all forces whether direct or indirect, and strive to build China into a powerful socialist country."[29] Again, the "powerful" character of Mao's statement should take precedent over the "socialist" one. This was a simple, yet profound, restatement of China's central objective—to become a global power.

To achieve great power status, Mao espoused learning from foreign nations how best to build China's national power. He reiterated the need to learn from foreign countries and cultures, even those of the imperialists. "Our policy is to learn from the strong points of all nations and all countries, learn all that is genuinely good in the political, economic, scientific and technological fields and in literature and art. But we must learn with an analytical and critical eye, not blindly, and we mustn't copy everything indiscriminately and transplant mechanically."[30] Rather than acquiring foreign equipment and technologies blindly, Mao encouraged the pragmatic application of foreign goods and ideas to the Chinese context.[31]

Western scholars often credit Mao's successor, reformist leader Deng Xiaoping, with promoting and enacting the transformational Four Modernizations in China, which emphasized the need to strengthen China's agriculture, industry, science and technology, and defense. But in 1956 Mao had already noted the central relationship between economics and national defense in his work *On the Ten Major Relationships*. Ever the realist, Mao wrote, "National defense is indispensable." Mao understood the role of the economy in national defense. "Only with the faster growth of economic construction can there be more progress in defense construction." He always prioritized national defense development over economic development, however: "We must strengthen our national defense, and for that purpose we must first of all strengthen our work in economic construction." At the end of this 1956 work, Mao again advocated for China to become a global power: "We must do our best to mobilize all positive factors, both inside and outside the Party, both at home and abroad, both direct and indirect, and build China into a powerful socialist country."[32] Mao's long-term objective was building the PRC in a comprehensive manner into a global power; moreover, the Chinese leadership supported this objective.

In 1956 the Eighth National CPC Congress convened. It was the first National CPC Congress after the establishment of the People's Republic and may, therefore, be viewed with particular significance. Mao's opening statement was unambiguous about China's central objectives: "To achieve a lasting peace in the world, we must further develop our friendship and cooperation with the fraternal countries in the camp of socialism and strengthen our solidarity with all peace-loving countries." Again, Mao emphasized the objectives of international unity and international peace, the latter of which would safeguard Chinese security and, therefore, CPC authority. Mao also reiterated some aspects of the 1949 Common Program: "We must endeavor to establish normal diplomatic relations on the basis of mutual respect for territorial integrity and sovereignty, and equality and mutual benefit, with all countries willing to live peacefully together with us." But he introduced a new and significant objective as well: "We must give active support to the national independence and liberation movements in countries in Asia, Africa, and Latin America as well as to the peace movement and righteous struggles in all countries throughout the world."[33] The Chinese government also made explicit reference to establishing a "beachhead in Africa," according to the CIA.[34] While Liu Shaoqi introduced the concept of colonial and semicolonial countries of the world in 1949, Mao's statement at the Eighth National CPC Congress made one of the earliest references to "active support [to the] national independence and liberation movements [in] Asia, Africa, and Latin America" as a policy.[35] This objective fully supported one of China's four central objectives, namely international unity. It also clarified the type of international unity the Chinese sought: unity that restructured the world with China as a global power.

Liu Shaoqi presented a report to the Eighth National CPC Congress that restated one of Mao's objectives from *On People's Democratic Dictatorship*: "In order to build our country into a great Socialist State, we must not only unite with all the forces at home that can be united with; we must also strive to bring about all favorable international conditions and unite with all forces throughout the world that can be united with."[36] Here was another top Communist official citing international unity as an objective in 1956. These pronouncements demonstrated the importance of international unity and were part and parcel to China's paramount objective of becoming a global power. But Liu also added a condition that cut across all four central objectives by enunciating the desire to create "all favorable international conditions" for the People's Republic. By creating "favorable international conditions," China could maintain national security and the CPC could maintain authority; the Chinese could seek international unity; and China could develop its economic and scientific communities. Therefore, keeping the international environment favorable in the long term allowed China to develop into a great world power (or "strong" and "prosperous," in Communist phraseology), which was the central objective.

Another top Chinese Communist official who exerted tremendous influence over Chinese policymaking was Premier Zhou Enlai.[37] Zhou, who as aforementioned concurrently held the post of foreign minister for a period, reiterated China's desire for international unity in 1955.[38] At the Afro-Asian Bandung Conference in 1955, which was organized with China in mind, Zhou mirrored Mao's and Liu's earlier calls to create a united front.[39] "The Chinese Delegation has come here to seek common ground, not to create divergence," Zhou proclaimed in his memorable supplementary opening speech.[40] Moreover, at one of the Political Committee meetings, Zhou asserted, "We should leave aside our different ideologies, our different state systems and the international obligations which we have assumed by joining this side or that side. We should instead settle all questions which may arise amongst us on the basis of common peace and cooperation."[41] Clearly, Zhou was attempting to create international unity—again, one of China's central objectives.

Zhou understood well the importance of international unity for China's growth to great power status. He also knew the relationship between the international situation and building a strong China: "We all recognize that Socialist construction and Socialist transformation are gigantic and arduous tasks. Therefore, at home, we need the strength of a united people; and abroad, we need a peaceful international environment." While the Socialist aims of Zhou's statement should not be overlooked, there was a clear association between building internal strength and maintaining external tranquility, much as there is today. Moreover, Zhou perceived Asia, Africa, and Latin America to be central to China's objective of creating international unity and maintaining a peaceful international situation. "We sympathize with and support all the peoples and countries of Asia, Africa and Central and South America in their struggle to achieve or safeguard their national independence." Later in 1955 Zhou made a direct correlation between the two. "Their victory will strengthen the forces for peace and deal a blow to the forces of war."[42] By creating such favorable conditions, Zhou advocated for a strong and prosperous China globally—the central objective envisioned by Mao prior to the establishment of the People's Republic.

The continuity of messages derived from China's top leaders—Mao Zedong, Liu Shaoqi, and Zhou Enlai—was a significant indication of China's central objectives. At their heart was China's desire to become a great world power. To attain this status, Beijing's leaders recognized that the PRC required national security, central authority, international unity, and economic and scientific development. "By acting in Africa, China contribute[d] to her own strategic [and] economic ... aims."[43] Yet Communist China also had other objectives, objectives of lesser importance.

"The immediate purpose of Red China in Africa, to eliminate Western and particularly American influence, seems clearer than its longer-term goals."[44] In contrast to its central objectives, however, China's secondary objectives were short term and regional: "The short-range objectives [were] much more bound to particular situations."[45] Without discounting their significance, the secondary objectives should be viewed as subsidiary to China's central objectives because they contributed to and, in some cases, furthered the central objectives. This is the same today. Moreover, they represented goals that were more immediately tangible. Because of this tangibility, however, some analysts have tended to overemphasize China's secondary interests while overlooking the central objectives; this is still true today. This simple variation of analytical emphasis results in remarkably different conclusions as to the motives and intentions of Chinese actions in Africa.

According to Yu, the three Chinese objectives in Africa were anti-imperialism, anti-revisionism, and Asian-African unity.[46] Yu did not misread the statements of Communist China's leaders. For example, while Zhou Enlai was in Ghana on his ten-nation tour from 1963 to 1964, he stated, "Imperialism is the enemy of the people of the world and the enemy of world peace. In order to defend world peace and promote the cause of human progress, the people of Asia, Africa and Latin America should unite, the people of various continents of the world should unite, all peace-loving peoples and countries should unite, to wage a resolute struggle against the imperialist policies of aggression and war."[47] Apparent from Zhou's statement, anti-imperialism was one of China's objectives. But, in itself, anti-imperialism was *secondary* compared to China's central objective of creating international unity, with China as a world leader. Identifying anti-imperialism as an end in itself overlooks China's long-term, strategic objectives.

Another secondary objective was China's campaign to secure international recognition and support.[48] This campaign was intimately related to Communist China's goal of Asian-African unity as well as purportedly achieving political objectives in the developing world in general.[49] According to this objective, China sought to gain recognition from newly formed African countries as the sole legitimate government of China and to take over the ROC's permanent seat on the UN Security Council (UNSC).[50] This was a tangible objective for Beijing, and time was on the side of the larger and more influential Communist nation vis-à-vis the island republic of the ROC. From the strategic perspective, however, gaining international recognition and the permanent UNSC seat was ephemeral compared to China's central objectives. As stated in the 1949 Common Program, being identified as the sole legitimate government of the Chinese people was a part of the PRC's objectives, but it represented only a small part of the larger objective of becoming a strong and prosperous Chinese nation.

Anti-revisionism, or the Sino-Soviet conflict, may be considered another secondary Communist Chinese objective.[51] Sinologists often cite the ideological aspects of China's foreign policy when referring to the Maoist period, including in Africa.[52] Mao himself was repeatedly perceived as a radical Communist firebrand.[53] The secondary objective of replacing "Moscow as leader of and spokesman for socialist countries" was a political aim for China.[54] However, the primary rationale for the Chinese-Soviet riff was not ideological but strategic. Located geographically on the same Eurasian landmass, the two historically proud and geographically large nations, with similar aspirations of becoming great world powers, were bound to clash. Throughout his life, however, Mao's statements of Chinese objectives were realist and pragmatic. With an expanding ballistic missile and nuclear warfighting capability, the Soviet Union was the only true threat to China, despite the many accusations of U.S. aggression.[55] If anything, the Communist ideological battle between China and the Soviet Union served to deter and confuse outside observers, but it was not an end in itself.[56]

Another notable secondary objective centered specifically on the contest for sole Chinese representation worldwide. Although the PRC-ROC battle was present throughout the world, it served as a prime example of an overemphasized Chinese objective, especially in Africa. Journalist John K. Cooley described China's manipulative aims in this manner: "What Peking ultimately demand[ed] from Africans, as from Asians, [was] choice: choice between Peking and Taiwan, between Peking and Moscow, and certainly between East and West."[57] Cooley was accurate in his analysis of Communist Chinese persuasion techniques, but he failed to elucidate China's strategic objectives. Writing from a more contemporary context, Professor Ian Taylor was correct when he wrote, "[T]he PRC *vs.* [italics in original] ROC theme should not be exaggerated when examining Beijing's behaviour on the [African] continent."[58] Clearly, the Communist government desired sole representation of the Chinese people throughout Africa and the rest of the world. But, once again, this secondary objective was part and parcel of China's central objective of becoming a strong and prosperous global power.

Many of Communist China's secondary objectives complemented its central objectives. While not citing any Chinese authorities directly, Professor Joseph Smaldone summarized some of China's secondary objectives: "[T]o gain international recognition and influence; to achieve a position of leadership among third-world nations; to win the mantle of ideological guide in the Communist world; and to undermine Western influence in the international system."[59] China's secondary objectives were short-term goals targeted specifically at certain countries and regions. Putting the central and secondary relationships into perspective, Chinese author Chang Ya-chun wrote pragmatically, "Politics is the object of Peiping's association with African countries, who look for economic benefit in their dealings with Red China."[60] This is quite the same for China in Africa today. Chinese pragmatism outweighed strictly ideological considerations during the Maoist era. And Communist China's central objectives demonstrated pragmatic strategic planning.

Clearly, then, China's secondary interests were a part of its central objectives, which were long term and strategic. "With a view toward a long-range goal of leadership of the Afro-Asian community, Peking consistently stresse[d] the great similarity between its suffering under the heavy hand of imperialism and that of the other Afro-Asian states."[61] Analyzing China's operations on the African continent with one or the other lens leads us to drastically different conclusions. Taking an example from a different part of the world, "Neutralism and nonalignment, as the Chinese recognized a decade ago, may be acceptable ways of securing China's long-term interests in Asia without excessive costs and risks."[62] Were one to perceive China's desire for nonalignment in Asia from the narrow perspective as a peace among neighbors objective, one would overlook the true intent of Beijing's leaders—namely to promote demilitarization and, therefore, to dominate strategically the Asian region. Secondary objectives were not insignificant; rather, these objectives were simply more superficial and more ephemeral. Thus, if prudent, one must analyze Chinese policies from a strategic perspective. Accordingly, China's central objectives should take precedence over all others.

In the final analysis, China's central objective—in Africa as elsewhere in the world—is to become a world power. Thus, its national security is paramount and essential, as is the authority of the CPC. Forming international unity as well as economic and scientific development were part and parcel of China's central objective as well. And Africa fits squarely in to China's long-term objectives.

Two

ORGANIZATIONS

To attain its objectives in Africa, China used several different organizations domestically and internationally. Since the focus of the book is China in Africa, Chinese organizations dealing with political, military, and strategic relations in Africa are most relevant to us here. Some of the organizations were strictly governmental, others were openly government sponsored, and still others were front organizations. Whatever its size or composition, however, each organization served a unique purpose (or multiple purposes) in furthering the objectives of China in Africa.

Many Chinese organizations helped in achieving its central objectives. From official to unofficial, economic to social, clandestine to overt, China's organizations covered a wide spectrum of missions and operations.[1] To gain influence in Africa, however, China used a unique and distinct group of organizations. In order to gain a better understanding of how China sought to achieve its objectives in Africa, one must understand the history, roles, and functions of these organizations.[2] No single organization performed all functions for China in Africa. Beijing's leaders used a diverse group of organizations to operate in the diverse environments on the African continent.

With much history and influence, the New China News Agency (NCNA) was a significant Chinese organization in Africa. The Red China News Agency was founded in Ruijin, Jiangxi Province, in 1931.[3] Six years later, the word "New" was substituted for the word "Red" after "Japan invaded China and the Communist formed a united front with the Nationalists."[4] "In the early 1940s NCNA began foreign broadcasts in English, and before the end of World War II it had started daily Morse transmissions overseas, putting heavy emphasis on the

Communist war effort against Japan—the common enemy of the English-speaking world."[5] In 1949, the same year the PRC was established, the NCNA became an official state organization.[6] Thus, the NCNA drew its lineage from the formidable Communist Party days. Because of its history, the NCNA was instrumental in furthering China's domestic and international objectives. The same is true today.

For the Chinese leadership, the NCNA acted as an exclusive communication channel to the outside world. The "NCNA [had] an exalted status in the Chinese Communist apparatus because it [had] the monopoly over the flow of public information within China and between China and the outside world."[7] In other words, the NCNA was "the primary PRC vehicle for the collection and dissemination of news at home and abroad."[8] Because of its functions as an intelligence collection organization and information-providing source, the NCNA played a significant role in Chinese policymaking. Professor Maochun Yu noted the importance of information control in the contemporary CPC context: "Censorship has always been a vital part of Chinese government policy. The survival of the Communist regime requires belief in the Party's infallibility. Pointing out anything negative about reality in China is viewed as a threat to the power of the Communist Party, a power that must be ruthlessly maintained by total control of the media."[9] The CPC leaders, therefore, understood the importance of direct operational control over their state-run media organization, much as they do today, especially in the context of Internet-based social media.

The global reach of the NCNA made it a desirable and useful organization in Africa. From Chile and Mexico in the Americas to Sweden and France in Western Europe, Japan and Laos in East Asia to Syria and Yemen in the Middle East, China located the NCNA in countries and regions around the world at a time when that country did not maintain official diplomatic relations with many nation-states, including the United States. In 1966 the NCNA had forty-nine locations overseas.[10] By 1972, intelligence scholar Jeffrey T. Richelson reported, the NCNA had "ninety-plus foreign bureaus employ[ing] three hundred workers."[11] The precise number and location of NCNA personnel overseas were unknown. In Africa in 1966 NCNA personnel were believed to be present in Algeria, the Central African Republic, Congo-Brazzaville, Ethiopia, Ghana, Guinea, Kenya, Mali, Morocco, Senegal, Somalia, Sudan, Tanzania, Tunisia, Uganda, the United Arab Republic (present-day Egypt and Syria), and Zambia.[12] Based on the presence of its many overseas NCNA offices, Africa was clearly a continent of interest to China and its leaders.

The overseas NCNA staffs varied in terms of size and composition. "Each of the NCNA overseas bureaus [was] staffed by at least two persons."[13] This minimum number of overseas personnel was a result of circumstances, especially the lack of trained and qualified personnel. At the same time, however, the NCNA may have intentionally chosen this small footprint globally to maintain a discreet and clandestine structure. But NCNA personnel were not always in isolation abroad. "Extremely close cooperation exist[ed] among NCNA, Radio Peking and the *People's Daily*, the Central Committee's newspapers." This close cooperation served to enhance the presence of NCNA personnel: "As part of the government machinery, NCNA personnel [were] interchangeable with those of other offices such as the Ministry of Foreign Affairs and the Ministry of Foreign Trade."[14] This interchangeability resulted in expanded influence: NCNA personnel could be called up to perform different roles in different circumstances.[15]

As China's primary news agency, the NCNA performed many legal and overt functions. "Much of NCNA's work involve[d] the simple collection of unclassified documents—newspapers, magazines, books, technical journals. Within its resources, Peking [was] as assiduous in the collection of overt intelligence as any other major power. But the main thrust of NCNA's activities [was] of a diplomatic or intelligence nature, as can be seen from the operations of its busier correspondents."[16] China benefited from NCNA's overt role as a news organization. "Assuming the role of foreign correspondents, NCNA reporters interview[ed] key government officials or members of significant opposition groups in Africa, Latin America, and the Middle East to probe their attitudes toward closer relations with China."[17] Playing the role of news reporter gave NCNA personnel cover and access to persons of influence in countries around the world. "In Africa, in fact, a pattern evolved by which NCNA correspondents arrived first, and diplomatic relations followed."[18] According to the biography of Tung Chi-ping, who was a Chinese assistant cultural attaché in Burundi who defected to the United States in May 1964, this was in fact PRC protocol. "In the first step [to penetrate Africa], a 'correspondent' of the official New China News Agency [was] assigned to a country."[19] The three case studies in this book illustrate that this indeed was the pattern.

Professor Alan Liu described the role of the NCNA personnel abroad in another manner: "Using a military metaphor, as Chinese Communist leaders love[d] to do, NCNA correspondents [were] scouts, not troop commanders."[20] NCNA personnel served as the advance guard for China's objectives. Moreover, they performed tangible operations abroad—as only a physical presence in foreign countries could. "While Radio Peking broadcast[ed] to the masses in [Africa, Latin America, and the Middle East], NCNA men translate[d] propaganda into concrete actions and, through their contact with elite groups, synchronize[d] the latter's activities with China's objectives."[21] And these functions were, in most instances, overt and legal.

The NCNA also performed covert functions abroad. In 1964 the CIA acknowledged as much, stating that all NCNA offices "probably conduct some undercover activity."[22] According to Wang Chia-yu, a candid Chinese writer, moreover, "NCNA personnel stationed abroad [were] engaged in various kinds of political activities other than press work." For example, "NCNA correspondents overseas, with the agency's foreign offices as headquarters, [were] conducting activities of cultural infiltration, political united front, and subversion." The three case studies in this book illustrate these types of activities. Furthermore, "NCNA personnel maintain[ed] contacts and liaison with the so-called 'cultural friendship associations' and distribute[d] propaganda materials in countries where they [were] stationed." From the financial perspective, "NCNA personnel transmit[ted] money and other forms of Peiping's assistance to local Communist and leftist organizations. They also assist[ed] in negotiations and settlement of trade transactions."[23] There was purported to be a military section of the NCNA as well. These NCNA personnel held the utmost loyalty to the CPC and received specialized training in foreign languages.[24] While their specific functions in the field were unclear, the military section played a significant role in Chinese operations. From its name, one might deduce that personnel performed military or security assistance-type functions overseas. "Overseas branch offices of NCNA [therefore, had] become principal footholds for Peiping espionage and subversive operations."[25]

From its rural beginning in the Chinese countryside to its expansive presence around the world, the NCNA served at the behest of the Chinese government. It was both a news gatherer and a newsmaker. "In short, the Chinese [grand] strategy of people's diplomacy in the Third World, designed [in part] to organize the underdeveloped nations into an anti-U.S. united front, [was] spearheaded by NCNA."[26] Moreover, as stated by CPC propagandist Liu Ting-yi on the NCNA's twentieth anniversary in 1957, the "NCNA, like the party, the government, the army, and the courts, is a weapon of class struggle."[27] The NCNA was an active and significant influence organization for China, especially in Africa.[28]

Also furthering China's objectives in Africa, the International Liaison Department (ILD) was established in May 1951 at the first CPC Central Committee meeting to study intelligence and the security system.[29] Located within the Central Committee of the Communist Party, the ILD was a Chinese organization that performed various international functions. Moreover, the ILD jointly supervised the relations of overseas friendship and cultural organizations, specifically in Africa.[30]

The ILD performed military-related functions by funding, training, and supplying arms to out-of-power Communist and revolutionary groups in Africa. "The ILD was not, however, indiscriminate; it generally supported only those groups it believed could substantially influence events and refused to support groups simply for diversionary or terroristic purposes."[31] Beijing's leaders prioritized targets for influence. This prioritization demonstrated the realistic and pragmatic nature of Chinese planners. With limited resources, China could not organize, fund, train, arm, and supply all revolutionary groups in Africa, so it carefully chose groups and organizations that it believed could be influential with Chinese support. Moreover, the Chinese were flexible with their covert operations. For example, the ILD, as a policymaking organization, may have utilized the International Equipment Division of the General Rear Services Department of the People's Liberation Army (PLA). This division was known to be "responsible for supplying arms to foreign allies and insurgent groups."[32]

In the political realm, the ILD developed relationships with Communist and revolutionary groups, as well as with Socialist parties, Social Democratic parties, labor parties, and the various political parties in the nations of the developing world. In a contemporary interview, a spokesperson for the ILD said, "At present, the CPC is maintaining contacts in different forms with over 200 political parties of more than 100 countries, which include not only communist parties, but socialist parties, social democratic parties, labor parties and other parties of developed and developing countries." Apparently, the ILD continues its operations in a similar manner today.[33] At the same time, the ILD provided support and supervision to specific Chinese mass organizations that developed relationships with foreign labor and with women's, youth, and student groups.[34] These overt functions added legitimacy to the ILD. By doing so, the organization could operate within legal and political constraints of wary nations. Furthermore, overt political operations allowed the ILD to gain firsthand knowledge of and contact with potential supporters of covert, military-related operations. The ILD multiplied China's reach overseas, particularly in Africa.

The ILD was an organization that assisted in directing and coordinating Chinese activities abroad. Unlike the NCNA, the ILD was a readily identifiable governmental organization and, therefore, was bound by its governmental association with the government in Beijing, whereas the NCNA could pass as another news agency within the international media realm. According to a contemporary ILD spokesperson, "The CPC has a long history of developing its relations with parties in Africa."[35] Although analysts of China in Africa often overlooked it, the ILD was a central means for China to further its objectives in Africa.

Another Chinese organization that operated in Africa was the Commission for Cultural Relations with Foreign Countries (CCRFC), created in February 1958. While a discrepancy exists, whether or not it was organized under the guise of the foreign ministry or the state council, the CCRFC performed intelligence work for China.[36] According to journalists David Wise and Thomas Ross, for example, the CCRFC was organized to encompass the "proliferating intelligence functions of the Foreign Ministry."[37] In this capacity, the CCRFC was similar to the NCNA. Moreover, it was "responsible for the Association for Cultural Relations with Foreign Countries together with the appropriate departments of the Ministry of Foreign Affairs, and, wherever present, the Chinese Institute for International Relations and the Chinese People's Institute for Foreign Affairs.[38] These oversight and managerial functions explain why the CCRFC jointly supervised the overseas friendship and cultural organizations along with the ILD. According to the CIA as early as 1966, the CCRFC was "responsible for carrying out the cultural exchange program."[39]

The Commission's structure revealed its emphasis and broad reach. The Commission comprised eleven divisions, total. Seven were regional divisions, "two of which were established in 1964 to handle the growing Chinese Communist activities in Africa and Latin America."[40] A separate division handled Chinese participation in international cultural conferences. The remaining three divisions were functional. They included a propaganda division, with sections for translating Chinese materials, presenting exhibits, and distributing films and periodicals; a foreign aid division that handled the construction of cultural facilities such as stadiums; and a human resources division for recruitment, training, and assignment of personnel abroad.[41] As will be illustrated in this book's three case studies, all of the CCRFC's functions were used in Africa, for both short-term and long-term effects.

Performing functions related to the CCRFC, the Chinese People's Association for Cultural Relations with Foreign Countries (CPACRFC) was founded in May 1954 with the aim of fostering relations between the Chinese people and the peoples of other lands by increasing cultural contacts.[42] Among its various functions, the CPACRFC sponsored the exchange of cultural delegations; sponsored the visits of writers, artists, and scientists; and held exhibitions and commemoration meetings of outstanding cultural figures of different ages and different countries.[43] These cultural exchanges exposed foreign peoples to the Chinese cultural achievements and allowed for ample communications opportunities to exchange words and ideas, as well as other politically oriented operations. Political relations were allowed to originate and flourish. Because the CPACRFC predated the CCRFC, the latter was more of a coordinating body while the former was an operational organization.

Both CCRFC and CPACRFC were created to target a similar group of individuals as the ILD, but they did so in different manners. The latter focused on the political and military means, while the former focused on social and cultural aspects. By using different approaches to achieve the same end, China had multiple means for gaining influence abroad—especially in the diverse countries of Africa.

Like its Communist counterpart, the Soviet Union, China utilized a "worldwide galaxy" of front organizations in Africa. In general, it created front organizations to supplement the work of local Communist or left-leaning political parties "for reaching specialized objectives."[44] As Professor Robert Bass wrote in 1960, "The fronts remain essentially what they have always been: auxiliary weapons. Their function is not so much to implement foreign policy as to make official Communist policy more acceptable and effective."[45] Moreover, as Professor William Kintner noted, "Fronts are weapons created to attack objectives which cannot be assaulted directly by the Communist party."[46] Fronts were "a means of exerting [Soviet or Communist Chinese] influence on the peoples of the world and as a 'front' for penetration and propaganda."[47] Thus, China created various types of front organizations to function in different ways to attain its objectives in Africa. While some of them may have been directly under the mechanical control of Beijing, others may have simply included the presence of Communist Chinese agents, who exerted influence on the organization and its activities.[48]

A front organization directly under the mechanical control of China was the China-Africa People's Friendship Association (CAPFA). Established on 12 April 1960 on the initiative of seventeen national people's organizations, the CAPFA was created to assist directly in the coordination of Communist China's various friendship associations with Africa.[49] Other Chinese front organizations were the Islamic Association of People's China, "headed by Burhan Shahidi, a Moslem by persuasion and a Uighur by birth," and the Albanian Union of Working Youth, which "occasionally act[ed] for the Chinese in East Africa, Libya, Algeria, Tunisia, and Morocco."[50] Other Communist Chinese fronts included the China Democratic

League and the Kuomintang Revolutionary Committee. "The League [had] set as its major objective the unity of 'the broad masses of intelligentsia, enlightened industrialists and businessmen and democratic overseas Chinese to strive for the realization of the common program of the CPPC and the fulfillment of the new democratic revolution.'"[51] All of these front organizations served specific purposes to further Chinese objectives in Africa. China also used organizations not directly under its control.

One prominent multinational organization used by China in Africa to further its objectives was the Afro-Asian People's Solidarity Organization (AAPSO). Established on 3 January 1958, "AAPSO was formed as the result of an initiative first put forward at the Conference for the Relaxation of International Tensions, held in New Delhi in April 1955."[52] At the New Delhi Conference, the Soviets intended to exploit the subsequent Bandung Conference image and extend its scope.[53] Ostensibly, the goal of the AAPSO was in its name: solidarity among African and Asian peoples. In reality, however, the AAPSO was a complex organization promoting anticolonialism and anti-imperialism, both of which were secondary objectives of Communist China in Africa.[54] These objectives were also those of the Soviet Union, and may be viewed from a strategic perspective as a restructuring of the international system.

The AAPSO was organized in a hierarchical fashion.[55] The AAPSO Conference comprised delegations from all member organizations, which included national solidarity committees, ruling political parties, opposition political parties, and national liberation movements, as well as observers from "fraternal organizations."[56] The term "fraternal organizations" should be understood in Communist terminology, meaning those sympathetic to the cause, including the interest of the PRC. The role of the conference was policymaking and election of the executive committee and permanent secretariat. Also performing policymaking functions was the AAPSO Council, which comprised one voting member from each national organization, additional representatives of national organizations, and, again, observers from fraternal organizations. The conference was intended to meet biannually and the council, annually.

The senior decision-making bodies of the AAPSO included the executive committee, the permanent secretariat, the fund committee, and the control committee. The executive committee provided administrative supervision over the permanent secretariat and all financial matters. It comprised twenty-seven members from specific countries designated by the conference and met semiannually. The permanent secretariat, which was in permanent session in Cairo, comprised a secretary general and eleven national secretaries selected by member organizations in specific countries designated by the conference. It included functional staff such as youth and women's groups. The permanent secretariat performed administrative functions and implemented policy. Meeting on a quarterly basis, the fund committee comprised seven designated members of the executive committee. It was used to satisfy the needs of member organizations in the struggle against imperialism. Finally, the control committee was an exclusive body comprising three designated members of the executive committee. Meeting semiannually, it examined the accounts of the permanent secretariat prior to each meeting of the executive committee.[57]

With its overarching organizational reach, the AAPSO served many political functions for China (and, parenthetically, for the Soviet Union). China used the AAPSO "to contact students and arrange further education for them in China, and to contact and finance nationalist movements."[58] Moreover, China used AAPSO headquarters in Cairo to develop relations with individuals and organizations throughout the African continent, particularly those national liberation movements leaning toward Mao's call for national liberation.[59] "The permanent secretariat [of the AAPSO] offered China contacts and information, an opportunity for the Chinese secretary to meet African representatives of national solidarity committees and liberation movements which had dealings with the Cairo office."[60] To help "satisfy the needs" of member organizations, the AAPSO fund committee channeled money, training, and arms to liberation groups throughout Africa.[61] The fund committee, along with the other organs of the AAPSO, thus acted as a conduit for Chinese operations in Africa. Significantly, as early as 1963 the CIA noted the "predominance of Chinese influence" in the AAPSO, which was reflected in pro-Communist Chinese views among its left-wing members in Africa.[62]

Another multinational organization influenced by China was the Organization of African Unity (OAU), which was formed in May 1963 as a result of the First Conference of Independent African States and Governments.[63] The OAU included a secretariat for supervisory and administrative purposes; specialized commissions for specific functional roles (such as economic, social, education and cultural); the council of ministers for supervisory roles over the secretariat and the various commissions; the assembly for supreme decision making; and various other bodies for miscellaneous purposes.[64] As a whole, the OAU was Africa's first continent-wide intergovernmental organization that was intended to perform both continental and international relations functions. China used its relations with the OAU to further its national interests in Africa.

Most pertinent to Chinese activities in Africa was the OAU's liberation committee (also known as the African Liberation Committee, or ALC).[65] In its original conception, the ALC represented all of the nonwhite states on the African continent in 1963. The Committee of Nine included Algeria, Ethiopia, Guinea, Nigeria, Senegal, Tanganyika, Uganda, the UAR, and Congo-Kinshasa (present-day Zaire). Somalia and Zambia were added later.[66] According to journalist Richard T. Gibson, moreover, "The O.A.U. had given the A.L.C. two specific objectives: first, the establishment of a liberation budget to finance the struggle for African freedom; and second, the co-ordination of the struggle on a territorial and interterritorial basis, beginning with the elimination of rival parties and the formation of united fronts."[67] The latter objective sounded strikingly similar to China's united front objective, internationally. Similarly, Professor John Markakis wrote that the ALC was established "for the purpose of coordinating and channelling O.A.U. assistance to African nationalist organisations in the few remaining areas still under colonial rule."[68] Contrary to Chinese interests, however, the ALC sought "to remove the external influences which might result from dependence on Communist countries for aid and which exacerbated western Opposition to nationalist struggles."[69] Nevertheless, while not a member nation of the OAU or the ALC, China exerted influence by providing political and military assistance indirectly; via bilateral friendship organizations or other fronts, funds, arms, and equipment were channeled to the ALC.

Headquartered in Dar es Salaam, Tanzania, the ALC performed both financial and military services for liberation movements across the continent. In 1975 journalist Milton Viorst wrote, "For a decade Dar es Salaam has been the hub of the liberation movements aimed at the white-dominated countries of Southern Africa." And Dar es Salaam happened also to be where China focused much of its efforts from the beginning of its activities in greater Eastern Africa. On the financial side, funds were dispersed according to competing interests. "Most of the money [was] transmitted by assessments from African governments, the rest from friendly states and private sources outside."[70] In the following case studies, one should bear in mind that Chinese interests may at times have been contrary to the local African interests. Subsequently, actions may have been taken that the PRC opposed but could not prevent. The ALC's funds were not a part of the regular OAU budget.[71] From the military perspective, the ALC "supervise[d] the operation of the guerrilla training camps in Tanzania and Zambia, and distribute[d] weapons and ammunition, most of it from China."[72] Or, as Markakis wrote, "According to statements by staff members the Committee [was] in contact with and provide[d] assistance to embattled nationalists in every remaining colonial territory [in Africa]."[73] While expansive in its reach across the African continent, the ALC's services were more useful from a qualitative rather than a quantitative perspective. In other words, "The material and financial aid which the liberation movements [were] receiving from the Committee [were] small but crucial for their day to day operation. Liberation movements aspire[d] for recognition by the Committee because this enhance[d] their status and offer[ed] them prospects of a base from which to operate their struggle."[74] Thus the ALC was another of the many organizations that China could exploit in Africa.[75]

Without official diplomatic relations with anyone on the continent in 1955, China first gained a foothold, then influence, through the use of a variety of organizations, governmental and nongovernmental. China's approach was mostly indirect, through both overt and covert means. It used a flexible approach on the continent that required such freedom of action—the flexibility to conduct unhindered strategic operations on short notice. The organizations furthering Chinese interests varied from region to region, yet they all had the ability to affect tangibly the targeted individuals and organizations. China's actions began in North Africa.

PART II

NORTHERN EXPOSURE

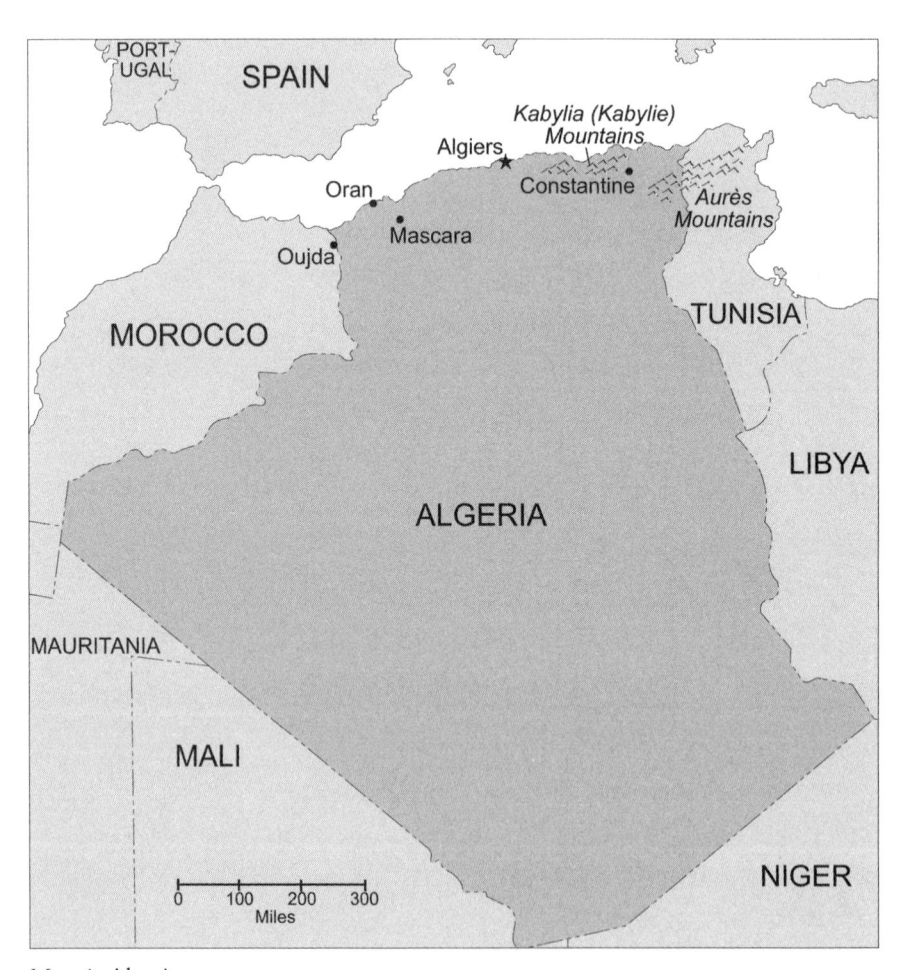

Map 1. Algeria

Three

INITIAL ENTRY

The conditions leading up to Communist China's arrival in Algeria reflected the influences of Algeria's political culture, its colonial history, and its cultural identification. The climate of rising Algerian nationalism was fueled by Algerian experiences in the Second World War as well as by direct contact with the French political scene in the early twentieth century. The French Communist Party, in particular, left an indelible mark on the course of Algerian nationalism.

The earliest indication of Algerian nationalism was the North African Star (Étoile Nord Africaine, ENA). Hadj Ali Abd el Qader, a member of the Central Committee of the French Communist Party, founded the ENA in Paris in 1926.[1] Leadership of the ENA quickly passed to Messali Hadj, an Arab from western Algeria who later became the recognizable figure of Algerian nationalism until his death. Born in the ancient city of Tlemçen in 1898, Hadj was educated along traditional lines in Koranic schools and was a member of the Derkawa Brotherhood. He moved to France in his early twenties and was drafted into the French army. After demobilization, he remained in France where he joined the Communist Party.[2] Until it burst on the Algerian political scene in 1936 the ENA, renamed the Algerian People's Party (Parti du Peuple Algérien, PPA), was under direct French Communist tutelage and, later, was a close associate of the French Communist Party. The Communists provided material and moral support to early Algerian nationalists. More important, the French Communist Party laid an organizational foundation for and taught activities of agitation and propaganda to the ENA, the PPA, and subsequent Algerian nationalist organizations.[3]

France's losses as a result of the Second World War were both material and psychological. During the war, France was forced to draw from the Algerian population and economy to support its war efforts. While the Algerian nationalist movement was "divided and demoralized" at this time, the 1942 Allied landing in North Africa gave the movement newfound inspiration. "Algerian leaders drew new hope and greater confidence from the perception that a greatly weakened France was now dependent upon a far more powerful United States; that [the] United States had coauthored the Atlantic Charter, which called for the liberation of subject people."[4] Historian Alistair Horne emphasizes the Muslim perspective on the outcome of the Second World War: "The Second World War came, and with it France's crushing defeat in 1940. To Muslim minds, particularly sensitive to prestige and baraka [special grace or good fortune], the humiliation made a deep impression."[5] By the end of the war, the use of Algerians in the French army also contributed to the growing dissatisfaction with the French presence in Algeria and a corresponding rise in Algerian nationalism.[6] Furthermore, adding to the potentially volatile situation, in "1945 Algeria was essentially governed as it had been at the turn of the century, when the secessionist impulse had run strong."[7] France's hold on Algeria, therefore, became more tenuous entering the postwar period.

Algerian nationalist organizations multiplied in the postwar environment. Alistair Horne states it clearly: "In broad terms, three separate strands of Algerian nationalism have been defined, each identified with a particular leader. There was the religious movement, as embodied by the Association des Ulema of Sheikh Abdul-hamid Ben Badis; the revolutionaries following Messali Hadj; and finally the liberals of Ferhat Abbis [sic]."[8] First, in 1945 Ferhat Abbas created the Democratic Union for the Algerian Manifesto (Union Démocratique du Manifeste Algérien, UDMA), which represented a less radical brand of Algerian nationalism than the PPA. One year later, in 1946, the Movement for the Triumph of Democratic Liberties (Mouvement pour le Triomphe des Libertés Démocratiques, MTLD) was created as an outgrowth of the then-outlawed PPA.[9] The MTLD was created to pursue Algerian independence in electoral politics. As Professor John Ruedy noted, however, "it was decided to continue the PPA at a secret level for the purposes of cultivating the movement's nationalistic purity and quietly communicating to Algerians that, although public statements might of necessity change from time to time, the goal of absolute independence within an Arab-Islamic framework remained unaltered."[10] Professor Alf Andrew Heggoy, citing an anonymous observer in an unpublished French document, provided a probable description of the underground Special Organization (Organisation Spéciale, OS). He described three types of tactical cells—planning, adaptation, and action; he also provided an organizational chart.[11] Political organizations were therefore present and active in Algeria a decade before Communist China's first contact with Algerians.

The most relevant Algerian nationalist organization was the OS, which was created within the MTLD and parallel to the secret PPA. As Ruedy writes, "Its mission was to explore the possibilities for revolutionary action."[12] Nationalist leader Hocine Ait Ahmed created the OS in 1947, and subsequently led it; in 1949 revolutionary nationalist leader Ahmed Ben Bella took control of the OS. From 1947 to 1950 the OS conducted "terrorist operations when political protest through legal channels was suppressed by authorities."[13] The roughly 1,000 to 1,500 OS fighters were trained in guerrilla warfare in the Algerian mountains.[14] In terms of recruitment, "[t]he object was to recruit young men of little or no political connection in order not to compromise the political action of the movement."[15] Note the emphasis on young men here, as China would target the same group in its own activities. "Its most notable exploit was the robbery, in 1949, of the Oran Post Office, from which it seized 3,000,000 francs with which to build up its treasury."[16] In March 1950 French colonial police were able to uncover and break up the OS, resulting in hundreds of members, including Ben Bella, arrested and sent to prison. While in prison OS members demonstrated their propaganda skills by going on hunger strikes and publicly exposing French use of torture. Despite French success at breaking up the OS, remnants of the organization remained. "[B]ecause it was a carefully compartmentalized secret organization, many sections survived intact. . . . The organization was decapitated, but many local cell members escaped notice and simply waited for leaders to contact them, and for an occasion to reorganize."[17] The OS was a demonstrably resilient militant wing of Algerian nationalism.

The occasion for OS reorganization came shortly after its apparent demise. Within two years of French success, numerous OS members, including Ben Bella, escaped from prison and relocated either back to Algeria or to Cairo. "That some went to Cairo is important because it helped strengthen Arab influences."[18] Therefore, it may not have been a coincidence that China began its African exploits in Cairo. Former members of the OS formed the Revolutionary Committee of Unity and Action (Comité Révolutionnaire d'Unité et d'Action, CRUA) sometime in 1954. The young group of revolutionaries originated in small towns and villages in the Constantine area, scene of Algerian uprisings in 1871 and 1945. Notably, the common denominator among CRUA members was service in the French army.[19] Although they had military backgrounds, they also drew inspiration from the printed works of the French resistance.[20] The CRUA eventually mutated into the National Liberation Front (Front de Libération Nationale, FLN).

As the Algerian nationalist movement gained momentum, China's foray into North African politics was initiated at the Bandung Conference in April 1955. According to Alistair Horne, the FLN gained an invitation to the conference after "energetic lobbying. . . . Although the Algerians, with no recognised government behind them, attended as 'unofficial' delegates, their presence at Bandung was sufficient to achieve a notable victory on the international scene."[21] Delegates from Egypt to the 1955 conference first introduced Communist China to the independence struggle in French Algeria. The Egyptians introduced a resolution on French North Africa, including Algeria, during the conference.[22] The conference delegates later "adopted unanimously an Egyptian motion proclaiming Algeria's right of independence, and called upon France to implement this forthwith."[23] In his speech at the closing session, moreover, Chinese premier Zhou Enlai declared that China extended its "full sympathy and support to the struggle of the people of Algeria, Morocco and Tunisia for self-determination and independence."[24] From this initial contact at Bandung, China began to play a more active and pragmatic role in Algerian affairs.

To gain access to and understand the situation in Algeria, China established relations with two North African countries: Egypt and Morocco. As scholar W. A. C. Adie wrote, "China's positions in Egypt, Morocco and later Iraq were mainly important as means of access to Algeria."[25] After the Bandung Conference, China moved aggressively to establish relations with Egypt.[26] While the Bandung Conference was ostensibly held to promote peace and stability in Asia and Africa, China successfully exploited the forum to promote its strategic interests worldwide, especially on the African continent. Thus, China's first contact with Egypt at Bandung helped spur direct interaction with African people across the continent.

Through its initial contact with Africans at Bandung, China used a series of contacts and agreements with Egypt to gain access to the African continent. PRC–Egypt talks on cultural cooperation were held in May 1955, a month after Bandung. In 1956 China sent cultural missions to Ethiopia, Morocco, Sudan, and Tunisia.[27] On 15 April 1956, a formal agreement on cultural cooperation was signed between Beijing and Cairo. Soon thereafter, Cairo withdrew recognition of Nationalist China (the Republic of China on Taiwan) and established full diplomatic relations with Communist China on 30 May 1956. In August the

Chinese negotiated to purchase Egyptian cotton, and Egypt negotiated to purchase Chinese steel. By October, China and Egypt agreed to a three-year trade agreement including a most-favored-nation clause and a provision for opening a Chinese trade office in Cairo and an Egyptian trade office in Beijing. In the same year, a Chinese commercial exhibition was held in Cairo, the Beijing Opera Company toured the Middle East, and a large hajj mission went to Mecca.[28] "From Cairo, China's diplomats observed the situation on the continent."[29] Thus, Cairo became China's first base from which it would assess and operate on the African continent.[30]

China exploited its presence in Egypt to further strategic objectives. The operations of one Chinese individual illustrated Cairo's geographic importance. "After the establishment of the Cairo Embassy in 1956, the Commercial Officer, Chan Hsiang-Kang, succeeded in establishing trade relations with Tunisia, Libya, Nigeria, Ghana, Ethiopia and Tanganyika in 1957."[31] Chan benefited from Egypt's geographic position and, later, the presence of numerous African nationalist leaders in Cairo. In December 1957 the establishment of the permanent secretariat of the AAPSO in Cairo "gave the Chinese a base from which to make direct contacts with dissidents from both North and Tropical Africa, without going through the European Communist Parties or the Soviet-controlled international front organizations, such as the WPC [World Peace Council] and WFTU."[32] Moreover, China contributed annual funds to the AAPSO, demonstrating its commitment to African nationalism. "The Cairo Embassy thus became the first basis for Chinese activity in Africa."[33] And China used whatever means available to further its interests in Africa.

Relations between Egypt and China became strained because of the latter's support of Iraq and Syria. Because of its diverse presence in Egypt, however, China was in a position to formally squabble with Egypt while maintaining contacts with informal groups in Cairo. For example, the NCNA established its first office on the African continent in Cairo in 1958.[34] Although the PRC moved elsewhere to enter the Algerian battlefield, Cairo would always remain a strategic location for Chinese operations on the African continent. As Professor Donald Klein wrote in 1964, "Abundant if inferential evidence suggests that the Cairo embassy is the pivotal mission for at least North Africa, and very possibly all of Africa and the Middle East. For example, a high percentage of the innumerable delegations visiting Africa from Peking transit Cairo."[35] In the summer of 1958, moreover, the *Peking Review* wrote, "Chen Chia-kung, China's Ambassador to Cairo called on Premier Nkrumah of Ghana during the latter's recent state visit to the United Arab Republic. They discussed questions relating to the promotion of friendly relations and trade between the two countries."[36] Thus, Cairo was used to contact countries and groups throughout the African continent.

West of Egypt and Algeria was Morocco, independent since 1956. Prior to gaining its independence, the territory played an instrumental role in establishing French colonial power in Africa, and this fact was not lost on Chinese decision makers. "Morocco was the key-stone of the arch and without it [French] colonial fabric in Africa was likely to fall to pieces at the moment of completion."[37] In light of French colonial possessions south of the Sahara, Morocco was termed the cornerstone of French colonial Africa.[38] With the same strategic perspective, China understood Morocco's importance vis-à-vis Europe, the Middle East, and indeed the rest of the African continent.

Like the flurry of diplomacy with Egypt, China quickly established relations with Morocco. "Trade agreements between the PRC and Morocco were signed on October 13, 1957, and on October 27, 1958, and finally full diplomatic relations were established on November 1, 1958."[39] As scholars Richard Lowenthal and Wei Liang-Tsai both attested, thereafter Morocco became one of Beijing's major trading partners in Africa.[40] While Lowenthal and Wei were correct, Communist China's trade with Morocco was not as significant as Morocco's strategic location west of Algeria. "In [1957] cultural and trade contacts were established with Morocco, and through Morocco and other channels China extended financial and other aid, plus training, to the *Front de Liberation* (F.L.N.) [italics in original] in Algeria."[41] This was the first strategic operation to exert Chinese influence on Algeria's war of independence.

Further analyses of Chinese intentions in Morocco reveal a common theme, namely Morocco as a western point of entry into Algeria. According to journalist Fritz Schatten, after establishing full diplomatic relations with Morocco, "China was more interested in Algeria than Morocco." Due to geographic circumstance, Morocco was "the only State in North Africa which offered Peking any chance of exerting influence on the Algerian war." China's "diplomatic activity was concentrated largely in the strategically placed Peking consulates in Tangiers, and in Oujda on the Moroccan-Algerian border."[42] In October 1958 Mehdi Ben Barka, president of the Consultative Assembly of Morocco, accepted an invitation from Liu Shaoqi, chair of the standing committee of the Chinese National People's Congress (NPC), to visit Communist China. The invitation was extended through a Chinese trade delegation visiting Morocco.[43] Numerous sources indicated that the Chinese used Oujda "as a base to support the Algerians against the French."[44]

According to Lowenthal, the Chinese consulate in Oujda was the "principal base of exiled FLN forces in Morocco."[45] After the Moroccan government banned the Communist Party in 1959, China was willing to cease contact with any of its members in order to continue providing military assistance to Algerian nationalists. "Thus, support for revolutionary activity in Algeria received priority [over the global Communist movement]."[46] Time and again in Africa, China prioritized its strategic ends over ideological pursuits. And Chinese activities in Morocco and Egypt laid the path for China to influence the Algerian war for independence. Supporting Algerian independence served China's great power ambitions. Thus, China's actions in Africa were from the very beginning more than revolutionary—they were designed for pragmatic, long-term strategic effect.

Four

SUPPORTING INDEPENDENCE

From the onset, Algerians aligned with China politically. "The War of Independence contributed to a set of beliefs that emphasized Algeria's identification with the newly independent, less developed countries."[1] Like in other wars of national liberation, during the war the Algerians used guerrilla techniques.[2] China exploited the existing situation to support the Algerian independence movement, particularly the existence of the FLN. Created in October 1954, the FLN was an outgrowth of Ahmed Ben Bella's CRUA based in Cairo.[3] The leaders of the Algerian independence movement were a group of nine CRUA leaders known as the historical chiefs (*chefs historiques*). They included Ait Ahmed, Ben Bella, Rabah Bitat, Mohamed Boudiaf, Moustafa Ben Boulaid, Mourad Didouch, Mohamed Khider, Belkacem Krim, and Larbi Ben M'Hidi. Thus, the leadership of the Algerian Revolution was experienced and recognizable.

The CRUA organized a military network in Algeria comprising six military regions (or *wilaya*). The leaders of these military regions and their followers became known as the internals. Ben Bella, Khider, and Ait Ahmed formed the external delegation in Cairo "to gain foreign support for the rebellion and to acquire arms, supplies, and funds for the *wilaya* commanders."[4] The renamed FLN took responsibility for the political direction of the CRUA; the National Liberation Army (Armée de Libération Nationale, ALN) was the FLN's military wing. "The contribution of the CRUA leaders lay mainly in their development of unity and cohesion rather than in their organizational creations. They had infused preexisting structures with a new sense of purpose and cooperation."[5] Experienced political and military organizations were present when China began assisting Algerian independence.[6]

Another significant organization related to the independence movement was the Political and Administrative Organization (Organization Politique et Administrative, OPA). Located in rural and urban environments, OPA cells performed financial and administrative duties; they also disseminated FLN propaganda and supplied intelligence reports. Known as "the backbone of the nationalist movement," the OPA's primary duty was "to undermine the French administration at every level, gradually replacing it with officials and institutions of the revolutionary party."[7] As a result, the OPA helped manage and sustain the Algerian nationalist movement while also carrying out significant portions of the FLN's operations. Such an organization benefited China's strategic activities on the ground.

In China's initial ploy, Premier Zhou Enlai called for negotiations in June 1956 between France and the Algerian resistance on the basis of full recognition of the national aspiration of the Algerian people.[8] "Peking regarded the Algerian *Front de la Libération Nationale* (FLN) [italics in original] as an avant-garde anti-colonialist movement and sought to shape it, along the lines of the Viet-Minh movement in Indo-China, into an instrument of revolutionary strategy against France and against the West generally."[9] The leaders of the FLN, it was believed, decided on an "Indochinese discussion" as well.[10] Reports also speculated that captured French Algerian soldiers in Vietnam were being converted into Algerian revolutionaries. Without citing any source directly, Alistair Horne wrote, "Employing subtlest techniques of psychological warfare, the Viet-Minh suggestively quizzed the Algerians captured there: 'Since you are such good soldiers, why do you fight for the colonialists? Why don't you fight for yourselves and get yourselves a country of your own?'"[11] Nevertheless, Zhou's action was an example of China communicating directly and publicly to the Algerian people, only about a year after the Bandung Conference, to attempt to shape the strategic environment.

China also communicated its message through public demonstrations. For example, in November 1957 China celebrated a "national day of solidarity with the Algerian people."[12] Utilizing the First Afro-Asian People's Solidarity Conference, which was held in Cairo from 26 December 1957 to 1 January 1958, China demonstrated its ability to communicate through international organizations as well.[13] At the conference, the Chinese delegation reaffirmed its country's support for the Algerian people. Two months later, on 30 March 1958 (designated Algeria Day by the Afro-Asian People's Solidarity Conference), China held its Support Algeria demonstration.[14] The event, "which included a mass rally and exhibition of maps and photographs, and statements from Chinese leaders," was held in

Beijing.[15] A resolution adopted at the rally pledged "full support for the just cause of the people of Algeria and of Africa as a whole in their efforts to secure and safeguard their national independence."[16]

On hand during the rally was Burhan Shahidi, chair of the Islamic Association of People's China, who stated, "[T]he Chinese people regard the Algerian people's struggle and victories as their own."[17] Kuo Mo-jo, member of the Chinese-African Solidarity Committee and a Chinese peace leader, was also on hand. In Beijing, Premier Zhou Enlai and Foreign Minister Chen Yi received Ibrahim Ghafa of the FLN and Atef Daniel of the Arab People's Conference. In this four-month span, Communist China used mass rallies and public statements to demonstrate full Chinese support for Algerian independence in addition to making direct contact with the FLN. These events may be discounted as simple actions. It is clear, however, that China used these planned demonstrations to influence relations with Algeria. China's verbal and moral support demonstrated to the Algerians the nature of Chinese intentions, adding a psychological element to Chinese activities. China provided multiple forms of public support, both in China and in Africa. China's leaders were clearly interested in supporting independence in Algeria.

Chinese material support began a month later.[18] In April 1958 China sent 500,000 yuan via the All-China Federation of Trade Unions (ACFTU), Islamic Association of People's China, and the Asian Solidarity Committee to the FLN, according to multiple sources.[19] In an article published in the *Peking Review* that same month, China gave additional moral support to the Algerian cause. It stated, "Now North Africa is in the forefront against colonialism. Fighting heroically, Algeria has become their beacon light in this struggle."[20] Although meager, Chinese financial contributions combined with publicly communicated support served useful purposes. China's political support for the Algerian cause became immediately tangible later that same year.

China was the first Communist country to offer to establish official diplomatic relations with the Provisional Government of the Algerian Republic (Gouvernement Provisionel de la République Algérienne, or GPRA) after its formation by Ferhat Abbas in the autumn of 1958. The provisional government was created on 18–19 September 1958; Beijing granted recognition on 22 September.[21] China recognized the newly formed GPRA after Foreign Minister Chen Yi informed Foreign Minister Mohamed Lamine Debaghine of Algeria of the decision in a message on 22 September 1958. In greetings sent to Premier Ferhat Abbas, Premier Zhou Enlai declared, "As in the past the Chinese people will firmly stand by the heroic and indomitable Algerian people."[22] Giving the GPRA immediate recognition was part of China's overall approach to Algeria and Africa in general. Public support for and acknowledgment of the newly created Algerian government was a psychological boost for the Algerians, even if they did not expect formal diplomatic recognition. This type of Chinese public support was essential for China, given its meager national resources for international relations.

By the end of the year, Beijing and the GPRA began face-to-face diplomatic engagements. An Algerian ministerial delegation led by Ben Yossef Ben Khedda arrived in Beijing on 3 December 1958.[23] On 5 December a mass rally was staged in Beijing where Burhan Shahidi, once again, voiced Chinese support for the Algerian struggle.[24] China reinforced the need to continue armed struggle, providing both verbal and moral support to the Algerian independence cause. At a 7 December banquet in honor of the Algerian government delegation, moreover, Vice Premier and Foreign Minister Chen Yi pledged Communist China's full support for the Algerian people's struggle for national independence.[25] Prior to the arrival of the Algerian delegation, Minister of Information Mohammed Yazid suggested that the delegation, invited by China, would negotiate for material support, including the possibility of military supplies.[26] Notably, Mahmoud Sherif, minister of armaments and supplies, was one of the delegates sent to China. While in China, the Algerian delegation spent an entire day with officers and men of an infantry division of the PLA stationed near the capital.[27] According to UN sources, the most likely Chinese supply route to Algeria would be by sea in neutral ships to remote landing points in Tunisia or Morocco, and then by land across Algeria's extensive frontiers.[28] While specific evidence of Chinese assistance was not revealed, Ben Khedda's visit illustrated a recurrent form of Chinese influence, communications, and negotiations through exchange visits to China. Algerian visits to China allowed the Chinese to, as in dynastic times, manipulate the environment to suit their objectives.

After a second visit of the Algerian delegation to China in the same month, the fruit of Chinese activities was a Sino-Algerian communiqué, signed on 20 December 1958. The Algerian delegation was in China for a total of sixteen days.[29] Signed by Foreign Minister Chen Yi and Minister Sherif, the communiqué stated, "During the talks, the two parties studied concrete methods to strengthen relations between the two countries and affirmed the principle of establishing diplomatic and cultural relations between the two countries." The communiqué concluded by indicating "their determination to further strengthen friendly co-operation between the two countries."[30] Evidence of "concrete methods" occurred on the last day of the Algerian delegation's stay in China, when it made a two-hour visit to a

Beijing gymnasium. The Algerian minister of armaments and supplies revealed that his government would send a football team and other "sportsmen" to China.[31] Understanding the nature of sports in Communist countries—athletes often were military personnel—this Algerian delegation to China most likely comprised members of the ALN. The same day the joint communiqué was signed, a reception for the UAR ambassador to China, Hassan Ragab, was held in honor of the visiting Algerian delegation. Chen Yi gave a speech at the reception, saying, "The Algerian people's struggle against French imperialism is a component part of the anti-imperialist struggle of the Arab and African peoples."[32] Here, a high-level Chinese official acknowledged the connection between Egypt and Algeria (i.e., the unity of North Africa). Furthermore, with this joint communiqué China laid the foundation for future activities in Algeria.

By the end of 1958, according to one observer, "Active support for the FLN . . . now became the heart of Red China's African policy."[33] Circumstantial evidence indicated that China was already active in its security assistance to the Algerian independence movement. Wei Liang-Tsai reported, "Algerian soldiers were trained in China, and between 1959 and 1962, when France agreed to grant independence to Algeria, the PRC supplied arms worth about $10 million to the Algerians."[34] More specifically, China allegedly financed Algerian arms purchases in the Middle East and Europe by "an interest-free loan" method and trained selected Algerian officers in China, as early as spring 1959.[35] In October 1959 Iraqi president Kassem announced that he had sent ten planeloads of arms and £500,000 to the Algerians via Libya.[36] General Kassem "also indicated that the Chinese had given other aid to the Algerians of which he had no personal knowledge."[37] While more specific evidence would offer a detailed assessment of Chinese operations, clearly China was intent on providing the FLN with whatever support was needed—from weapons and equipment to funds and training—to achieve independence. China's support for Algerian independence was indicative of its perception of Africa—strategic and long term in nature. Within five years of the Bandung Conference, China was an active player in African affairs.

In 1959 China communicated indirectly through international forums, as well as by way of assistance to the Algerian people and government. The Afro-Asian Youth Conference opened in Cairo on 2 February 1959.[38] Liu Hsi-yan, head of the Chinese delegation, noted that this was the first time numerous youth from Asia and Africa had come together. Zhou Enlai sent a message of greetings to the conference, hoping it would make a contribution to Afro-Asian unity much as the Bandung Conference and the Afro-Asian People's Solidarity Conference had done. Thus began the persistent Chinese targeting of Algerian youth. The following month the Chinese Red Cross Society sent 15,000 yuan to the Moroccan Red Crescent Society and 10,000 yuan to the Tunisian Red Crescent Society "as contributions to the Algerian refugees now in exile in those countries."[39] While this assistance was relatively small, it conveyed China's continual intention of assisting Algerians inside and outside Algeria. Later in the year, on 18 September 1959, Zhou Enlai sent a message of greetings to Premier Ferhat Abbas on the first anniversary of the founding of the Algerian provisional government. The message reiterated Chinese support for the Algerian people's struggle for national independence.[40] China did not relent in its support for Algerian independence.

Also in 1959, an Algerian military delegation "headed by Omar Oussedik, Secretary of State, and an experienced guerilla fighter" arrived in Beijing on 29 March.[41] At the invitation of Minister of National Defense Marshal Peng Tehhuai, the delegation was in China until May, touring military academies and installations (presumably to gain a better understanding of PLA training and doctrine). Chen Yi and Mahmoud Sherif signed a Sino-Algerian communiqué on 6 April 1959.[42] Although the communiqué was not explicit, the fact that the minister of armaments and supply cosigned the document was an indication of Chinese objectives. Notably, in March Tunisian president Habib Bourguiba had stated that he would not oppose China supplying arms to the FLN.[43] With reference to cross-border arms transfers, Heggoy wrote, "Still later the ALN-FLN sent young recruits to their sanctuaries in Tunisia and in Morocco. There they were able to train the men and keep them out of the hands of the various French institutions of counterrevolutionary education."[44] And in April the military mission of ten FLN officers led by Omar Oussedik told the Belgian News Agency that twenty Algerians were being trained as pilots in China.[45]

About the same time, a mass rally was held in Beijing for Support Algeria Week (5–11 April 1959). On hand were members of the visiting Algerian military delegation, led by Oussedik. In his speech to the rally, Oussedik noted that the Chinese were helping "the Algerian people combat the coalition of imperialist powers."[46] Five hundred representatives of the PLA were also at the rally. Meanwhile, in May 1959 the Algerian military delegation completed its monthlong visit to China, having visited eastern, southern, and northeastern China. "In a farewell message, its leader Omar Oussedik declared that his delegation was returning home with far richer experience and a new firmer determination to battle the French colonialists."[47] According to Western reports in autumn 1959, China had spent somewhere between $4 million and $10 million for weapons, propaganda, and administration for Algerian rebels.[48] In December 1959 China received another Algerian military delegation in Beijing. "This delegation, led by Armaments Minister Sherif, and Social Minister Ben Chedda, had a number of discussions with prominent generals of the Peking Defence Ministry. Before long a second FLN delegation arrived in Peking."[49] The repeated Algerian military delegation visits to China reinforced Chinese support to the Algerian cause and helped the Algerian guerrillas enhance their capabilities. Through a combination of exchange visits and material and financial support, China demonstrated its strategic interests in Algeria—and in Africa.

While providing material assistance, China continued to communicate to the Algerian people. On 17 November 1959 a General Union of Algerian Workers delegation visited Beijing to discuss means to assist Algeria in the war against France: Rahmoune Dekkar, secretary of the General Union of Algerian Workers (Union Générale des Travailleurs Algériens, or UGTA); Mohamed Bernon, member of the executive committee; and Pierre Namat, member of the agricultural committee.[50] Zhou Enlai and Liu Chang-sheng, vice chair of the ACFTU, invited the delegation to China. On 31 December 1959 Liu Ningyi, president of the ACFTU, sent a letter to the secretariat of the Foreign Mission of the General Union of Algerian Workers, paying respect to the fifth anniversary of the Algerian people's war against France.[51] Finally, the ACFTU and Chinese National Women's Federation sent "medicines and children's clothing worth fifty thousand yuan" in December 1959 in response to a worldwide appeal to provide help for Algerian refugees. The appeal was issued the previous September by a committee for solidarity with the workers and people of Algeria at the conference of the International Trade Union in solidarity with the people of Algeria.[52]

On China's designated Algeria Day on 30 March 1960, the Chinese Committee for Afro-Asian Solidarity issued a special statement of support, as did organizations of workers, women, and youth. Paying respect to their "Algerian brothers," the messages stated that Algeria was at "the forefront of the struggle against imperialism and colonialism."[53] With personal visits, messages, and distribution of funds, China combined its means of influence in support of Algeria. China emphasized an empathetic message to the Algerian people, repeatedly calling for Algerian independence. China was demonstrating its commitment not only to Algeria, but also to Africa.

Meanwhile, China continued to assist the Algerians militarily. In 1964 Adie reported that Chinese equipment had been found on the battlefield in Algeria early in 1960.[54] In spring 1960 another high-level Algerian delegation visited

China and was received by Chairman Mao.[55] Led by Vice Premier and Minister of Foreign Affairs Krim Belkacem, the GPRA delegation was met at the airport by Vice Premier Ho Lung, Senior General Lo Jui-ching, who was concurrently vice premier and chief of the General Staff of the PLA, Vice Premier Hsi Chung-hsun, and other "leading government officials and leaders of popular Chinese organizations."[56] At a banquet for the Algerian delegation, Vice Premier Ho Lung declared, "[T]he Chinese people have always stood firmly by the African peoples in their struggle for national independence, and will continue to stand shoulder to shoulder with them in the future to bring the struggle against imperialism and colonialism to its conclusion."[57] The senior-level Algerian visit to China was a significant milestone in Sino-Algerian relations, given Mao's presence. China conferred its highest level of political support to date to the Algerian independence movement.

A report following the Algerian delegation's visit to China hinted at additional military assistance to the FLN. "The Algerians have sent a mission of three high-ranking members of the Provisional Government to Communist China to discuss material aid . . . for nationalist guerrilla forces in Algeria."[58] Another communiqué in May affirmed China's support continued for Algeria and Algeria's "full support" for China's recovery of Taiwan. The communiqué also stated, "The two parties studied various ways to enhance friendly co-operation between China and Algeria."[59] (Significantly, the director of the West Asian and African Department of the foreign ministry, Ho Ying, took part in the talks with the Algerian delegation. Ho would later become ambassador to Tanganyika and, subsequently, to Tanzania.) That same day Krim Belkacem thanked China for its "tangible aid" and "material sacrifices."[60] As China continued its support for Algerian independence, for the first time Algeria voiced its support for Chinese interests.

U.S. analysis at the time recognized Chinese actions in the region. "In Africa, the USIA [U.S. Information Agency] reported, Red China [was] concentrating on 'anti-colonialist' propaganda and support of the Algerian Nationalist movement. Chinese Communist diplomatic missions have been set up in Morocco and Guinea, it said."[61] Left unsaid was that both missions served as transit points for Chinese activities in Algeria. By July 1960 China had become the first Communist government to accept permanent representation from the GPRA, offering the Algerians even closer relations with the Chinese.[62] In the same month Feng Chih-tan, a Chinese commentator, likened the Algerian struggle to the Chinese struggle, specifically citing the peasant aspects of both. "Without the active participation of this huge peasant force, there could be no powerful national independence movement in Africa. The war for national independence in Algeria, for instance, is basically a peasant war."[63] Through this public pronouncement China created a sense of commonality—a shared strategic understanding—between the two countries, thereby furthering its influence in Algeria, specifically, and in Africa, as a whole.

A U.S. report in the summer of 1960 indicated the intimacy of the PRC-FLN relationship. "A close relationship is developing between Communist China and the government in exile of the Algerian rebels [of] the FLN, in Tunis."[64] The same article referred to Chinese "technicians" and "specialists" flooding into North Africa. "Chinese technicians and specialists in various fields are flooding into Libya, Tunisia, Morocco and the newly independent nations to the south. They are promoting trade, cultural and scientific and technical exchanges at every level, with special emphasis on students and young intellectuals."[65] Chinese technicians and specialists were in various North African countries and served as another means of communicating the Chinese message to the African people, as well as gaining intelligence on the local environments. This was the first tangible evidence of China's strategic presence in Africa.

In September 1960 Chairman Liu Shaoqi, Premier Zhou, and Vice Premier and Foreign Minister Chen Yi sent greetings to leaders of the GPRA on occasion of the second anniversary of its establishment.[66] Premier Zhou noted that the "militant friendship" and cooperation between the two peoples was being "continuously developed and consolidated," and Premier Ferhat Abbas accepted Premier Zhou's invitation to visit the PRC for National Day celebrations. The continual reciprocation of visits demonstrated the intimacy of the relations of the two governments. At about the same time, China sent a military mission to Cairo, creating speculation that China might offer large-scale military assistance to the FLN. General Chang Tsung-hsun, deputy chief of staff of the army, led the military mission. Other members of the delegation included Lieutenant General Liu Shao-wen of the PLA, Rear Admiral Chang Yuan-upei of the navy, Major General Wut Sung-hsien of the air force, Major General Teng Chia-tai of the army, and numerous other high-ranking army officers.[67] From Cairo, China developed and furthered its relations with the Algerian independence movement. From China, China continued to support Algeria as well.

An Algerian delegation led by Premier Ferhat Abbas visited China from 29 September to 6 October 1960, attending the eleventh anniversary of the founding of the PRC. The Algerian delegation included Minister of Interior Bentobal Lakdar, Director of the Premier's Office Benyakia Mohamed, Director of Political

Affairs (Ministry of Information) Boumendjel Ahmed, and Director of Political Affairs (Ministry of Interior) Khene Lamine.[68] On the evening of 29 September the delegation attended a banquet in its honor where Premier Zhou voiced Chinese support for the Algerians. Premier Zhou stated, "We will do everything we can to support the Algerian people's struggle for national liberation." He later added in the speech, "We have done so and will continue to do so in the future."[69] In reply, Premier Abbas stated Algeria's intention, like China's, to spread its revolution throughout the region: "We will then turn to our neighbors, asking them to participate more actively, to the brother countries, to the Arab countries, and to all free peoples who cannot allow an explosive situation liable to endanger world peace to continue."[70] Algerian and Chinese interests had united. China had developed close ties with an African counterpart. On 30 September Chairman Mao and Chairman Liu received Premier Abbas and the delegation in Beijing. At the invitation of the CAPFA, a twenty-four-member Algerian art troupe attended the National Day celebration.[71] Significantly, this was the first African art troupe to visit Communist China.

Later, China and Algeria signed a joint communiqué on 5 October, which stated, "The Chinese Government reiterated its firm stand of rendering unfailing assistance and support to the just struggle of the Algerian people." In reply, the Algerian government voiced support to China. The Algerian side "expressed full support for the Chinese people's just struggle to liberate their own territory," adding, "The two parties further studied various ways for promoting the relations of friendship and co-operation between the two countries."[72] The joint communiqué was a clear indication of the strong bilateral relationship between China and Algeria.

In his farewell speech at the Beijing airport on 6 October, Premier Abbas concluded, "We are returning home with the conviction that the People's Republic of China stands resolutely by the Algerian people against imperialism and that it will not cease to support the Algerian people, materially and morally, until they attain independence."[73] And in an interview with an Italian Communist newspaper at the end of the month, Premier Abbas said China would provide "multiform aid" to the Algerian rebels. Abbas further stated that China could provide assistance "on a material and on a diplomatic plane."[74] Ferhat's September visit to China confirmed the status and direction of relations. Both visits communicated the same message of public mutual support, and China once again agreed to support Algerian independence, politically and materially.

To demonstrate China's level of development, China participated in the October 1960 International Fair in Tunis with a 2,160-square-meter pavilion of industrial and agricultural exhibits. The Algerian minister of state, Said Mohamadi, visited the Chinese pavilion and endorsed China's development path in the visitor's book.[75] Once again China used an international venue to influence Algerian leadership. On 1 November seven Chinese people's organizations sponsored a rally to commemorate the sixth anniversary of the Algerian Revolution. Vice Premier Chen Yi and Chairman of the Chinese Committee for Afro-Asian Solidarity Liao Cheng-chih were both present. Notable speakers at the rally included Burhan Shahidi, vice chair of the Chinese Committee for Afro-Asian Solidarity and vice president of the CAPFA; Li Chieh-po, vice president of the ACFTU; Rafa Abdel Madjid, head of the visiting Algerian art troupe; Malan Tanko Yakasai, a national organizer of the Northern Elements Progressive Union of Nigeria; Alao Aka Bushorun, a trade union worker from Nigeria; and Ahmed Mohammed Kheil, a Sudanese "peace champion."[76]

Also in November 1960, astute observers in Tunis predicted that China's "multiform aid" to the FLN would consist of arms, money, and technicians. Algerians quoted Mao Zedong as saying that China would provide "multiform and growing help" to the FLN.[77] These same observers expected Communist technicians to help breach the frontier line that was isolating the interior of Algeria from nationalist arms and men in Tunisia. In addition, the technicians would serve as ideological warfare counselors. In my opinion, this should be interpreted as guerrilla warfare advisers rather than Communist political commissars. Although observers did not expect aid to arrive until the following year, the rumors of immediate Chinese aid to the FLN served to influence public perception of the strength of bilateral relations. In the same month, an NCNA correspondent made much of the fact that FLN officers were studying Mao's works and using Chinese guerrilla methods.[78] Also in that same month, Reuters claimed that China set up in Amoy and other parts of Fujian Province training centers for Chinese volunteers to work in Algeria.[79] Once again, China combined active public communications with handsome political and material support.

China continued to voice support for Algerian independence until it was achieved. On occasion of the National Day against Partition on 5 July 1961, China expressed full support for the Algerian people's recent resistance to the colonists' attempt to carve up their country. Chinese organizations, including the Committee for Afro-Asian Solidarity, the ACFTU, and the CAPFA, "declared that Sahara is the inalienable and sacred territory of Algeria and that the scheme of French imperialism to separate the Sahara from Algeria is a gross violation of and encroachment on the sovereignty and the territorial integrity of Algeria."[80] This was in concert with China's views on territorial integrity and sovereignty, which were embodiments of the Bandung Conference. Later in the year, on 18 September, Chairman Liu and Premier Zhou sent a greeting to Algerian premier Ben Youssef Ben Khedda on the third anniversary of the establishment of the GPRA. The message expressed confidence that the "militant friendship" between the two peoples would grow firmer with each passing day.[81] Furthermore, the following month a Chinese commentator describing the Algerian Revolution wrote, "The Chinese people along with the other peoples of the socialists countries, have extended [the Algerians] active support from the very beginning."[82] On 1 November Premier Zhou sent another message to Premier Ben Khedda on the anniversary of the beginning of the Algerian war. At a mass rally, Liu Ningyi, president of the ACFTU and vice chair of the Chinese Committee for Afro-Asian Solidarity, attended a celebration in Beijing for the same occasion.[83] Abderrahmane Kiouane, head of the GPRA diplomatic mission to China, also addressed the gathering. The repeated communications and mass rallies were Chinese attempts to convince Algerians—as well as all observant Africans—of China's firm support to Algerian independence.

China was, therefore, from 1955 onward, a staunch and active supporter of Algerian independence. According to the CIA, "The Chinese supplied approximately $15 million, beginning in 1959, to support Algerian nationalist military activity."[84] While the exact figure may be uncertain, it was clear that China provided material support—funds, arms, and equipment—as well as robust political support—communications in print, mass rallies, and exchange visits—to the FLN. In 1962 the Algerians finally achieved their goal of independence, this after consistent assistance from China.

Five

CLOSE AND MILITANT

On 20 March 1962 Premier Zhou sent a letter of congratulations to Premier Ben Khedda on occasion of the Algerian-French ceasefire agreement.[1] The letter read in part, "The conclusion of the agreement between Algeria and France is the result of armed struggle waged heroically by the Algerian people for more than seven years, and of their perseverance in negotiations on an equal footing and on the basis of armed struggle." A 20 March editorial in *People's Daily* commended the Algerians for using "the revolutionary double tactics of combining armed struggle with negotiations." In other words, they used armed struggle and "struggle through negotiations."[2] Zhou's letter continued, "The close and militant friendship between the Chinese and Algerian people is based on reliable foundations."[3] Thus, the PRC had believed armed struggle, and support thereof, was the key to success. Since 1956 China had provided multiform support to the Algerian cause, so the Chinese were pleased when the Algerians achieved independence from France in July 1962. On 3 July 1962 Chairman Liu and Premier Zhou sent a message to Premier Ben Khedda, congratulating him on Algeria's independence.[4] Foreign Minister Chen Yi sent a message to Foreign Minister Saad Dahlad, announcing China's decision to recognize independent Algeria.[5] The fruits of Chinese assistance bore fruit in North Africa, and China remained steadfast in its support of Algeria.

After Algeria formally gained independence in 1962, China continued its economic support of the regime, giving approximately $1.8 million that same year.[6] The Chinese Red Cross Society donated 20,679 yuan (about £3,000) to the Red Crescent Society of Algeria in response to its appeal.[7] The donation and a letter from the Chinese Red Cross were presented on 13 June 1962 in Beijing by

Peng Yen, secretary general of the Society, to Amor Soukhal, third secretary of the diplomatic mission of Algeria to China. Later that same month, two NCNA reporters who toured North Africa for more than two years published an article in the *Peking Review*. The article recounted a tour of the eastern front (along the Algerian-Tunisian border), interviews with former imprisoned Algerian women, and a tour of an ALN-run village.[8] The publication of such a report was meant to expose the worldwide public to independent Algeria, which was supported by China. Thus, China attempted to provide the Algerian government and people with financial and moral assistance. (Moral assistance was in terms of Chinese publishing and sympathizing with the human side of the Algerian struggle for independence.)

Chinese personnel traveled to Algeria soon after it gained independence, placing an emphasis on rebuilding the country. On 10 September 1962 Hsien Yi, chargé d'affaires ad interim of China to Algeria, arrived in Algeria.[9] In a press statement Hsien declared that the Chinese people had always sympathized with and resolutely supported the Algerian people. In a tangible show of support, nine thousand tons of Chinese wheat arrived in Bone in September 1962. Presented in response to an appeal by the Political Bureau of the FLN to help rebuild Algeria, the gift also included three thousand tons of rolled steel—for construction uses—and twenty-one tons of medical supplies.[10] In October 1962 Vice Minister of Defence Senior General Hsu Kuang-ta of the PRC attended independence celebrations and was warmly greeted by Houari Boumediene, senior member of the FLN.[11] That same month, on the eve of China's National Day celebration, "Foreign Minister Mohammed Khemisti said that admission of Communist China to the United Nations would be a basic plank in Algeria's foreign policy."[12] Khemisti was speaking at a reception to mark the PRC National Day. This was an early example of independent Algeria's support for China internationally, plain and simple. Similarly, observer Waverley Root associated Chinese military aid to the FLN with China's desire for Algerian gratitude in concrete form: "Chinese arms were supplied to the National Liberation Front during the Algerian revolution, and FLN leaders were received lavishly in Peking. Now that the recipients of Chinese aid and favor are in power, Peking hopes that gratitude will be shown in concrete form."[13] China did not need to request Algerian gratitude publicly, however, in light of the various communications, rallies, and visits between the two countries. In effect, China had created an environment in which Algeria would be favorable to Chinese interests.

Sino-Algerian exchange visits—communications in person—became regular after 1962. A five-member Chinese public health delegation visited Algeria in March 1963.[14] Two months later Premier Zhou received two delegations from Algeria.[15] They were a delegation of the General Union of Algerian Workers and a delegation of Algerian women. China was clearly targeting certain aspects of the Algerian population for influence: labor and women. In August 1963 Chairman Mao and Premier Zhou on separate occasions received a visiting Algerian journalists' delegation led by Meghraoui Mohamed, member of the Algerian Constituent National Assembly and of its foreign affairs and press committees.[16] By conferring time with an assembly member, China was providing legitimacy to the Algerian government—communicating a powerful message of political support.

In Algeria, President Ben Bella opened China's exhibition on economic construction on 31 August 1963. On display for four weeks in Algiers, more than 150,000 people viewed the exhibition, expressing their wish for closer Algeria-China friendship in the common struggle against imperialism and for strengthening of trade relations.[17] With this exhibition, China attempted to influence the Algerian population's perception of China's economic development capabilities. To influence other aspects of society, Algeria and China signed a cultural agreement for the exchange of books, artists, films, and radio programs on 12 September 1963.[18] This first treaty between Algeria and China was a conduit for close ties because it created direct Chinese communications channels to Algeria—in print, radio, and motion picture. On 9 October 1963 China offered Algeria a long-term loan of $50 million. The *New York Times*, among others, believed the loan to involve technical aid and shipments of machinery rather than cash.[19] The *Peking Review*, on the other hand, reported, "On 11 October 1963 it was announced that China agreed to extend long-term, interest-free loan to Algeria amounting to 250 million French francs (or 25,000 million old Francs)."[20] Chinese ambassador Tseng Tao made the offer in Algiers during a meeting with Minister of Foreign Affairs Abdellaziz Bouteflika. Thus, China was attempting to cement political and economic relations with Algeria at the same time that it attempted to communicate to and influence the Algerian population's attitude and the government's behavior.

Also in October 1963 an Algerian government delegation led by Minister of State Amar Ouzegane concluded a five-day goodwill visit to China. Interestingly, the *Peking Review* reported that the Algerians spent ten days in China.[21] The visit coincided with the Chinese aid offer. On an invitation by Vice Premier and Foreign Minister Chen Yi, the Algerian delegation attended China's National

Day celebrations in Beijing and visited Hangzhou, Shanghai, and Kunming. In a speech at Yunnan University, Minister of State Ouzegane mentioned how Chairman Mao's ideology on revolutionary war spread throughout Algerian towns and villages. Ouzegane's recognition of China's propaganda influence demonstrated the success of Chinese activities overseas. Accompanying Minister Ouzegane, Chen Yi spoke of the need to "take an active part in the revolution [and] firmly struggle against the enemy" to "contribute to the revolutionary cause of the people throughout the world."[22] Although the Algerians had achieved independence, it was significant that China continued to emphasize the call for change in the world, with particular focus on Africa.

In a separate trip later in the month, five Chinese delegations traveled to Algeria to participate in Algeria's National Day celebrations. On 27 October President Ben Bella received the Communist Party of China delegation led by Liu Ningyi, member of the Central Committee; the government delegation led by Fang Yi, vice chair of the State Planning Commission; and a military delegation led by General Li Chih-min, political commissar of the Military Academy of the PLA. Two other delegations on hand were a women's delegation and a youth and students' delegation. The multiple delegations revealed the close Sino-Algerian relations, where a variety of issues could be discussed. On 28 October 1963 the Sino-Algerian economic and technical cooperation agreement was signed in the hall of the People's Palace in Algiers. After signing the agreement, Minister of Foreign Affairs Bouteflika said, "Algeria considers this agreement a new page in the history of relations between the peoples of China and Algeria."[23] Although Bouteflika's statement may have been hyperbole, the economic and technical agreement certainly encompassed various significant aspects of their relations over time. And it solidified already intimate relations between the two countries.

On the eve of the second Algeria National Day and the ninth anniversary of the Algerian Revolution, Chinese leaders—Chairman Mao, Chairman Liu, Premier Zhou, and Chairman Chu Teh (of the Standing Committee of the NPC)—sent a joint message to the Algerian leaders hailing the Algerian Revolution and Sino-Algerian friendship. The message assured the Algerians that "the Chinese people [would] remain for ever their most reliable friends in the defense of their independence, building of their country and the development of their revolution."[24] Liao Cheng-chih, chair of the Communist Chinese Committee for Afro-Asian Solidarity, and Major Ben Djedid Chadli, head of the visiting Algerian military delegation, addressed a Beijing rally on 1 November. Although by this time statements on anniversaries were not novel, the Chinese message in this instance notably included both security and development issues. Examined in this manner the statement bears considerable weight while maintaining Chinese communication to the Algerian government and people.

At the end of the year, Schatten reported that Chinese propaganda on guerrilla warfare was widely distributed and received amongst the Algerian public. On 22 December 1963 an NCNA correspondent writing from Algiers "described how he had been left with the impression that Mao's work enjoyed wide popularity among the people." According to the correspondent, Mao's works on guerrilla warfare circulated underground, in prison, and among FLN guerrillas. "He also recalled how he had found four well-worn volumes of Mao's *Selected Works* in French and a copy of *Problems of Strategy in China's Revolutionary War*, copiously annotated in Arabic, in the political commissar's office in a barracks near the Moroccan border."[25] Mao's works served to educate the common or imprisoned Algerian and to assist in training Algerian militants.[26] China had influenced the Algerian people ideologically, on the ground, in Algeria.

Within one year of Algerian independence, it was believed that Algeria was becoming a base of operations for national liberation movements in Africa, as China intended. "In 1963 the [Algerian] government provided training to 1,000 guerrillas from Mozambique, South Africa, and Angola."[27] More broadly, a U.S. State Department report on the world situation submitted to the House Foreign Affairs Committee on 2 April 1964 listed Algeria, Angola, Ghana, Mali, and Zanzibar among "critical points" subject to Communist influence.[28] While difficult to corroborate in open sources, the activity of one Chinese official was significant: "Colonel Hu Pin-fu, the Chinese military attaché, had become one of the most active, if discreet, figures on the Algerian diplomatic scene by early 1964." Colonel Hu benefited from the cover provided by various technical specialists traveling to Algeria, and to North Africa in general. A Western source, while not mentioning Colonel Hu, made reference to Chinese experts and officers training the Algerian military and Moroccan rebels.[29] Taking into account Ouzegane's October 1963 visit to China, Algeria was becoming a base for revolution in Africa; this allowed China to use its resources across the African continent. Addressing the first Algerian congress in April 1964, President Ben Bella cited support for and aid to the liberation movements in Angola, Mozambique, Portuguese Guinea, and South Africa.[30] Furthermore, the Algerians, after fighting the French for eight years, had the expertise and equipment to support other groups seeking a guerrilla war against a European power. Algerian support of African liberation movements was in Chinese interests, primarily because it furthered the redistribution of power in Africa, which allowed for greater Chinese influence on the continent.

On a much-publicized visit, Premier Zhou traveled to several North and West African countries—including Algeria—between 21 December 1963 and 12 January 1964.[31] Premier Zhou and Foreign Minister Chen Yi arrived in Algiers on 21 December. In his welcoming speech, President Ben Bella recalled the mutual help between China and Algeria and between Asia and Africa in their common struggle for liberation. Thanking the Algerians for their hospitality, Premier Zhou replied, "In the protracted struggles against imperialism and colonialism, the Chinese and the Algerian peoples have always sympathized with and supported each other and formed a profound comradeship-in-arms."[32] As a show of hospitality, the *New York Times* reported, "President Ahmed Ben Bella of Algeria, grateful to Peking for aid rendered during his country's war for independence from France, wanted to bolster his credentials as a leader of a truly revolutionary government. Thus, Algeria staged the [only] full-dress welcome the 50-man Chinese delegation received in North Africa." This was, perhaps, also a sign of close military relations and support for national liberation movements in Africa. The importance of the military parade was more than symbolic due to the continuing Chinese assistance to Algeria. While Algeria was referred to as "the country most susceptible to Peking's influence" at the time, there was no reason to believe Algeria would act blindly in Chinese interests.[33] This was another reason for continued Chinese efforts in Algeria specifically, and in Africa as a whole.

Premier Zhou also made a nine-day trip to Albania during this tour of ten African countries.[34] The special relationship between China and Albania was known prior to this visit.[35] Significantly, although not overtly acknowledged, Czechoslovakian arms had been supplied to the FLN during the war, and Albania served as the transit country. As one commentator noted, "The importance of a Communist-controlled Mediterranean port for North African operations may indeed have contributed to the growth of Chinese interest in Albania."[36] In addition, Professor Jan Prybyla reported that the Albanian Union of Working Youth "occasionally act[ed] for the Chinese in East Africa, Libya, Algeria, Tunisia, and Morocco."[37] Within this broader context, Zhou's visit to Albania was not a sidetrip but rather an extension of China's influence in North Africa, with shared borders along the Mediterranean Sea. Algeria and North Africa were strategically important to China.

Thus, in 1964 communications in person through exchange visits continued, with Algerians visiting China. On 17 January Abderrachid Gherab, a leader of the FLN and a leading member of the General Financial Administration, and an Algerian jurists' delegation led by Ben Abdallah Abdessamad, president of the

Justice and Legislation Commission of the National Assembly, arrived in Beijing. Mao received them on 28 January, and two days later they left for Shanghai to tour the country.[38] At the end of January 1964 Minister of National Economy Bachir Boumaza raised the possibility that Algeria would sell oil to China. Minister Boumaza said Algeria would sell oil abroad to Brazil, Spain, and other countries "whose names I cannot cite."[39] Rather than allowing the French to exploit Saharan oil and natural gas, Boumaza said Algeria would exploit these resources on its own and with the help of foreign partners. Although a final resolution on this matter was not discovered, it is possible that the Algerians were attempting to coax non-French Western interests into exploring Algerian natural resources. And though China may not have had the technological capabilities to extract oil at the time, this was a significant political statement of Algerian support for long-term Chinese strategic interests.

While access to natural resources was important, China also continued to cultivate broad political relations with Algeria. Chairman Mao received an Algerian cultural delegation led by Malek Ben Nabi, adviser to the Ministry of National Orientation, and its deputy head Salih Ben Kobbi, director of the Cultural Department of the foreign ministry in April. During their stay, the Algerian delegation signed the 1964 executive plan for implementation of the Sino-Algerian cultural cooperation agreement and a Sino-Algerian radio and television cooperation agreement.[40] On 19 September China and Algeria signed a trade agreement, a payments agreement, and a protocol on economic and technical cooperation. Bachir Boumaza, minister of national economy and member of the Political Bureau of the FLN, led an economic delegation to Beijing. Mao received the Algerian delegation and Vice Premier Chen Yi hosted them as guests of honor at a banquet.[41] Codification of these agreements benefited China by broadening communications channels to Algeria, and elsewhere in Africa. The agreements also solidified China's political presence in Africa.

In October 1964 Chinese representatives attended anniversary celebrations in Algiers and eight Chinese people's organizations held a rally in Beijing. The Chinese representatives in Algeria included a government delegation headed by Chen Yi, member of the political bureau of the Central Committee of the Chinese Communist Party, vice premier, and foreign minister; a military delegation led by General Yang Yung, deputy chief of the General Staff of the PLA; and a youth delegation led by Wang Chao-hua, member of the secretariat of the Central Committee of the Communist Youth League and vice president of the All-China Youth Federation.[42] Reports at the time indicated that Algeria decided to use the aforementioned Chinese credits of $50 million for irrigating desert lands in southwest Algeria, experiments in rice- and tea-growing, and the construction of bicycles, chinaware, and shoe factories. Moreover, the *New York Times* reported that China was active on the cultural front as well, sending a team of doctors to Algeria and maintaining a large (but unofficial) military mission that had easy access to the Algerian defense minister.[43] On 3 June 1965 Algeria and China renewed their cultural exchange program. Under the program, Chinese writers, educators, athletes, and news reporters were to visit Algeria in 1965.[44] Exchange visits between the two countries continued apace, and the Algerians benefited from Chinese assistance. Clearly, Sino-Algerian relations were robust.

As relations matured, China began modifying its approach to Algeria. At the invitation of the General Staff of the PLA, Mahmoud Guenez led an Algerian militia delegation to China on 23 December 1964.[45] Chairman Mao received the delegation on 26 December. Earlier in the month, Amar Ouzegane, who had become minister of tourism, visited Beijing for one day. During his stay, Minister Ouzegane handed a letter from President Ben Bella to Chairman Liu, held talks with Premier Zhou and Vice Premier Chen Yi, and attended a banquet in his honor hosted by Chen Yi. Ouzegane had been minister of state in 1963.[46] In a speech at a banquet for the delegation, Mahmoud said the visit would further promote friendship between the Algerian and Chinese people: "Referring to the task of the militiamen, he declared that the formation of the Algerian militia showed that Algeria was determined to safeguard its national dignity and revolutionary gains and support the other peoples struggling for liberation and against colonialism, old and new."[47] The Algerian visit was a success: on 11 February 1965 the Algerian government signed an agreement with China to help equip Algeria's popular militia. The popular militia was used on auxiliary patrol duty in smaller towns and villages, and was actively engaged in fighting opposition guerrilla forces in the Kabylia and Aurès Mountains and the North Constantine region. Militia commander Mahmoud Guenez said the agreement covered "the supplying of some materials" to the militia forces, but gave no details. Colonel Hu Pin-fu, the Chinese military attaché in Algeria, called the newly signed agreement a contribution to the two countries' "common struggle against imperialism, colonialism, and neo-colonialism."[48] By shifting focus to assistance to Algeria's militia, China intended to ensure Algeria's independence and its own influence within the country. China was attempting to support the Algerian government as well as segments of the Algerian populace, as represented by the militia.

High-level Chinese political activities in Algeria continued the next month. From 30 to 31 March 1965 Premier Zhou visited Algeria via Albania, again visiting both countries on one trip. General Hsieh Fu-chih, vice premier of the State Council, and others accompanied Zhou. In addition to the aforementioned assistance to the militia, the *New York Times* reported that China had given the Algerian merchant marine a cargo ship as a gift.[49] Indicating its interest in Algeria's geographic position, Ogunsanwo reported that China donated a 13,000-ton freighter to the Algerian National Navigation Company and four transport aircraft to the Algerian government.[50] At the end of Zhou's visit, a joint communiqué was issued, wherein "the staunch fight against imperialism, colonialism and neo-colonialism" in Africa, Asia, and Latin America was reaffirmed as the main feature of the international situation.[51]

In April 1965 the *New York Times* reported that Premier Zhou was again in Algeria, and was going to Egypt.[52] Two months later, an Algerian delegation led by Mohamed Yazid, president of the Foreign Affairs Committee of the Algerian National Assembly, traveled to Beijing.[53] Chairman Liu Shaoqi received the delegation, and Yazid handed Chairman Liu a letter from President Ben Bella. That same month, the BBC reported that China gave one thousand tons of school equipment to the Algerian Ministry of Education and equipment to the Algerian militia.[54] The flurry of Chinese activity indicated close and steady relations with Algeria. China's support of Algeria covered a broad spectrum of areas: security, maritime-logistics, politics, and even education. But political changes in Algeria soon had direct effects on Sino-Algerian relations.

A coup d'état on 19 June 1965 removed Ben Bella from power, replacing him with Houari Boumediene. The change in government did not affect the Algerian government's support of anticolonial struggles in Africa or subsequent assistance to revolutionary groups and liberation movements in Africa.[55] Two weeks after the coup, on 5 July, Chairman Liu and Premier Zhou sent a message to Premier Boumediene, leader of the new Revolutionary Council of Algeria, on occasion of Algeria's third Independence Day. The message said in part, "The Chinese people have consistently supported the cause of Algeria's national liberation and the development of its national economy."[56] The ease with which China recognized Boumediene's regime signaled a continuation of Chinese policy in Algeria and an awareness of the local situation. It also indicated that China may have been aware of the coup prior to its occurrence.

Only two months after the coup, on 24 August, State Minister Rabah Bitat visited China. Minister Bitat attended a banquet hosted by Vice Premier Chen

Yi.[57] Conferring high-level respect, Chairman Mao and Chairman Liu received the visiting Algerian delegation on 27 August. The next day a joint communiqué was issued. Among the topics discussed, the communiqué expressed firm support for the national liberation movements and condemned imperialists for endangering freedom in Asia, Africa, and Latin America.[58] Before departing Beijing, Minister Bitat hosted a banquet for Chinese leaders, with Premier Zhou, Vice Premier Chen Yi, and Vice Premier Lo Jui-ching in attendance.[59] Clearly, Sino-Algerian relations remained close at the highest levels. And the emphasis on national liberation movements after the coup was evidence of Algeria's continued policy, as well as China's support for the same. Using Algeria as a springboard, therefore, Chinese influence moved beyond North Africa. Despite political changes in Algeria, China continued its overall approach to Africa.

The following month, from 8 to 9 September, Vice Premier and Foreign Minister Chen Yi visited Algeria, the first high-level visit after the coup. During his visit, Chen Yi met with Premier Boumediene and held talks with Minister of Foreign Affairs Bouteflika.[60] Later in the month, Ogunsanwo reported that Chinese "experts" arrived in Algiers to work on the first major project directly under the economic and technical cooperation agreement of 1963, an exhibition hall covering 37,000 square meters.[61] (In December 1966 Algeria and China signed an agreement under which China would build a large new exhibition hall in Algiers for an undisclosed cost.[62]) On 31 October Chairman Liu and Premier Zhou sent a message to Premier Boumediene greeting the eleventh anniversary of the Algerian Revolution. The next day Algerian chargé d'affaires ad interim Khouri Mohamed hosted an anniversary reception in Beijing, with Zhou, Chen Yi, and Vice Premier Li Hsien-nien in attendance. Extending congratulations, Chen Yi said, "There is a deep militant friendship between the Chinese and Algerian peoples."[63] The next month, China ordered four hundred trucks from the French Berliet Company's subsidiary in Algeria.[64] The following was an interesting side note about the trucks: "As in Morocco, China was interested in Berliet lorries and it was agreed that 400 of these would be shipped to China. The first batch of 40 was sent in April 1965."[65] Sino-Algerian relations were as close as they had been prior to the coup, and perhaps even closer.

China maintained its level of influence from Algeria and Beijing. On 10 January 1966 *El Moudjahid*, an Algerian paper, published commentary censuring imperialism and its followers for slanders against China. The commentary added that the Chinese people were friends of the African people.[66] From 20 to 24 April 1966 the secretariat of the Afro-Asian Journalists' Association met in Beijing.

Delegations from nineteen countries and areas attended, including those from Algeria and Tanzania. A representative from the Algerian delegation stated that the Algerian people would spare no effort to support the Congolese, Palestinian, Vietnamese, and other peoples fighting imperialism.[67] Significantly, China hosted the meeting, and an Algerian defended Chinese interests. Despite the change in regime the previous year, Algeria remained a staunch supporter of China's policy in Africa. China thus was able to maintain effective communications to the North African regime and its people.

China's message, from the very beginning in 1956, was always accompanied by tangible enticements. Reports of the amount of Chinese assistance to Algeria vary, depending on the source. For example, between 1954 and 1967, according to the CIA, the PRC gave Algeria $24 million in economic aid, second only to its aid to Guinea in Africa.[68] In April 1967, according to Algerian radio, China offered Algeria $2.5 million in hard currency as part of the interest-free loan promised in 1963.[69] This figure may be compared with another CIA figure, which stated that from 1954 to 1970 China gave Algeria $50 million in credits and grants, none of which was given in 1969 or 1970; also according to the CIA, between 1956 and 1971 China granted Algeria $98 million in economic aid extensions.[70] In contrast to the CIA reports, one scholar recorded $52 million in Chinese economic aid to Algeria from 1961 to 1964, along with an additional $40 million in 1971 alone.[71] Like the amount of Chinese assistance provided, the precise number of Communist Chinese present in Algeria was divergent as well. In 1968, for example, the CIA reported that in 1967 there were sixty Chinese economic technicians in Algeria.[72] This was the fifth-most Chinese in an African country at the time. Four years later, the CIA reported that the number of Chinese economic technicians in Algeria was two hundred.[73] China combined strong, consistent communications to Algeria—in print and in person—with tangible economic and security assistance. The next year the fruits of Chinese operations in Algeria ripened.

As reported in the *Washington Post*, in the February 1968 UNSC meetings Algerian ambassador Tewfik Bouattoura, acting in Chinese interests, "opened a campaign of psychological warfare" on behalf of China to obtain a seat in the UNSC.[74] Using deftness and secrecy, Bouattoura on multiple occasions brought up the point of representatives' credentials, which served to remind members that there had been no new members since 1948. Whether or not China advised Algeria on this diplomatic item was not the point. These procedural techniques forced U.S. ambassador Richard F. Pedersen, after hours of negotiations, to state that the United States did not have any reservations regarding the possibility of future debate of the Chinese representation question. Moreover, according to the *Washington Post* article, any member of the UNSC could, at any time, raise the question of the secretary general's report and seek to place it on the UNSC's agenda; the latter served to dramatize the fact that ten of fifteen UNSC members voted in the previous General Assembly to throw out Nationalist China and bring in Communist China. With the UN as the international venue, Algeria served as an agent of China.

After this incident, Chinese assistance to Algeria continued apace. A new Chinese medical team arrived in Algeria in August 1968 with more than fifty members.[75] This was their second tour of duty in the country. According to an article published in 1972, a Chinese medical team member, Dr. Shih Hsueh-min, performed acupuncture in Mascara, west Algeria, in 1968. Dr. Shih, the article stated, learned to speak the local language and taught acupuncture to an Algerian colleague.[76] Another Chinese medical team arrived in Algeria in August 1969, the third such team to assist in Algeria. As reported by the *Peking Review*, in eight months the Chinese medical team had treated more than 29,000 patients and performed more than 3,500 major and minor operations.[77] By sending small medical teams, China focused on addressing basic human needs, thus directly conveying a strong message of support to the Algerian people.

As the decade came to a close, China continued exchange visits to Algeria. On 28 October 1969 a Chinese government and military delegation led by Chen Shih-chu, commander of the engineer corps of the PLA, left Beijing for Algiers.[78] The delegation planned to attend National Day celebrations in Algiers. Chou Hua-min, member of the delegation and vice minister of foreign trade, left the same day for Algeria. On 1 November Nacereddine Haffad, chargé d'affaires ad interim of the Algerian embassy in China, hosted a reception in Beijing to mark the fifteenth anniversary of the Algerian Revolution. Vice Premier Hsieh Fu-chih of the State Council and Vice Chairman Kuo Mo-jo were among the guests.[79] The following October Premier Zhou sent a telegram to Premier Boumediene marking Algeria's National Day. The telegram read in part, "The Chinese and Algerian peoples have forged a profound militant friendship through the long common struggle against imperialism and colonialism."[80] Through military and economic visits as well as high-level communications, China continued to exert its influence in Algeria. The respect that China continually bestowed on Algeria was rewarded in 1971.

On 21 July 1971 an Algerian delegation arrived in China. Two days later Premier Zhou and Acting Foreign Minister Chi Peng-fei met with Minister of

Foreign Affairs Abdellaziz Bouteflika and other members of the delegation. In his speech at the opening banquet, Minister Bouteflika voiced strong support for Chinese rights over Taiwan and added that China and Algeria hold common views on international political issues.[81] Three days later Minister Bouteflika hosted a banquet attended by Premier Zhou, Vice Premier Li Hsien-nien, Acting Foreign Minister Chi, and Prime Minister Samdech Penn Nouth of Cambodia. Notably, Algeria supported China's interests and met with China's friends. On 27 July China and Algeria signed an economic and technical cooperation agreement in Beijing.[82] Vice Premier Li Hsien-nien attended the signing ceremony. In total, the Algerian delegation visited China from 20 July to 1 August, touring Beijing, Yenan, Xian, and Shanghai. It also visited factories, a people's commune, and "places of interest." Both sides had military representatives participating in discussions as well. Notable participants on the Chinese side during the visit included Yuan Hua-ping, head of the Armaments Department of the General Logistics of the PLA; Ho Ying, director of the West Asian and African Department of the foreign ministry; and Chen Mu-hua, vice minister of economic relations with foreign countries. On the Algerian side, significant participants included Chaieb Taleb-Bendiab, ambassador to China; Ambassador Omar Oussedik, general inspector of the Ministry of Foreign Affairs; Kamal Abdelrahim, major in the National People's Army; Mohamed Harireche, lieutenant in the National People's Army; and Mohamed Belaid, counselor of the Algerian embassy in Libya.[83]

The UN vote in favor of seating China was a major symbolic victory for Beijing, and a byproduct of its influence in Algeria. Part of its success could be attributed to the African bloc of nations. "At the United Nations General Assembly in 1970 six African states dropped their veto on Peking's entry, and more votes for the first time went to Peking than Taiwan. One year later, in October 1971, the long-awaited avalanche rolled. Peking received 76 votes out of 111, the two-thirds majority necessary to evict Taiwan from its seat. Of those 76 votes a crucial 26 were African. Mali and Algeria were Peking's sponsors, and a former Tanzanian ambassador to Peking led the floor."[84] Moreover, seventeen countries had sent a letter and memorandum to the UN secretary general requesting "restoration" of the lawful rights of China in the UN. Among the signatories were Algeria and Tanzania.[85] As a sponsor to the eventual vote and a signatory to the seventeen-nation letter, Algeria was clearly a staunch supporter of China. In the run-up to the vote, China was seen currying favor with the Algerians. One month before the vote, for example, Chinese experts traveled to Algeria to assist with public housing.[86] More than a decade of Chinese influence in Africa was eventually rewarded through Algerian support at the UN. This was a significant long-term political victory for China in Africa and the world.

After assisting the Algerians in their war for independence, China thanked Algeria for its assistance at the UN. On 31 October 1971 Premier Zhou sent a letter to Premier Boumediene greeting the country's National Day. The message thanked the Algerian government for efforts at the twenty-sixth session of the UN General Assembly for "restoring" China into the UN.[87] The next summer, Tung Pi-wu, acting chair of the People's Republic of China, and Premier Zhou sent another message to Premier Boumediene greeting the tenth anniversary of Algeria's independence. The message read in part, "The independence of Algeria is the result of the protracted armed struggle waged by her people and a brilliant example for the national-liberation movements in Africa." An exchange visit followed these written communications. At the invitation of the Algerian government, a Chinese government and military delegation arrived in Algiers. The delegation was headed by Minister of the First Ministry of Machine Building Li Shui-ching, with Deputy Commander of the Beijing Units of the PLA Kang Lin and ambassador to Algeria Lin Chung as deputy heads.[88] As China continued to reward Algeria for its support, Algeria remained allied with China internationally. According to a report in the *Rose El Youseef*, Algerian minister of foreign affairs Bouteflika said, "The current situation of foreign military presence in the Mediterranean runs counter to the liberation of our peoples and their aspirations for progress and advancement."[89] Minister Bouteflika emphasized the role of developing world nations in defending their own national interests. Much as had happened during his July 1971 visit, Bouteflika's statement conformed to Chinese interests. Sino-Algerian interests were shared and strategically aligned.

Later that year, China's influence continued in Algeria. From 31 October to 7 November, Minister of Commerce Layachi Yaker led an Algerian delegation to China.[90] In talks with the Chinese delegation led by Minister of Foreign Trade Pai Hsiang-kuo, the two parties discussed trade development as well as economic and technical cooperation. The two ministers signed a trade protocol for 1973 in accordance with the long-term Sino-Algerian trade agreement signed in Algiers in October 1972. The protocol dealt primarily with agricultural and industrial projects in Algeria. The next month, a youth delegation of the FLN visited China. Saadna Abdelkader, national secretary in charge of external relations of the FLN's youth organization, led the delegation.[91] At the end of the year, the *Peking Review* reported that a Chinese bank delegation had traveled to Algeria.[92] Chiao Pei-hsin, acting chair of the board of directors and general manager of the Bank of China, led the delegation. The next year, in May 1973, Vice Minister of National Defence Hsiao Ching-kuang hosted a banquet for a visiting Algerian delegation, led by Colonel Mohamed Ben-Ahmed, member of the Algerian Revolutionary Council. Guests of the Chinese Ministry of National Defense, the delegation visited Xinjiang with Kang Lin, deputy commander of the Beijing units of the PLA. Vice Chairman Yeh Chien-ying of the Central Military Committee of the Communist Party of China met the entire delegation on 9 May 1973.[93]

As China continued to influence Algeria, the two countries worked together to strengthen ties in Asia, Africa, and Latin America. On 4 February 1974 Minister of Foreign Affairs Bouteflika sent a letter to Foreign Minister Chi Peng-fei. The letter included an Algerian proposal to UN secretary general Kurt Waldheim to convene a special session of the General Assembly to discuss development, international economic relations, and the implications of a "new system of relations based on equality and the common interest of all states."[94] On 12 February Foreign Minister Chi sent a reply to Minister of Foreign Affairs Bouteflika expressing Chinese support for developing world struggles. Similarly, speaking at a banquet in honor of the visiting Algerian guests, Premier Zhou said, "Both China and Algeria belong to the Third World."[95] Two weeks later, Premier Boumediene visited China. On the first two nights, Chairman Mao and Premier Zhou received the visiting Algerian delegation, which conveyed a strong sense of Chinese support to Algeria.[96] During their stay Boumediene and the Algerian delegation visited a people's commune, a university, and historical and cultural sites in Beijing and Shanghai.[97] Notable participants during discussions on China's side included Ho Ying, vice minister of foreign affairs; Li Ta, deputy chief of the General Staff of the PLA; and Tsao Ke-chiang, director of the West Asian and North African Department of the Ministry of Foreign Affairs. On the Algerian side, notable participants included Ahmed Taleb, minister of information and culture; Mohamed Benyahin, minister of higher education and scientific research; and Mouloud Kassim, minister of general education and religious affairs. Thus, China and Algeria voiced the same political message of developing world and international unity. Bilateral relations were at the highest point to date.

By this time Algeria was considered a base for Chinese activities and influence in Africa. In March 1974, for example, the central African country of Burundi moved closer to the Arabs and Chinese than to the Soviets. A substantial number of Burundi military officers were trained in Communist and Arab countries, including sixty in Algeria and ten in Egypt. Jack Anderson, writing in the *Washington Post*, reported that regular shipments of arms and munitions to Burundi arrived from Algeria on Algerian planes.[98] China was using Algeria as a conduit to other parts of the continent. But these activities were in concert with political ties between China and Algeria. On 1 November 1974 Algerian ambassador to China Chaieb Taleb-Bendiab hosted a reception to celebrate the twentieth anniversary of the Algerian armed revolution. Hsu Hsiang-chien, vice chair of the Standing Committee of the NPC, Chi Peng-fei, minister of foreign affairs, and other leading government officials attended the reception. In Algeria a Chinese government delegation, a PLA military goodwill delegation, a Beijing Opera troupe, and a men's basketball team from Jilin Province all attended celebrations.[99] Finally, on 9 September 1976 Premier Boumediene sent a message to President Hua Kuo-feng expressing grief at the death of Mao. The letter stated, quite simply, "He set an example for the third world."[100] Boumediene's message confirmed how closely aligned the two countries had become since ties were first formed in 1955 at the Bandung Conference.

For more than two decades, China used various means to initiate, cultivate, and influence its relations with Algeria. For example, from 1971 to 1975 Algeria drew $15 million in economic aid from Communist China, according to the CIA.[101] In 1971 China distributed portions of $40 million in aid to Algeria.[102] From 1955 to 1976, according to the *Africa Contemporary Record*, twenty-five Algerian military personnel trained in China.[103] The varied Chinese activities helped Algeria to gain independence, furthered ties on the African continent, and advanced China's aims to become a world power. Algeria was one of China's closest and earliest allies in Africa. Sino-Algerian relations were broad-based, politically, economically, and strategically. China sought a foothold in Africa, and it gained a firm one in Algeria, for the long term.

PART III

NO GOLD

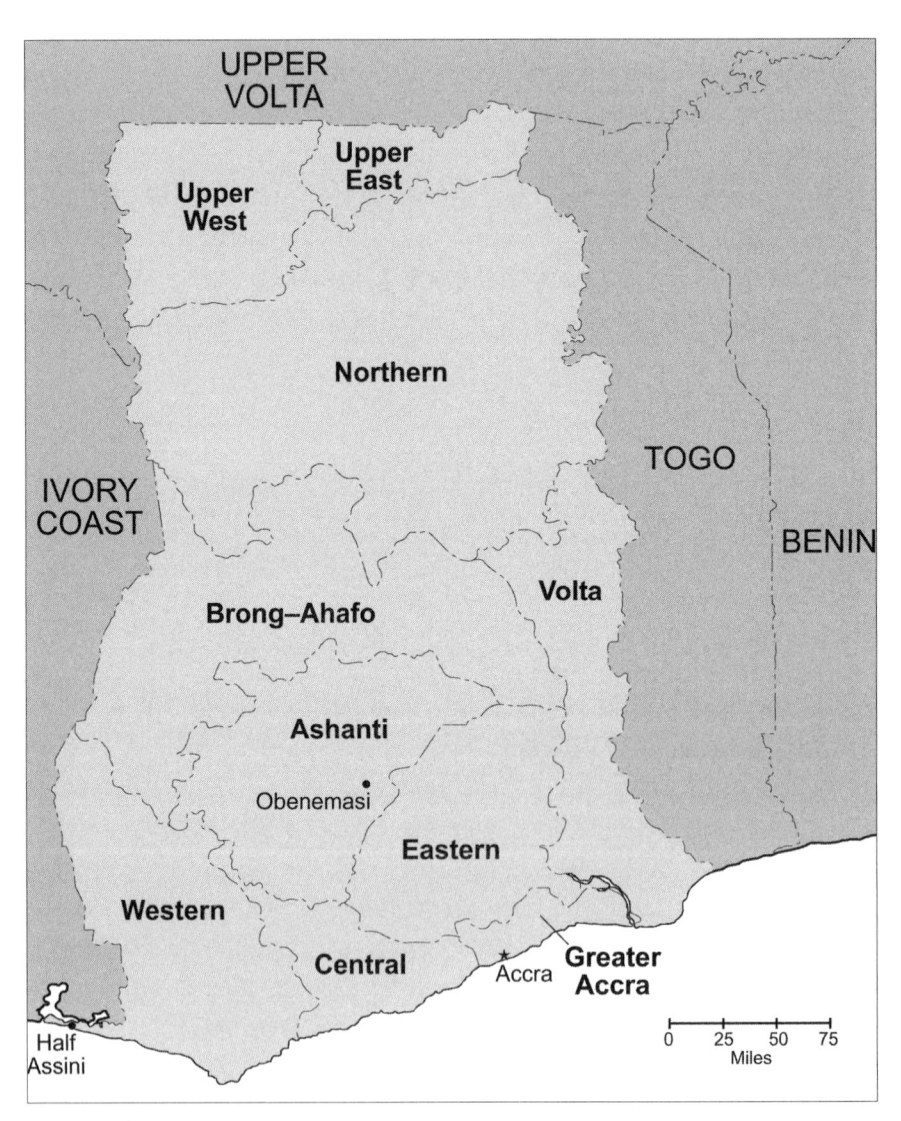

Map 2. Ghana

Six

RIPE FOR REVOLUTION?

In addition to North Africa, China also perceived West Africa as a strategically significant region of the African continent. Ghana, in particular, emerged as a politically active nation-state upon independence in 1957, and China took note. According to one analysis, Ghana (formerly the Gold Coast) was even a stable political entity prior to independence. "There was practically no specifically racial or religious animosity or conflict," for example, and "[t]here was no feudal aristocracy, warrior caste, compradore or white settler group." Moreover, the economic climate was considered positive and optimistic: "Economically the peoples of the Gold Coast had a higher real income than in comparable areas of the colonial and tropical world and a greater degree of economic security." Nevertheless, the same analysis concluded, "The effects of the [colonial] occupation on traditional social, economic, and agricultural systems were disruptive."[1] But these same British disruptions did not prevent the Gold Coast from possessing by 1957 a civil service, some of the best schools in Africa, a free press, an independent judiciary, and a freely elected parliament.[2] China found in West Africa an environment that diverged quite a bit from the environment in North Africa.

As the first leader of a newly independent African nation in West Africa, Kwame Nkrumah became known as "the elder statesman of tropical Africa"; he exerted tremendous political power in Ghana.[3] In order to understand the context upon the arrival of the Chinese, one must understand Nkrumah himself. A teacher by training, Nkrumah was educated in the United States (at Lincoln University and the University of Pennsylvania) as well as in the United Kingdom (at the London School of Economics, or LSE). Notably, while at the LSE Nkrumah helped organize "The Circle," a small secret society of African revolutionaries whose members included Jomo Kenyatta of Kenya. While he was in England Nkrumah attended Communist party meetings to "study their tactics."[4] It was the latter experience in London that would later contribute to an underlying conspiratorial mindset in Nkrumah.

While abroad, he became active in the West African Students' Union and the Pan-African Congress, and was a participant in the Communist-oriented Manchester Congress of 1945 (a Pan-African movement), where leadership of the movement passed to Africans.[5] By request of indigenous Gold Coast political leaders, Nkrumah returned to the Gold Coast in late 1947.[6] He created the Convention People's Party (CPP) in 1949, which was a significant organizational milestone for Nkrumah. Four years later, in 1953, Nkrumah organized the first pan-African conference in Africa in the Gold Coast (held in Kumasi).[7] Recalling the independent-minded Ashanti (or Asante) kingdom, it was no coincidence that the conference was held in Kumasi. Writing in 1955 Marxist-Leninist terminology, Nkrumah noted, "In the Convention People's Party no individual is greater than the Party and the principle of democratic centralism, that is, the subordinating of individual opinion to the decision of the majority, has always been the guiding principle in the formulation of the plans and policies of the Party."[8] Clearly, Nkrumah recognized the power of an organized political entity. Nkrumah also created the National Association of Socialist Students Organizations (NASSO) "to act as a cadre of party intellectuals charged with 'ideological and political education.'"[9] Africanist Colin Legum pointed out that NASSO owed much to The Circle in its organization.[10] NASSO was an organization that could be exploited by entities that desired political influence in Ghana—including China.

Nkrumah's latent ideology encompassed both Socialist and pan-African beliefs. Explaining pan-African ideology, Professor Robert Good wrote, "It [Pan-Africanism] differs from pan-Arabism in being based not upon the memory of historical unity, but upon the unity of color and resentment of racial prejudice; but it is similar to pan-Arabism in that—in its extremist form—it seeks a fundamental revision of the state system inherited from the colonial era."[11] Nkrumah's main themes of racial equality and political revolution were congruent with China's position on Afro-Asian unity, which emphasized Third World solidarity.[12] Both Nkrumah and China sought, in some form, the establishment of a new world order, an alteration of the international political landscape—to suit their respective interests.

More specifically, Nkrumah's ideology emulated the thinking of China's paramount leader, Mao Zedong. Chairman Mao's requirement for revolution was similar to Nkrumah's statement: "Freedom thus becomes a product of 'bitter and vigorous' struggle." Furthermore, Nkrumah leaned toward keeping the nation "mobilized for the 'struggle.'"[13] To carry out this struggle Nkrumah proposed using "positive action," described as adopting all legitimate and constitutional means to use the weapons of political agitation, newspaper, and educational campaigns, and, "as a last resort, the constitutional application of strikes, boycotts, and non-cooperation based on the principle of absolute non-violence, as used by Gandhi in India."[14] Mao's focus on the rural areas of the countryside was comparable to Nkrumah's program of "rural reconstruction" as well.[15] Inspired by Mao's revolutionary warfare strategy, Nkrumah himself later penned a similar pamphlet for distribution to African revolutionaries.[16] Thus, Nkrumah espoused political and military beliefs quite similar to those of Mao.[17]

Although Nkrumah's policies were characterized in many different ways, "there can be no question of his anticolonialism, his socialist approach to economic questions, his deep admiration for India's Nehru, and his determination to manipulate all issues—including the conflict between the Soviet Bloc and the West—to the betterment of Ghana's position."[18] Nkrumah was first a Ghanaian, arguing that African industrial and economic advancement was contingent on the destruction of the artificial boundaries created by the colonial powers, an argument similar to that of the Chinese.[19] Therefore, taken together, Ghana's policies under Nkrumah were "anti-neo-colonialism."[20] China had to face the forceful leadership of Nkrumah if it wished to gain traction in West Africa.

After gaining independence and organizing politically, Nkrumah and the CPP laid out a series of objectives. "Nkrumah and the CPP [had] three primary objectives—the creation of a modern unitary state, the development and diversification of Ghana's economy, and the extension of its influence throughout West Africa."[21] To achieve these objectives, the CPP mobilized its supporters, which "controlled virtually all trade-union, cooperative, and similar activities." Because "[b]oth administratively and ideologically the party was in charge," Nkrumah was in the position to exert substantial personal influence on the CPP's political direction.[22] Nkrumah's goal of extending influence throughout West Africa required both political and military action. Nkrumah may have perceived China as a useful resource to expand Ghanaian influence in West Africa.

During this period, Nkrumah and the CPP were forced to take into account the immediate postindependence domestic situation, including social and economic divisions. "Much of the Northern Region [was] generations behind the coastal areas in ways of the modern world. Moreover, some attachment to tribal customs and beliefs [could] be found among even the most educated and urbanized Ghanaians." The former was a legacy of colonial and geographic circumstance, while the latter was a fact of native life. Not surprisingly, in Ghana there were "deep-rooted regional and tribal loyalties." For example, based on their proud history and culture, the Ashanti were known to be "unruly." In addition, and important for future considerations of Ghana's political leadership, the Northern Territories were the location of "a large percentage of the army and police."[23] Thus, to accomplish CPP objectives Nkrumah was forced to deal with "the resistance of the traditional leaders in the Ashanti region and the Northern Territories."[24] Though Nkrumah was an outstanding political leader, he had to face the sociocultural realities in Ghana as well.

While there appeared to be social and economic divisions in Ghana, clear social, political, or economic fault lines did not exist throughout the country. At the time, Ghanaians perceived Nkrumah as a forceful, charismatic leader with a robust organizational apparatus (the CPP) to support him. By and large, however, Ghanaian society developed freely—with a polity that was fast becoming trained, educated, and attuned to the Western world. China faced quite different political circumstances in Ghana than in Algeria, which later would have direct implications on its activities in the former.

Unlike Algeria's outreach in 1955, initially "Nkrumah refused to recognise China after Ghana's independence in March 1957."[25] Although never fully explained, it appeared Nkrumah was focused on internal consolidation of power. British Gold Coast and British Togoland—part of the UN trust territories—united as the Kingdom of Ghana on 6 March 1957. Three years later, on 1 July 1960, the Republic of Ghana was created. According to one scholar, in its first five years Nkrumah's Ghana did not actively participate in Afro-Asian affairs.[26] Ghana was looking inward. China was actively interested and engaged in Ghanaian affairs, however. In this case, its active involvement connotes qualitative engagements, not necessarily quantitative ones.

While Ghana had not yet established relations with China, Nkrumah was in the early stages of contacting African nationalist movements. At the end of 1957, for example, Nkrumah invited the Cameroonian guerrilla movement Union of the Peoples of Cameroon (Union des Populations du Cameroun, or UPC) to move its headquarters from Cairo to Accra. "After his move to Accra, Dr. Moumie [of the UPC] was one of those who persuaded Nkrumah to establish close relations with the [Communist] Chinese, especially as regards national liberation movements and all anti-colonial forces operating in Africa."[27] Nkrumah's interest in supporting African national liberation movements led ultimately to Ghana's pursuit of relations with China, which he considered to be a great world power as early as 1957.[28]

Before establishing diplomatic relations, China first made contact with Ghana using an art troupe. On 6 March 1958 a Chinese acrobatic troupe visited Ghana for the first time and gave a special performance in Accra in honor of Ghana's first anniversary.[29] Prime Minister Nkrumah and other government officials were on hand for the performance. The troupe had been touring in the Middle East and Africa for six months and concluded with performances in Morocco. The troupe's visit was no doubt the result of efforts by the CCRFC. Two years later, in January 1960, it was learned that a deputy director of the CCRFC sponsored a similar Chinese acrobatic group in Khartoum, Sudan.[30] The troupe was scheduled to give six performances in Accra during the Conference of Independent African States.[31] The troupe gave a special performance on 16 April 1958 for the heads of delegations to the conference. As a means of influence, China used the troupe to shape the perception of China in the minds of African leaders, particularly Nkrumah, as well as to gain knowledge of the local environment.

Before China established diplomatic ties with Ghana, Nkrumah was in search of African unity. Nkrumah summoned the aforementioned Conference of Independent African States in Accra in April 1958. Delegates were from Ethiopia, Ghana, Liberia, Libya, Morocco, the Sudan, Tunisia, and the UAR, with a three-member delegation from the FLN and a delegation from Cameroon.[32] "Another dramatic event was the union between Ghana and Guinea that was proclaimed after the latter's break with France in 1958, and which in 1960 was extended to include Mali also."[33] On 23 November 1958 the Ghana-Guinea Union was created and shortly thereafter a Ghana-Guinea-Mali Union.[34] These events caught the eyes of China. According to one observer, China's "center of interest was Guinea, as a base for contact with dissidents from Tropical Africa and especially with the armed struggle in the Cameroun, and later in the Congo."[35] It is interesting to note that Guinea was known as "the front door to West Africa" since colonial times.[36] The relationship between Ghana and Guinea, then, appeared to be symbiotic. After examining Nkrumah's actions and his stated desire to play "a leading role" in African affairs, China was inclined to study the Ghanaian context further.[37]

The Ghana-Guinea-Mali Union signaled a possible opening for Chinese exploitation. "The radicals—Ghana, Guinea, and Mali—sought what may be called a systematic change in the order inherited from the colonial era which they deemed 'neo-colonial' and illegitimate." Furthermore, "The radical view produced a concurrence of interests with the communist world."[38] To gain influence in the region, the PRC cultivated ties with Guinea and Ghana to serve Chinese interests. In both Guinea and Ghana, Schatten later wrote, "the Chinese . . . obtained a foothold which enable[d] them to contact and influence the exiled leaders of various African extremists [sic] groups, now living in these countries, and in one or two cases they have succeeded in winning them over. This applie[d], in particular, to exiled politicians from the Ivory Coast Republic, the Portuguese territories, and some of the leaders of the terrorist wing of the UPC of Cameroon."[39] Indeed, the *New York Times* said, "Guinea has come in for Peiping's special attention. A cultural cooperation program was concluded between the former French colony and Communist China in June [1960]."[40] After the initial dance in West Africa, China gained awareness of the political situation and pursued closer relations with the Ghana-Guinea-Mali Union.

Although Ghana and China had not yet established relations, the former was already acting in PRC interests. At the UN in September 1958, the spokesperson for Ghana, Ako Adjei, voiced his opinion that Communist China should be admitted to the UN forthwith.[41] The level of Chinese influence was unclear, but Ghana was signaling to China its active political support. Guinea became independent on 2 October 1958. At the end of that year, China voiced its opinion in an international forum. The All-African People's Conference opened on 5 December 1958 in Accra, a result of Nkrumah's desire to "harness the widespread nationalist sentiments in Africa toward the achievement of a Pan-African goal, and to co-ordinate the efforts of various political groups throughout the continent."[42] In attendance was Yang Shuo, the Chinese delegate, who used his observer status to contact members of the numerous delegations. Thus, China was able to use the international conference as a means of extending influence into West Africa in general, and into Ghana in particular.

After the conference, China and Ghana began to communicate directly. On 6 March 1959, for example, Gamesu Kofi Amegbe and Moses Fairchild Gahoho addressed a Beijing audience on the second anniversary of Ghana's independence. Amegbe, not coincidentally secretary general of the Preparatory Committee of the All-African People's Conference, and Gahoho, publisher of the Ghanaian magazine *Pan-African Age*, spoke about "the struggles of African peoples for freedom and Ghana's achievements since independence."[43] The presence of a Ghanaian publisher in China was ideal for spreading Chinese influence in the print media. The next year, on 4 March 1960, Premier Zhou Enlai sent a message of greetings to the government and people of Ghana on occasion of the third anniversary of Ghana's independence.[44] Wishing the Ghanaians success, the message also expressed hope for further development of friendly relations between the two countries. This public communication signaled clearly China's intent to establish direct political relations with Ghana, which was meant to extend Chinese influence beyond its borders.

As China and Ghana came closer together politically, Nkrumah continued to advance his own interests. Thus, upon Nkrumah's request, the Bureau of African Affairs (BAA) was established on 17 March 1960 to study development in other parts of Africa and relate them back to Ghana, specifically "furthering the activities of all organisations working for the freedom and unity of Africa, and any other functions which the Minister may direct to be performed." As originally conceived, the BAA comprised a special bureau that handled so-called freedom fighters, activists, and agents of espionage in other African countries, and a research bureau that supported the special bureau. Unfortunately, Nkrumah's arrogance led to the ill treatment and alienation of African nationalists and foreign fighters in Ghana.[45] The BAA was "by statute a nongovernmental organization, designed to coordinate aid to freedom movements in dependent African territories, although it became headquarters for all nondiplomatic Ghanaian involvements in Africa, and a chief instrument of Ghana's Africa policy."[46] Considered to be nongovernmental, the BAA was much like Chinese organizations used to influence African affairs. But China would later discover that the BAA did not receive the resources necessary to achieve its objectives. This would become a continuous theme throughout Nkrumah's tenure because his political desires were not matched with physical resources.

Additional Chinese communications to Ghana occurred on 28 June 1960. Chairman Liu Shaoqi and Premier Zhou Enlai, in separate messages, congratulated Kwame Nkrumah and the people of Ghana on the establishment of the Republic of Ghana and Nkrumah's assumption of the office of the president.[47] Because of its size and youth, Ghana was grateful to receive such messages from China, messages that served as effective forms of Chinese influence to West Africa as a whole. This was the beginning of active Chinese involvement in the affairs of West Africa.

Seven

TOWARD REVOLUTIONARY FRIENDSHIP

Though beginning in a cautionary manner, Sino-Ghanaian relations moved quickly apace in the year of Africa, 1960. On 5 July China and Ghana established full diplomatic relations. China and Ghana agreed to establish diplomatic relations and exchange ambassadorial diplomatic representatives in a joint communiqué, and President Nkrumah accepted Chairman Liu Shaoqi's invitation to visit China.[1] Ghana became the second black African state to recognize Communist China, following the example of nearby Guinea. Notably, the previous week China's ambassador to Guinea, Ko Hua, attended celebrations in Accra marking the inauguration of the Ghana republic.

After being appointed China's ambassador to Ghana, Huang Hua presented his credentials to President Nkrumah in September 1960.[2] He had arrived in Accra on 25 August. According to Thompson, "By all accounts Huang Hua was exceedingly shrewd. A senior party official, he had headed the Western Europe and Africa divisions of the Ministry of Foreign Affairs in Peking before being accredited to Accra in 1960."[3] During his presentation, Ambassador Huang declared that Ghana and China faced "the common task of defending national independence and opposing imperialist aggression."[4] In response, President Nkrumah said it was gratifying to know that "in the fight for freedom and independence of all Africa, Ghana could count on the support of the Communist Chinese government and people."[5] Clearly, Ghana and China shared political interests from the onset, common perspectives of the world at large. By identifying common interests with Ghana, China used the domestic conditions in Ghana to cultivate expanded bilateral relations. Ambassador Huang later played a significant role in Beijing's diplomatic activities throughout the African continent.[6]

After establishing relations, China quickly sent personnel to Ghana. This could be contrasted with the situation in Algeria, where China sent personnel only after a period of time. On 4 August 1960 two Chinese diplomats and five officials arrived in Accra to open the first Chinese embassy in Ghana.[7] The size of the embassy was notable relative to the size and strategic importance of Ghana. Later in the year, Ghana again acted in Chinese interests, within a month of the establishment of full diplomatic relations, at the UN.

On 23 September 1960 President Nkrumah made the first major speech as an African leader before the fifteenth UN General Assembly.[8] Of his significant points, he asserted that China should be admitted to the UN to make it "more realistic and more effective and useful."[9] In October 1960 Ghana named Cobina Kessie, former ambassador to Liberia, as Ghana's first ambassador to Communist China.[10] Ghana was a vocal supporter of China from the onset.

In the same year, scholar Ernest W. Lefever reported the following within the BAA: "Nkrumah operated four 'freedom fighter' camps to train foreign nationals in the ideology and tactics of guerrilla warfare for eventual military operations against Rhodesia, the Portuguese provinces, and South Africa. These camps, begun in 1960 with the help of Russian and Chinese agents, were operated by Red Chinese instructors."[11] In return for Ghana's strong international support, China deepened its influence by training and arming African fighters in Ghana. By the end of the year, both China and Ghana had personnel in place to cultivate further relations. Moreover, China was working in Ghana to exploit the two countries' shared interests in Africa.

The first publicized Chinese visit to Ghana occurred the following year. In spring 1961 the CAPFA visited eight West African nations. Feng Chih-tan, a member of a delegation of the CAPFA that visited West Africa, first wrote about the visit in August 1961.[12] The delegation visited Dahomey, Ghana, Guinea, Mali, Niger, Senegal, Togo, and Upper Volta. The delegation's visits to Ghana, Guinea, and Mali should not have come as a surprise, due to the political union of these West African states. Liu Cheng-sheng, the president of the CAPFA, led the delegation. The CAFPA visit was touted ostensibly as a mutual friendship visit but, in fact, was an intelligence gathering and propaganda mission—to further Chinese influence in West Africa. For example, Feng Chih-tan, the author of *Glimpses of West Africa* who was a member of the CAPFA delegation, noted significant geographic and cultural aspects of each West African country. Notably, this was an English-language monograph published by Beijing. In Ghana specifically, Feng

Chih-tan mentioned the gold deposits and mines as well as the large production of cocoa, or "green gold." "Ghana is a country richly endowed by nature," Feng wrote, making reference to Ghana's diamonds, the world's third-largest source; manganese, for which Ghana is Africa's second-largest producer; and the large quantities of bauxite.[13] Unlike its operations in Algeria, which benefited initially from close contact to Algerians in Cairo, China gathered more information on Ghana before expanding its activities. By sending a friendship association to Ghana, China was able to operate under the guise of a friendly nongovernmental organization.

That summer it was revealed that Ghana had youth in China already. In June 1961 Oginga Odinga, Kenyan legislative council member, made reference to three thousand Ghanaian students who were attending colleges in Soviet Bloc countries and China.[14] While a majority of these students were in Soviet Bloc countries, this statement revealed that Ghanaian youth were in fact already in China. These mutual exchange visits served as a means of furthering China's strategic interests in Africa by influencing Ghanaians who were in China. Indeed, the Ghanaian students may have been studying guerrilla warfare. In July 1961 Chairman Liu Shaoqi and Premier Zhou Enlai "conveyed the Chinese people's warm greetings to the Ghanaian people on the first anniversary of the founding of the Republic of Ghana." At a reception in Beijing hosted by Ghanaian ambassador Cobina Kessie, Vice Premier Lo Jui-ching "acclaimed the continuous growth and consolidation" of the friendship between China and Ghana. In addition, "The Vice-Premier reaffirmed the support of the Chinese people for the anti-colonialist struggles of the peoples of Algeria, the Congo, Angola and other parts of Africa."[15] Liu and Zhou's communication once again conferred respect to Ghana, which served as a means of greater Chinese influence in West Africa. In addition, Lo's comments reinforced the nature of China-Ghana relations (growing) as well as Chinese aims in Africa (political and strategic). Soon, high-level Ghanaians would be visiting China, seeking benefits for the young West African nation.

The first Ghanaian official visit to China occurred in the summer of 1961. On 14 August President Nkrumah arrived in China.[16] In meetings with various high-ranking leaders such as Chairman Liu, Chairman Chu Teh, and Premier Zhou, two recurrent themes emerged: first, China and Ghana shared common interests in the struggle against imperialism and colonialism; and second, the two countries voiced a shared history.[17] The visit allowed Ghana and China to communicate their interests and intentions in person at the highest political levels. In addition, since it was the host nation, and in typical Chinese fashion, China was able to control the environmental setting as a means of influencing bilateral relations.

As a result of Nkrumah's visit, China and Ghana signed three agreements to develop economic and cultural cooperation. Under the Sino-Ghanaian Agreement on Economic and Technical Co-operation, China agreed to provide a twenty-year interest-free loan of 7 million Ghanaian pounds. The Sino-Ghanaian Trade and Payments Agreement fixed the annual volume of exports for both countries at 4 million Ghanaian pounds. Finally, the Cultural Co-operation Agreement covered science and education, arts, medicine, and public health issues between the two countries.[18] The favorable terms of the agreements were a means of enhancing Chinese political influence on Ghana. For example, the economic and technical agreement provided non-interest-bearing credit of £7 million for five years, from 1 July 1962 to 30 June 1967. (The economic and technical agreement provided non-interest-bearing credit of nearly $20 million over five years, from 1 July 1962 to 30 June 1967.) Ghana agreed to repay China in equal installments of export goods or third-country currency during the ten-year period from 1 July 1971 to 30 June 1981. Specific projects cited included an integrated textile and knitwear factory and an enamelware and chinaware factory. In other words, China would supply Ghana with technical assistance and complete sets of "equipment, machinery and materials, technical and other goods."[19] Meanwhile, the cultural cooperation codified China's channel to the broader West African region. Ogunsanwo reported "Ghanaians would also be trained in China to man [the development] projects."[20]

This gave the Chinese another opportunity to influence Ghanaians directly in person. The Sino-Ghanaian joint communiqué was signed at the end of the visit in Beijing on 18 August 1961.[21] After the signing of the friendship treaty, President Nkrumah said he hoped the treaty would "strengthen relations not only between Ghana and China, but also between Africa and China."[22] Zhou and Nkrumah signed the Sino-Ghanaian Treaty of Friendship on 18 August 1961; that treaty remained in force for ten years.[23] Once again, Ghana was publicly reaffirming its allegiance to the PRC and, at the same time, furthering Chinese interests in Africa. Along the same lines as Nkrumah's statement, in September 1961 the *Peking Review* published a brief article entitled "China and Africa." It read in full, "Chinese and African peoples have established a militant friendship in the struggle against their common enemy, imperialism. The Chinese people have always shown the deepest sympathy for and resolutely supported the African peoples in their patriotic struggle for national liberation against imperialism and colonialism. They have demonstrated these sentiments in various ways."[24] The militant, anti-imperialistic message was not novel for a Chinese publication. But, read in light of Nkrumah's recent visit to Beijing and his statements, China was intentionally targeting Ghana for influence in West Africa and Africa as a whole.

China used multiple means of influence to further its interests in Ghana. For example, an exhibition devoted to China's economic construction opened in Accra while President Nkrumah was in China. "The exhibition, the second of its kind ever held in West Africa, opened on August 10."[25] The *Peking Review* reported that the 3,800 exhibits included heavy and light industry, agriculture and culture, as well as education and publication. Like the exhibition later held in Algiers in 1963, the exhibits, particularly the cultural and educational exhibits, were meant to shape perceptions of China, targeting a wide African audience. "More Ghana visitors from places far away from Accra as well as people from Nigeria, Togoland and Niger came to see the exhibition."[26]

China's economic construction exhibition in Accra "aroused tremendous interest among the Ghanaian people." The Ghanaian people voiced their friendship for the Chinese and "expressed deep sympathy and support" for China by denouncing U.S. obstruction of Chinese efforts at the UN. In a specific example of China's ideological aims, Mao's works were available at the exhibition and "sold out as fast as they came in." The exhibition contributed to the broader relationship between the African and Chinese people. One visitor said, "Seeds of friendship planted in the soil of Africa are taking firm root."[27] The optimism of the exhibition was realized three months later.

Relations between Ghana and China became more tangible later that same year. In November 1961 Minister of Foreign Trade Yeh Chi-chuang and Krobo Edusei, head of a visiting Ghanaian trade delegation, signed the protocol of a trade and payments agreement for one year in Beijing. "Letters on trade, economic and technical cooperation, and cultural co-operation were also exchanged."[28] During its five-day visit to China, the Ghanaian trade delegation met Premier Zhou, which conferred high-level political respect to the Ghanaian delegation. The next year the *Peking Review* reported that Joseph Y. C. Amegashie, a Ghanaian craftsman, had presented a carved wooden tray to Premier Zhou through the Chinese embassy in Accra.[29] The motif of the carving on the tray was a Ghanaian traditional dance. According to the *Peking Review*, Amegashie presented his work in appreciation of China's exhibition in Accra the previous year. This human-interest story demonstrated China's success in communicating directly to the Ghanaian people.

The Treaty of Friendship between China and Ghana that was signed in Beijing in 1961 came into force with the exchange of the instruments of ratification on 28 March 1962 in Accra.[30] But China was already furthering political ties with Ghana. After an eight-week tour of Africa, a Chinese table tennis team of three men and three women returned home in June 1962.[31] The team visited Ghana, Guinea, Mali, Sudan, and the UAR, competing with local teams and giving exhibition matches. Notably, the team visited the three-country union—Guinea, Mali, and Ghana. The six-member team, although small in size, was nevertheless significant as a means of influencing African public perception of China.

By the end of the year, China was engaged in economic assistance to Ghana. In October 1962 Ghana and China signed the protocol of the agreement on economic and technical cooperation.[32] Under the protocol, China agreed to supply Ghana with complete sets of equipment and building material as well as technical assistance to build industrial projects and to develop paddy rice cultivation, freshwater fisheries, and handicraft industries.[33] Chinese technical assistance was a conduit to expand political influence in Ghana. In addition, *Jeune Afrique* reported that "[p]art of the Chinese loan to Ghana was to be used for two complete arms factories making grenades and mines—items suitable for use by 'freedom fighters.'"[34] Therefore, "Chinese activities began in October 1962, when Beijing provided a loan for the construction of two arms factories; Ghana, however, never used the funds."[35] During this period, from 1963 to 1964, Chinese ambassador Huang Hua was considered one of the most influential diplomats in Accra. His influence resulted in negotiations that created additional opportunities for China in Ghana. It was notable that one individual could perform so much in a country like Ghana.

Ghana and China continued to deepen relations as Chinese influence in the country grew. In January 1963 a Ghanaian government friendship delegation visited China. Led by Minister of Justice Kofi Asante Ofori-Atta, the delegation visited Hangzhou and Beijing; Premier Zhou, Chairman Liu, Vice Premier Chen Yi, and other high-ranking officials received the delegation.[36] The following month, on 27 February, a photographic exhibition devoted to Communist China's public health and sanitation work opened in Ghana.[37] This exhibition was yet another forum for the Chinese to influence the Ghanaian people directly. And, in a related example, Chinese radio reported in June 1963 that a five-member Guinean women's delegation completed a visit to China and returned to Africa.[38] Although the *Washington Post* reported the delegation to be from Guinea, its targeting of West African women was an indication of China's intentional approach.

Alongside exchange visits, the Chinese leadership continued to communicate publicly to the Ghanaian leadership. On 18 August 1963, the second anniversary of the Sino-Ghanaian Treaty of Friendship, Chairman Liu and Premier Zhou exchanged greetings with President Nkrumah. The same day, chargé d'affaires ad interim Jacob Charles Bonney hosted a reception in Beijing. In attendance were Premier Zhou and Vice Premier Li Hsien-nien. In a toast describing Sino-Ghanaian friendship, Li said that in the past two years (1961 and 1962) "frequent and amicable exchanges" had greatly promoted mutual understanding and friendship and the two parties were effectively cooperating in the economic and technical fields.[39] China had gained a better understanding of Ghana through exchange visits. Moreover, China's recognition of Ghana on significant anniversary dates served to create a climate conducive for further Chinese influence in and through Ghana.

Outside the official channels of government communications, China was also engaged in frequent public communications with the Ghanaian people. In October 1963 Chinese and Ghanaian trade unions issued a joint statement in Beijing. The National Committee of the Agricultural and Forestry Workers Trade Union of China and the Union of General Agricultural Workers of Trade Union Congress (Ghana) stated, "Both sides unanimously recognized imperialism as the source of war and enemy of national liberation and world peace, and held that independence and peace can be won only when resolute struggle is waged against imperialism and colonialism."[40] China targeted the labor group here for political opportunity. It also explored opportunities in international venues. In November 1963, for example, the African Journalists Conference convened in Accra. Over one hundred delegates from thirty-six countries attended the meeting organized by the Pan-African Journalists Union. Summarizing the message of the conference, the *Peking Review* stated, "Journalists are fighters. There must be the closest collaboration between the press and the cause of freedom in Africa. Journalists will give the fullest support to the national-liberation movements on the continent."[41] The conference was an ideal forum for China to communicate its political message to the African media. Clearly, China did not rely on formal governmental channels.

Nevertheless, China did continue to communicate officially with Ghana through its highest political channels. For example, Chairman Mao sent a message on 9 January 1964 to President Nkrumah extending his regards after Nkrumah escaped an assassination attempt.[42] On 2 January a constable assigned to the presidential guard fired five shots at President Nkrumah.[43] This assassination attempt "heightened [Nkrumah's] distress and his determination to reconstruct Ghana along Socialist lines."[44]

That same month Premier Zhou arrived in Ghana for an official visit. Coincidentally, Zhou had arrived the day before the revolution in Zanzibar.[45] During his stay, Zhou visited President Nkrumah at Fort Christianborg (present-day Osu Castle), where he had been holed up since the 2 January assassination attempt. On 12 January, according to published reports, Zhou handed a message to President Nkrumah directly from Chairman Mao. In this message, Mao congratulated Nkrumah for surviving the assassination attempt (the second in eighteen months) and blamed the attempts on imperialists and reactionaries.[46] Later in his visit, Zhou toured a government-run printing press, a government-owned distillery, and Tema harbor.[47] Both the printing press and harbor were significant targets of Chinese political and strategic influence. Garrison reported, "Speaking at a state dinner for Premier Chou En-lai President Nkrumah reiterated Ghana's support for Communist China's entry into the United Nations."[48] Nkrumah also proclaimed, "[T]he surest road to the welfare and happiness of the people lies in Socialism."[49] Clearly, Ghana had become a full supporter of China's international political agenda.[50]

After his return to China, Premier Zhou's five-nation tour of North and West Africa was characterized as an international propaganda success. "The net propaganda gain for Peking has been more than was expected here at the start of the tour."[51] In a joint communiqué issued at the end of Zhou's visit to Ghana, moreover, the two countries insisted that "African countries needed to heighten their vigilance against neo-colonialist intrigues" within their borders.[52] Mao's insistence of Western participation in Nkrumah's assassination attempts created additional intrigue. While in Ghana, Zhou offered a Chinese recommendation to Nkrumah: "In 1964 . . . [Zhou] Enlai advised Nkrumah that his new development plan, replete with soaring projects for the industrialization of Ghana, was too ambitious."[53] Put simply, Zhou pointed out that Ghana was laying the wrong emphasis on industrial development and neglecting the agricultural sector. To assist Ghana in the agricultural sphere, in February 1964, after Zhou's departure, Ambassador Huang Hua offered to send Chinese agricultural experts to increase Ghana's rice production, with the goal of self-sufficiency within two years.[54] The experts arrived in August 1964. Thus, China successfully persuaded Nkrumah of Ghana's need for agricultural expertise. Notably, PLA soldiers were known for being farmers as well, so the possibility of sending agricultural specialists as a cover was not beyond the realm of possibility. Nkrumah, however, was not always so tolerant of China's political advice.

The congruence of Ghanaian and Chinese political interests directed animosity toward their mutual enemy, the United States. In early February 1964

Ghanaians marched, in an organized group, against the U.S. embassy in Accra. At the same time, Ghana's government-controlled press attacked the U.S. government.[55] Ghanaians staged protests outside the U.S. embassy in Accra opposing "American rumor-mongering and other subversive activities" against the Ghanaian government.[56] This public demonstration reflected the political influence of Chinese activities and revealed once again that Ghana was in lockstep with China internationally. In the same month, a new united Ghanaian trade union, the Federation of Revolutionary Trade Unions (FRTU), was formed. In its first communiqué, it called on the Ghanaian people to be vigilant against "U.S. intervention and sabotage of the revolution."[57] Here, China was successful in targeting Ghanaian labor for political purposes—to publish a message serving the political interests of China.

A U.S. assessment at the time noted Ghana as a critical Communist point in Africa, although it did not point directly at Chinese influence. A U.S. State Department report on the world situation submitted to the House Foreign Affairs Committee on 2 April 1964 listed Algeria, Angola, Ghana, Mali, and Zanzibar among "critical points" subject to Communist influence.[58] Further demonstrating Chinese influence in Africa, on 13 April 1964 in Beijing, a mass rally was held to voice China's support for the South African people's struggle and for national liberation. The main speaker was Mao Tun, vice chair of the Chinese Committee for Afro-Asian Solidarity. Guest speakers included Malek Ben Nabi, head of an Algerian cultural delegation, and Miraji Mpatani Ali of Zanzibar.[59] The convergence of Chinese-targeted countries at a mass rally revealed the web of Chinese activities throughout the African continent.

High-level Chinese political leadership continued to communicate publicly to the Ghanaian leadership. But it was notable that the communications occurred on sporadic occasions, perhaps signaling waning enthusiasm on the part of Ghana. On 30 June 1964, the eve of the fourth anniversary of the founding of Ghana and its army, Chairman Liu and Premier Zhou sent a joint message of greetings to President Nkrumah. On 1 July in Beijing, the Ghanaian ambassador Joe-Fio N. Meyer held a National Day reception with Zhou and Vice Premier Li Hsien-nien among the guests.[60] Meanwhile, in terms of economic assistance, China granted an interest-free loan of $22.4 million to Ghana under an economic and technical cooperation agreement signed on 15 July 1964.[61] Although serious utilization of the Chinese loans did not begin until 1965, from 1961 to 1964 one analysis recorded a total of $40 million in Chinese economic aid to Ghana.[62] In mid-August 1964 Beijing and Accra celebrated the third anniversary of the 1961

Treaty of Friendship. In Beijing the Ghanaian ambassador held a reception attended by Vice Premier Chen Yi and Vice Foreign Minister Tseng Yung-chuan. In Accra the chargé d'affaires ad interim, Wang Yi-mu, also held a reception.[63] Although both events were significant, the Beijing reception was notable for its absence of Premier Zhou. Sino-Ghanaian relations continued to develop, but apparently without the same level of enthusiasm as at the onset.

Chinese activity in Ghana continued in earnest after codification of another agreement, this one with strategic ramifications across Africa. In 1964 "the two countries signed a secret agreement for the provision of military equipment and advisers for Ghana's 'freedom fighters.'"[64] According to one analysis, Ghana did not have sufficient capabilities at the time to train foreign fighters and therefore sought Chinese security assistance. This was illustrated earlier in the year when the director of the BAA traveled to Dar es Salaam to arrange for twenty-five militants to train in Tanzania. Notably, "Most of the men had already received some training in Peking, and all were educated." The Ghanaian official was eventually forced to ask the Algerians to give the militants advanced training. The director of the BAA, A. K. Barden, had to endure "humiliation" for having to ask the Algerians for assistance.[65] Notably, by this time the Algerians had been influenced by the Chinese.

China acted with haste after the covert security agreement was signed. In October 1964 a five-member team of Chinese guerilla warfare experts arrived at a training camp in Half Assini, a village near the Ghana–Ivory Coast border.[66] The instructors made several initial recommendations for improvement.[67] Shortly thereafter, the same Chinese security team inaugurated a twenty-day course that consisted of training in the manufacture and use of explosives, guerilla tactics, and "basic guiding and thinking on armed struggle."[68] Chinese instructors remained in Ghana while Nkrumah was in power, "although training was suspended for a short time in 1965 while preparations were made for the meeting of the OAU in Accra."[69] China, thus, was directly involved in the strategic affairs of Africa from its base of operations in Ghana.

During the same period, from October to November 1964, a newspaper in Senegal, *Afrique Nouvelle*, reported that China had supported the anti-government party in Niger, the Sawaba party. Notably, China assisted through its embassies in Ghana and Algeria.[70] Ogunsanwo reported that "the Chinese had continued to help the Cameroun U.P.C. based in Accra. . . . Their aid had partly been channelled through the Afro-Asian Solidarity Fund and partly had consisted of the training of Camerounians in guerrilla tactics in China."[71] China clearly was intent on furthering Ghana as its base of operations (not unlike Algeria), from whence it could support liberation and guerrilla movements across Africa.

At the end of the year, Ghana was again acting in Chinese political interests at the UN. In December 1964 Ghana associated itself formally with a request that the UN General Assembly consider the question of UN membership for China.[72] Ghana became the eighth such country to make the request. Algeria, Burundi, Congo-Brazzaville, Cuba, Guinea, Indonesia, and Mali had previously endorsed the request. Simultaneously, in that same month Camp Half Assini was closed down due to its proximity to the border, distance from Accra, and poor lines of communications—specifically, the condition of the roads.[73] At the same time, a replacement camp was created at Obenemasi, the site of an abandoned goldmine. By January 1965 multiple sources reported that Camp Obenemasi had 210 students and 17 Chinese instructors. China was in sole charge of the camp in Obenemasi.[74] The CIA reported that 8 specialists in guerrilla warfare and sabotage arrived in Accra on 30 December 1964.[75]

Similar to Camp Half Assini, training at Camp Obenemasi included guerrilla warfare, explosives, and weapons, but also the use of telecommunications equipment and battlefield first aid. The Chinese program in Ghana attracted Africans from many parts of the continent, including Angola, Cameroon, Congo-Kinshasa, Gabon, Malawi, Niger, Nigeria, Rwanda, Tanzania, Upper Volta (present-day Burkina Faso), and Zambia. Conversely, a large, disparate number of African youths were trained in China at three secret training centers: Harbin in Manchuria, Nanjing on the Yangtze River, and an unidentified place in Shantung Province on the North China coast. Africans were from Algeria, Angola, Benin, Cameroon, Congo-Brazzaville, Congo-Kinshasa, Guinea, Ivory Coast, Kenya, Madagascar, Mozambique, Nigeria, South Africa, and Zanzibar. The guerrilla warfare course in China lasted from 7 October 1964 until 13 February 1965 and was described by one of the participants from Ghana as "a 90-day course in theory and practice . . . arduous and intensive."[76] Thus, China was heavily engaged in the covert security assistance to Africans in Africa as well as in China.

With the amount of Chinese activity channeled to and through Ghana, the public began to voice its suspicion. In March 1965, for example, while visiting the United States, President Maurice Yaméogo of Upper Volta (present-day Burkina Faso) accused President Nkrumah of sending "subversives" to neighboring countries, of attempting to impose "arbitrary socialism" on the rest of Africa, and of maintaining close ties with China.[77] Based on the available data, he was correct on all counts. In a similar development in January the following year, President

Yaméogo declared a state of emergency and accused the former president of the Upper Volta National Assembly of having tried to hand over the country to neighboring Ghana and Communist China.[78] Furthermore, a report in March 1965 stated that President Diori Hamani of Niger charged China with trying to subvert democracy in Africa: "Diori said Peking smuggled [Communist-trained Africans] into Niger by way of Ghana and that his country would seek outside aid if the Communist infiltration increases."[79] Notably, here, an African head of state identified Ghana as a transit point for Chinese-trained African fighters to other parts of Africa. And again, in August 1965 President Hamani noted, "Young Africans, particularly intellectuals, are offered voyages to Red China, where they are indoctrinated with a political-military type of Communist ideology."[80] China was targeting West Africa through Ghana—to further its political interests in Africa.

After five years of formal relations with China, Ghana had become a base of operations. According to a CIA assessment, "The Chinese consider[ed] Ghana a base country for exporting 'revolution' to West and Central Africa."[81] Thomas Ofcansky's assertion was, therefore, not surprising: "Students from many other African nations, including, Zaire, Niger, Cameroon, Fernando Po, Tanzania, Zambia, Rwanda, Togo, Côte d'Ivoire, Burkina, Gabon, Nigeria, and Guinea, also received intelligence training from the Chinese in Ghana."[82] In addition to training Ghanaians in Ghana and in China, China had begun sending arms to Ghana. In March 1965, for example, the CIA stated, "The first known Chinese arms shipment to Ghana [was] believed to have arrived in late March. The shipment included 40 truckloads of small arms and some heavier equipment."[83] China was active in Ghana, but the activity focused mainly on the training and arming of African fighters. China's relations with Ghana had become one-sided.

Meanwhile, China continued to send public messages to Ghana. "On the occasion of Ghana's National Day [in March 1965], Chairman Liu and Premier Zhou sent a joint message of greetings to President Kwame Nkrumah." Ghanaian ambassador to China Joe-Fio N. Meyer hosted a reception in Beijing on 6 March to celebrate, with Zhou and Vice Premier Li Hsien-nien in attendance. Meyer described Ghana's achievements, the importance of African unity, and the disruptive efforts of imperialists, neo-colonialists, and their agents. "He pointed out that the imperialists were groundlessly accusing Ghana of engaging in subversive activities in other African countries."[84]

At about the same time (between February and April 1965), a Chinese NPC delegation toured West Africa. The delegation toured the Central African Republic, Ghana, Guinea, and Mali.[85] According to one observer, the purpose was to generate goodwill toward China and "to solicit support for keeping the Soviet Union out of Algiers [for the Second Afro-Asian People's Solidarity Conference]."[86] But the NPC delegation visit coincided with a high degree of Chinese activity in Ghana. In early May 1965 China and Ghana "pledged their determination to strengthen further the existing bonds of friendship and mutual understanding," according to a Beijing broadcast at the end of talks between Premier Zhou and Kojo Botsio, foreign minister of Ghana.[87] At about the same time, moreover, a new course at Camp Obenemasi started with fifty students from Niger.[88] Between May and June 1965, a PRC vice foreign minister visited the Central African Republic, Congo-Brazzaville, Ghana, Guinea, Mali, and Morocco.[89] On 5 May 1965 Liu Ningyi, vice chair of the Standing Committee, reported to that committee on the NPC delegation's recent visit to five African countries, including Ghana. In his report, Vice Chairman Liu stated that President Nkrumah expressed the view that the success of the Chinese Communist Party and the liberation of China had "dealt imperialism its biggest blow."[90] Nkrumah's strong support for China was not novel. The absence of Chinese praise for Ghana, however, was a significant indicator of the state of relations between the two countries.

Events in the second half of 1965 foreshadowed the looming fate of Nkrumah. After the June 1965 coup in Algiers, Nkrumah received an intelligence report, purportedly from a Russian source, of Chinese complicity in the coup; after hearing this report, he placed Chinese activities at the training camps under the supervision of a trusted general.[91] Although the Protocol on Dispatching Military Experts by the government of China to Ghana was signed in August 1965, Sino-Ghanaian relations were not positive.[92] With suspicion planted in his mind, Nkrumah began to doubt Chinese intentions in Ghana. The reorganization of his intelligence organization, seen in this light, was significant. The BAA was newly reorganized in October 1965 to comprise four departments, as well as an African Affairs Center (the Center) and a press branch. The Center had been opened in 1959 and had housed foreign fighters from across Africa. By February 1966 the Center had 136 residents. As originally conceived, the BAA was to evaluate residents and to recommend the most trusted and militant for training, sometimes by Chinese instructors, and sent for operations around Africa. "It was the duty of the Bureau to maintain a steady influx of Freedom Fighters into Ghana and members of the staff prepared annual estimates covering how many should be recruited and at what cost." The annual cost of the Center's activities was approximately £50,890 in 1959, £100,000 in 1963, and £127,000 in 1964.[93] But with the new security environment, the BAA's reorganization demonstrated Nkrumah's distrust of China, specifically its advisers in Ghana.

In some sense, China could perceive that political conditions in Ghana were not in Nkrumah's favor. In late 1965 China finally convinced Nkrumah to form a people's militia, which might have maintained his hold on power.[94] In December 1965 Nkrumah announced his intention to set up a people's militia.[95] China had on multiple occasions recommended to Nkrumah to establish a militia, and the militia was eventually created, but its organization lacked funds and the army resisted it. Even if the militia was given time and resources, it was too little, too late. In early 1966 an armed revolt occurred in nearby Equatorial Guinea. "A press release issued [in] Accra, capital of Ghana, and signed by Jesus Mba Ovono, Secretary-General of the People's Idea of Equatorial Guinea, announced: Our first groups of the future liberation army of Equatorial Guinea have taken positions in the mountain of Rio Muni and started military operations against the Spanish colonists."[96] Ghana had become a base of operations for African radicals and guerrilla groups, but the external Chinese support it had received would soon come back to haunt Nkrumah.

Eight

REVOLUTION DERAILED

Sino-Ghanaian relations began cautiously and moved quickly in the direction of covert security assistance. The one-sided nature of relations was the demise of close relations between Nkrumah's Ghana and Communist China. On 24 February 1966 a coup d'état removed Nkrumah from power and changed the country's foreign and security policy. The Ghanaian army "toppled the Nkrumah regime while Nkrumah was out of the country on a fatuous mission to end the Vietnam war."[1] It became clear that the coup was timed to coincide with Nkrumah's absence from the country, to include a visit to China. According to General Joseph Ankrah in a 23 February nationwide radio address, the coup was planned in Kumasi three weeks before it took place and was carried out without any aid from outside Ghana.[2] Kumasi was the traditional capital of the Ashanti, who were known to be unruly in the early days of Gold Coast independence. But a Western report indicated that planning for the coup began months in advance. J. W. K. Harley, commissioner of police, and Colonel Emmanuel K. Kotoka, commander of the Second Brigade in Kumasi, organized and led a small group of young army and like-minded police officers.[3] General Ankrah, Ghana's new military leader in the newly formed National Liberation Council (NLC), was not included in the deliberations until the last moment because he did not have any units under his command, according to this report. "The National Liberation Council, as the military government was styled, could count on the intelligentsia and on the traditional rulers, both of which groups had been alienated from the Nkrumah regime."[4] The latter group—traditional rulers, many from the inland region like Kumasi—was particularly helpful because of the rulers' roles in society prior to British rule and in the creation of the modern nation-state. Because China developed such close relations with Nkrumah, it would find it difficult to forge new ties with post-Nkrumah Ghana.

Without a doubt, the coup altered the nature and character of Ghana's relations with foreign countries, Communist nations in particular. "Over 1,000 Russians, East Europeans, and Chinese were promptly expelled after the coup. They included 665 Soviet and 52 Chinese technicians, security advisers, and 'freedom fighter' instructors. The technicians included men in fishing and construction."[5]

After the coup, a copy of Nkrumah's *Strategy and Tactics of Revolutionary Warfare with Particular Reference to the African Revolution* was found in Nkrumah's residence at Fort Christiansborg.[6] According to the post-Nkrumah government, the book was based on guerrilla warfare courses given by Chinese instructors at Camp Obenemasi and included chapters devoted to a people's militia.[7] The influence of Chinese doctrine and tactics was exposed. Along the same lines, the Nkrumah Institute of Economics and Political Science (or the Winneba Ideological Institute) housed over three hundred Chinese publications in its library.[8] The presence of Chinese publications was indicative of certain amounts of influence on Nkrumah's government, but that influence was unable to prevent the NLC from gaining power. Yet Nkrumah remained defiant.

On 25 February 1966, a day after the coup in Ghana, President Nkrumah issued a statement in Beijing. He called on Ghanaians to "remain calm, but firm in determination and resistance." That same day, the CIA reported a meeting between Premier Zhou and President Nkrumah. According to the CIA, "Chou told Nkrumah China [would] solve [the] Ghana coup with military operations mounted out of Guinea." The report continued, "Nkrumah further stated the Chinese Communists will send arms, ammunition, and train guerillas in Guinea. They will, in addition, broadcast from Radio Conakry to stir up internal Ghana [*sic*] sentiment to support Nkrumah and to oppose the National Liberation Council."[9] Although China's commitment to Nkrumah was overemphasized, the report described potential active Chinese support of Nkrumah. Before leaving Beijing on 28 February, Nkrumah issued another statement dismissing the rebellion and vowing to stamp it out. He also expressed thanks to China, with Chairman Liu, Premier Zhou, and Vice Chairman of the Standing Committee of the NPC Lin Feng seeing him off.[10] Clearly, this was a show of high-level Chinese political support for Nkrumah.

In Ghana events occurred rapidly to remove Chinese influence. On 28 February and 1 March, the Chinese embassy in Accra sent two notes to Ghanaian authorities because of Ghanaian troop search and attacks on Chinese experts. The *Peking Review* later reported that a group of Chinese experts and embassy staff, numbering 125, returned to China on 5 March.[11] Four days after the coup, moreover, Ghana sent a diplomatic note to the Chinese embassy requesting all Chinese technical experts working in Ghana to leave immediately.[12] As a result, "Ghana expelled 430 Chinese nationals, including three intelligence officers and thirteen guerrilla warfare specialists."[13] Also in early March 1966, four Chinese technical advisers were beaten after being arrested for not having Ghanaian identity cards. The *New York Times* described the four as "experts supervising the construction of a textile plant."[14] At the time, the Chinese embassy in Accra delivered three additional notes (on 6, 15, and 19 March) to the Ghanaian foreign ministry to protest moves taken by Ghanaian authorities to "worsen relations" between the two countries.[15] The *Peking Review* never directly identified the relationship between the Chinese embassy in Accra and the Nkrumah regime. Notably, however, in early 1966, "The Chinese chargé d'affaires came to [Nkrumah's] headquarters with an oral message from [Zhou] Enlai advising him to drop the visit as he 'needed to look after the situation at home.'"[16] Had Nkrumah acted on Zhou's advice—as he had with regards to Ghana's agricultural policy—the fate of Ghana might have been altered.

Nevertheless, after his removal from power Nkrumah was "entrusted with the leadership of the Government and Democratic party of Guinea" under the Guinean constitution. According to a provision in the Guinean constitution, all Africans who were "instruments of the African revolution" became citizens of Guinea. Ambassador Abdoulaye Diallo of Guinea clarified this point on 4 March 1966. Mr. Nkrumah, Ambassador Diallo stated, was given "all the rights and duties" of the Guinea presidency but Sekou Toure remained the chief executive of Guinea.[17] Thus, Nkrumah had been given what amounted to an honorary presidency in Guinea. Affording Nkrumah this honorary position in Guinea, if seen in light of the aforementioned CIA report on Chinese assistance, was a threat to the new NLC government in Ghana. Meanwhile, China's activities throughout West Africa were being exposed.

According to President Felix Houphouet-Boigny of Ivory Coast in a publicized April 1966 interview, China used two forms of expansion in Africa. One was the continuous subversion of existing governments through Chinese political agitators and instructors in guerrilla warfare and sabotage; the other was corruption of politicians and officials and economic aid projects whose nature would give Beijing a start toward control of vital industries and increase the number of

Chinese working in key countries.[18] President Houphouet-Boigny was describing China's activities in Ghana and elsewhere on the continent. These Chinese activities, according to Houphouet-Boigny, were the pattern followed in Ghana before the overthrow of Nkrumah. Notably, Nkrumah and Houphouet-Boigny had met face to face in 1957, charting different paths to independence. Houphouet-Boigny sought close association with France prior to and after Ivory Coast gained independence in 1960; Nkrumah sought the opposite with Britain.[19] President Houphouet-Boigny also made the following comments about future Chinese objectives in Africa: the PRC aim was "to obtain either open or covert control of governments and their economies rather than wholesale conversion of the African masses to Communism." He warned, "Africa, underpopulated Africa, is their long-term goal and we must be alive to the danger."[20] The president of Ivory Coast had articulated the means and pattern of Chinese influence in African countries. China had worked diligently and pragmatically to further its influence in Africa, but now its activities were being exposed.

The relationship between the new Ghanaian government—the NLC—and China continued to deteriorate, as might have been expected after the coup. In early April 1966 the new Ghanaian government of General Ankrah accused China of sending "a substantial quantity of arms to Guinea," where Nkrumah had taken refuge, to help Nkrumah carry out a counterrevolution in Ghana.[21] China responded mutedly through communication at an international forum. From 27 June to 9 July 1966 in Beijing, representatives of writers of Asian and African countries attended the Emergency Meeting of Afro-Asian Writers in support of the Vietnamese people against American imperialist aggression.[22] The Resolution on the Ghana Coup, published by the Emergency Meeting, denounced the military coup and expressed support to Nkrumah. It also condemned the delivery of African nationalists from Ghana to Fernando Poo (present-day Bioko in Equatorial Guinea) and Portuguese Guinea (present-day Guinea-Bissau).[23] The new Ghanaian government was removing Ghana as a Chinese base of operations in Africa. On 17 July Chairman Mao received delegates and observers (from international organizations) to the Emergency Meeting of Afro-Asian Writers. Among the delegates were Armah and J. Biki of Ghana and Yahya Mohamed Hassani and Mohamed Ali Hemedi of Tanzania.[24] While they were not government representatives, Armah and Biki were Ghanaians who nevertheless had direct ties to China.

The NLC continued its purge of Chinese influence within Ghana throughout the remainder of the year. In September 1966 the *Washington Post* reported that the new Ghanaian military government notified China, as well as the Soviet Union and eight Eastern European countries, of its intent to renegotiate trade agreements signed by ousted president Nkrumah. The reasons for renegotiating were not disclosed, but General Ankrah said he would remove all aspects of the treaties "not in the best interest of Ghana."[25] This implied, of course, that there were aspects of treaties that were not in the interest of Ghana—the Protocol on Dispatching Military Experts by the government of China to Ghana as an example. Responding to NLC actions, on 1 October 1966 the PRC embassy in Accra delivered a note to the Ghanaian ministry of foreign affairs lodging "the most serious protest" with the Ghanaian authorities against their anti-Chinese policy.[26] At the end of the month, the Chinese embassy in Accra delivered a note to the Ghanaian foreign ministry protesting Ghana's unilateral suspension of relations between the two countries.[27] Ultimately, China announced that it was withdrawing all its embassy personnel from Accra. It blamed Ghana for unilaterally disrupting diplomatic relations, according to the NCNA.[28] A PRC note also said an aide-mémoire dated 20 October from the Ghanaian ministry of foreign affairs had informed the Chinese embassy that Ghana was suspending relations between the two countries.[29] All embassy staff would withdraw by 5 November 1966.[30]

Although it was successful ridding Ghana of Chinese interference, the NLC suspected the worst from Communist countries. In February 1967 Ghana accused the Soviet Union, China, and Cuba of attempting to restore Nkrumah to power by subverting the regime.[31] The deputy chair of the NLC, J. W. K. Harley, charged the Soviet and Chinese embassies in Conakry, Guinea, with supplying funds to aid in subverting Nkrumah's successors. Notably, Lefever regarded J. W. K. Harley as coauthor of the 1966 coup, because he had been intelligence chief and police commissioner.[32] Furthermore, Harley said the Russians had given Nkrumah $200,000 and the Chinese, $1.4 million. Harley displayed Russian, Czech, and American arms and explosives as evidence. Harley continued his charges, noting that Nkrumah had tried to smuggle arms to Ghana but failed. Instead, according to Harley, Nkrumah decided to hire terrorists and open bases in Nigeria and Dahomey (present-day Benin). While Harley's accusations may have been exaggerated, his evidence demonstrated not only Nkrumah's determination, but also the extent to which the Chinese were interested in maintaining a militant presence in Ghana.[33] But Chinese attempts were to no avail.

In some respects, the numbers reveal the nature of Sino-Ghanaian relations. Between 1954 and 1967, Ghana received $3.5 million in economic aid from China.[34] The CIA reported that there were no Chinese economic technicians in Ghana at the end of 1967. From 1954 to 1970, according to the CIA, China gave Ghana $40 million in credits and grants, none of which was in 1969 or 1970.[35] But, clearly, these numbers do not completely describe China's relations with Ghana. Some funds were used to convert Ghana into a covert base of operations. Ghana's role as a covert operations base was altered because of the coup. The NLC understood Nkrumah's past relations with China and attempted to prevent a similar rise again in Ghana as well as elsewhere in West Africa.

Between 1968 and 1970, relations between Ghana and China were at their lowest point. By this time China, it seemed, was content to focus its attention elsewhere in Africa. At the same time, it was learning from its experiences in Ghana, which was of value elsewhere in Africa. (Specifically, it had learned that the ramifications of coups against African strongmen could negatively affect bilateral relations.) Moreover, Chinese personnel had benefited from their West African experiences. For example, on 31 January 1972 the Chinese representative to the UN and former ambassador to Ghana, Huang Hua, made a statement on Africa at the special UNSC meeting. He pointed out that holding the meeting in Africa (Addis Ababa, Ethiopia) was a victory for African countries struggling to win and safeguard national independence.[36] Huang's experience while serving in Ghana gave him firsthand knowledge of the African political environment. This experience was a byproduct of Chinese activities in Ghana. Thus, despite the negative turn in Sino-Ghanaian relations, China had gained valuable experiences in Ghana.

After six years Ghana and China decided to restore relations in 1972. On 29 February 1972 China and Ghana issued a joint press communiqué on the resumption of diplomatic relations between the two countries. Yang Chi-liang, ambassador to Nigeria, and Major General N. A. Aferi, commissioner for foreign affairs, signed the communiqué in Lagos.[37] The six-year respite had allowed Accra time to reconsider its relations with the outside world; it also allowed the perception of China in West Africa to alter. But all the while the Chinese continued to pursue their interests elsewhere in Africa.

Using the UN as an international forum for public communications, China expressed its opinion of security in Africa. In the same vein as Huang Hua's statement, Chinese representative Chang Yung-kuan spoke at a UN Special Committee on Decolonization meeting on 1 March 1972. He noted the excellent situation on the African continent in favor of the national liberation movements.[38] China had been removed from Ghana, but it was intent on furthering its interests elsewhere on the continent.

Meanwhile, also in 1972, Ghana began its Feed Yourself program that focused on generating an increasing effort to raise more food crops, even in urban areas.[39] By this time, Communist Chinese farm experts had replaced Nationalist Chinese ones, who had temporarily made a presence in the country, demonstrating that Beijing's recommendations for a focused agricultural policy in Ghana were in fact correct. Kwame Nkrumah died in April 1972; there was no fanfare.[40] The muted response from China symbolized its desire to focus on a new chapter in relations with Ghana, which maintained an important political role in West Africa.

Chinese efforts were rewarded at the end of the year. From 8 to 9 September 1972 a Ghanaian trade and goodwill mission visited China.[41] Kodjo Barney Agbo, member of the succeeding government National Redemption Council and Commissioner for Industries of Ghana, led the delegation with Roving Ambassador Joseph Emmanuel Appiah as the deputy. While in China, the Ghanaian delegation met with Minister of Foreign Trade Pai Hsiang-kuo, Vice Foreign Minister Ho Ying, Vice Minister of Economic Relations with Foreign Countries Chen Mu-hua, and others. While some of the Chinese participants (notably Ho Ying) had prior experience in Africa, China set the meeting at mid-level, focusing on trade and economic relations. China was not replaying its policies during Nkrumah's rule. The following year the new Chinese policy with Ghana achieved a success. In late March 1973 China renewed an interest-free loan made during Nkrumah's regime for construction of irrigation facilities, chemical complexes, a cotton complex, and a textile factory.[42] Later that same year, China also helped construct a cement factory. In 1974 it donated agricultural machines and sports equipment to Ghana. One year later, "China's current programme in Ghana involve[d] a contribution toward the development of the Dawkenya scheme irrigating 1,200 acres; and the construction of a 50-mile canal from the Volta lake to the Accra plains."[43]

Similar to the Chinese muted response to Nkrumah's death, the Ghanaian government did not issue a formal, public message upon Mao's death in September 1976. The lack of public communications in both cases signified a desire to move past previous relations. Ghana no longer acted as a Chinese base of operations; rather, China was able to begin afresh bilateral relations in this critical West African nation.

PART IV

EASTERN JEWEL

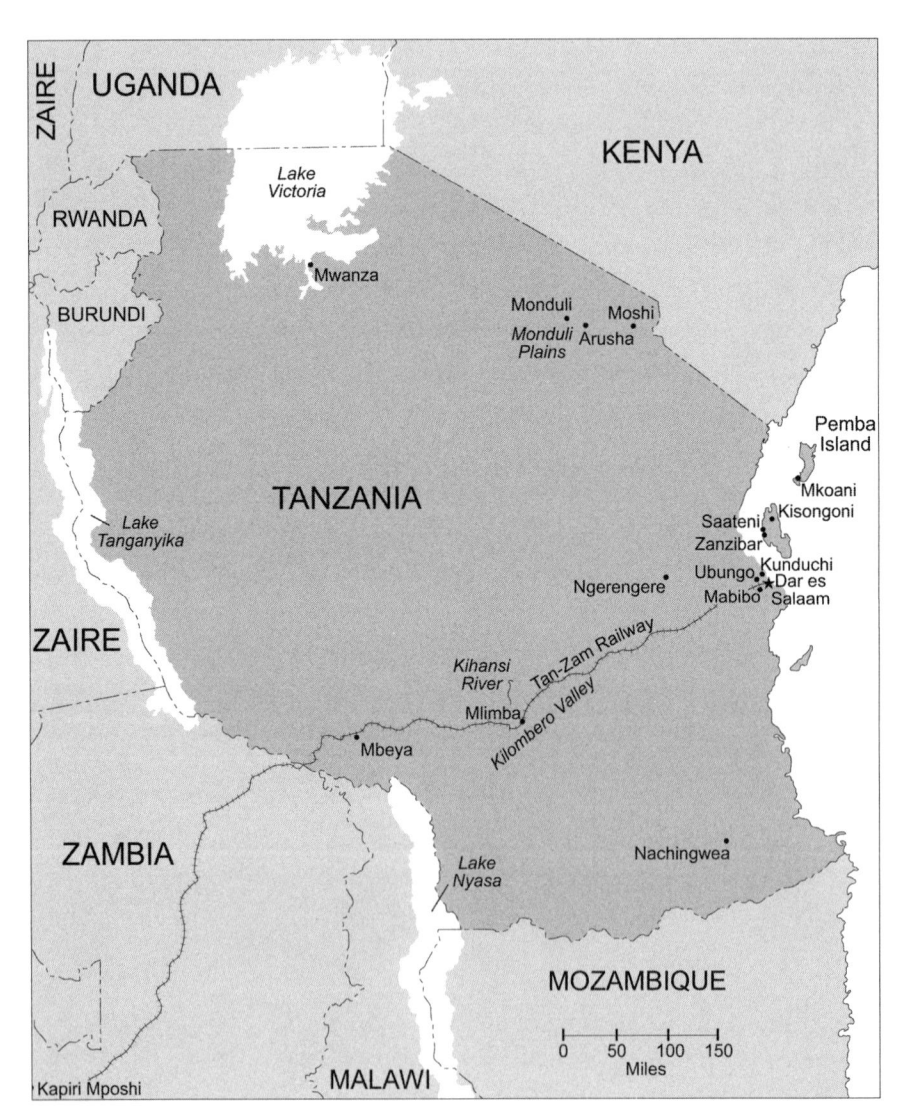

Map 3. Tanzania

Nine

INDEPENDENCE AND REVOLUTION

On the other side of the African continent, China found a different geographic and historic environment. "One of the most important results of the [Second World] war in so far as the internal administration of East Africa as a whole was concerned, was the revival of the idea of closer co-operation between the three territories" of Kenya, Uganda, and Tanganyika. While Britain preferred to control its territories together, the context of local domestic situations did not allow such control. In the postwar years, despite cultivation of natural and mineral resources, the standard of living of the majority of the African population in Tanganyika remained low and the supply of public services was limited.[1] In Zanzibar the Second World War and the return of prosperity produced, as scholar Anthony Clayton put it, "a sense of purpose uniting all the islands' inhabitants, in particular ending much of the bitterness between Arabs and Asians. . . . In the immediate post-war years the general arousal of nationalist and anti-colonial sentiments, [moreover], carried a particular local significance in Zanzibar, due to Arab resentment at British policies in Egypt and Palestine."[2] This sentiment in Zanzibar persisted and extended onto the mainland—to the benefit of Chinese interests in East Africa before their arrival.

In response to European policies and programs, natives in Tanganyika and Zanzibar organized to improve social, political, and economic conditions. According to Professor Abdin Chande, the Muslims in the region played a particularly important role in anticolonial organizations. "Some of this anticolonial resistance became channeled into organizational activities by Muslim groups responding to the socioeconomic inequalities."[3] In 1922, for example, the Tanganyika Territory African Civil Service Association (TTACSA) was established in Tanga to fight for the privileges of African civil servants. That same decade TTACSA's successor, the Tanganyika African Association (TAA), was set up in Dar es Salaam. The governor of Tanganyika Territory (1925–1931), Sir Donald Cameron, supported the creation of the TAA to provide Africans with more means of developing self-reliance and responsibility.[4] "After World War II, the TAA became increasingly political and began to develop into a national movement with branches in different parts of the country."[5] In Zanzibar the African Association for Immigrant Workers—known simply as the African Association—was formed in 1934. The African Association had roots in football teams of young Africans that appeared in the late 1920s. In 1931 all the teams converged to form the African Sports Club that toured Tanganyika.[6] The African Association eventually corresponded with the TAA; these groups later held two joint meetings. For the Chinese, these early political organizations laid a solid foundation for potential exploitation as independence approached.

In the immediate period before independence, additional political organizations were created. The Tanganyika African National Union (TANU) was established in 1954 "to succeed TAA as a national political organization," creating a pro-independence movement for the first time.[7] In 1946 the words "Tanganyika, African, national, and union" were linked together in India by a small band of Tanganyikans who had served on the King's African Rifles in Burma.[8] The All-Muslim National Union of Tanganyika (AMNUT) was formed in 1957 and acted as a Muslim pressure group in Dar es Salaam. Not all organizations, however, cooperated with one another. For example, "AMNUT was roundly denounced by Muslim leaders who were strong supporters of TANU."[9] Meanwhile, on Zanzibar in December 1955 members of the Arab Association, formed at the turn of the century to represent Arabs, created a new Zanzibar Nationalist Party (ZNP).[10] The ZNP was created in a time (between 1952 and 1960) when Zanzibar was considered "a land of almost pathological communal suspicion" due to ethnic, political, and economic divisions.[11] Thus, social and political fault lines existed on Zanzibar but were less prevalent on the mainland. Julius Nyerere, soon to be president of Tanganyika, understood religion's impact: "Nyerere was apprehensive that the highly emotional subject of Muslim educational backwardness might create dissension and disunity in the country; therefore, to keep Muslim demands at bay, he kept on insisting that Tanzania's politics knows no religion."[12] The newly created political organizations were means through which the native population could voice grievances, which were of notable political interest to China.

Communist China used radio communications to initiate contact with East Africa. China may have been interested in the region because of recent events. In April 1959 the alliance in Zanzibar strengthened between African-dominated Afro-Shirazi Party (ASP) and the ZNP, brought about by Pan-African Freedom Movement for East and Central Africa (PAFMECA), headed by Nyerere. In June 1959 broadcasts from China in English were "bombarding East and Central Africa ... with a strong, clear signal." The clarity of the radio signal was particularly notable at the time. "Everyone who has heard the Peiping radio in this area marvel[ed] at how clearly it [came] in." The Chinese message to the East African audience was simple: "Listeners in Zanzibar ... heard glowing descriptions of industrial and agricultural progress under the Communist regime."[13] After these initial broadcasts, Beijing promoted communications in person. For example, Abdul Rahman Mohamed (also known as "Babu"), secretary general of the ZNP, visited China in January 1960.[14] Vice Premier Chen Yi received Babu in Beijing. As the first known visit of a Zanzibari official to China, this marked the beginning of China's attempts to contact and cultivate relations with influential individuals on the island. Later in the year, on 24 July 1960, Chairman Mao Zedong, Chairman Liu Shaoqi, and Premier Zhou Enlai received Latin American and African guests who were visiting Beijing.[15] Among the guests was another ZNP group, a delegation led by Miraz Shaalab Abdulla. Typical of its operations on the continent, China cultivated ties with various members of the same group in Zanzibar.

China targeted certain segments of the Zanzibari society. In June 1960 the ACFTU sent a cable to the Zanzibar and Pemba Federation of Labor, backing the Zanzibar workers' fight against the establishment of a U.S. rocket base in their country.[16] Predominately African oriented, the ASP supported the Zanzibar and Pemba Federation of Labor, comprising 9 unions with over 3,000 members as well as 2 other unions with about 1,200 members, together. By directing operations at the ASP, China had begun cultivating ties with the second major ethnic group on the island, Africans. China had contacts with Babu and Miraz Shaalab Abdulla of the ZNP, the Arab-dominated party. Around the same time, the Chinese National Women's Federation also conveyed its public and political support in a cable to the Department of Women of the ZNP. This demonstrated another example of Chinese targeting a specific group.

Meanwhile, Chinese radio communications continued to flood the East African airwaves. By September 1960 Chinese radio broadcasts to Africa totaled seventy hours a week in English, Portuguese, and French. This was an early demonstration of Chinese foreign language exploitation capabilities. Because of the presence of several hundred Chinese traders, radio broadcasts to Zanzibar included a few hours each week in Cantonese as well. A possible explanation for intense Chinese radio propaganda could be found in U.S. activities there. "Chinese Communist influence in Zanzibar forced a change in United States plans to establish a satellite tracking station there." U.S. Project Courier was a military project linked to a U.S. civilian plan to set up a satellite observation post. China cultivated its contacts in Zanzibar to influence decision making on the plan. "The Communist Chinese offered twenty-five free trips to Peiping to members of the ZNP. About twenty [were] there [by September 1960] for visits of three or four months."[17] Interestingly, the *New York Times* reported that Chinese contacts with Zanzibaris had been mostly among the island's 47,000 Arabs. Nevertheless, by offering Zanzibaris a visit to China, Beijing influenced Zanzibari public perceptions and, therefore, may have affected local attitudes towards U.S. activities on the island.

By December 1960 it was clear that China was targeting and cultivating contacts in Zanzibar for political purposes. Zanzibar, it was believed, "had become a launching pad for a Communist assault on the African continent—backed jointly by Moscow, Peiping and Prague, with an assist from President Gamal Abdel Nasser's United Arab Republic."[18] According to Anthony Clayton, China's interest in Zanzibar "had been aroused by the events of 1961."[19] Two contentious elections, campaign violence, and rioting occurred in 1961—all of which contributed to an unstable, divisive environment in Zanzibar that was advantageous to Chinese interests and activities in the region.

Chinese attention soon turned to mainland East Africa. Tanganyika gained independence on 9 December 1961. Different sources reported that Huang Hua, Chinese ambassador to Ghana, attended independence celebrations.[20] Shen Su, a PRC commentator, described the event in this manner: "On December 9, a young African officer lit a big Uhuru (Freedom) torch atop the snow-capped Kilimanjaro, Africa's highest mountain, to celebrate the independence of Tanganyika—the latest among the African states to shake off colonial rule."[21] Later, Ambassador Huang handled negotiations that led to the establishment of relations between China and Tanganyika.[22] The Chinese began communicating directly to the Tanganyikan people in the immediate post-independence period.

According to the *Peking Review*, the Chinese people greeted Tanganyika's independence "after years of brutal colonial rule." That publication reported that on 11 December Premier Zhou and Foreign Minister Chen Yi sent messages to Tanganyikan president Julius Nyerere "extending warm congratulations on the establishment of diplomatic relations." A 12 December *People's Daily* editorial also stated, "The people of China and Tanganyika, both having suffered under imperialism and colonialism, have always sympathized with and supported each other." China created an immediate shared historical bond between the two nations, laying the foundation for further influence. The editorial continued by declaring that "the Tanganyikan people will certainly have the sympathetic support of the 650 million Chinese people in their continued struggle against imperialism, in upholding national independence and building their homeland." Supporting Communist China's rights in the UN, the *Peking Review* reported that President Nyerere said in return, "[T]here is only one China in the world which we recognize and that is the People's Republic of China which truly represents the Chinese people."[23] After receiving Chinese support, therefore, Tanganyika gave support to China in return. Chinese activities were cemented with the establishment of a diplomatic mission in Dar es Salaam on 24 January 1962.[24]

By that time, Chinese attention was directed simultaneously to the mainland and to Zanzibar. In July 1962 Chinese journalists demanded immediate release of Babu, secretary general of ZNP and publisher of the pro-Communist *Zanews*, and other Zanzibaris arrested by British colonial authorities in Zanzibar.[25] "Closely connected with [the ZNP] headquarters was *Zanews*, a cyclostyled publication completely taken up with Chinese agitation and propaganda and unquestionably controlled and financed by the New China News Agency, some of its issues have contained only material provided by this agency. Numerous other publishing ventures were closely connected with Zanews and the objective behind this organization was to keep East Africa steadily supplied with Chinese communist propaganda material."[26] Furthermore, Clayton made clear Babu was no friend of the West. "In 1962 Babu instigated the burning of the British Information Office and other acts of sabotage in protest against Britain's refusal to grant immediate independence, for which he was arrested on a charge of sedition and sentenced to fifteen months in prison."[27] Notably, Babu had visited China in January 1960.[28] In addition, "As General Secretary of the Z.N.P. [Babu] organised and edited a daily broadsheet Zanews which proclaimed that it was an agent for the New China News Agency. At this time the Z.N.P. was in receipt of a number of scholarships for study in Communist countries." The All-China Journalists' Association (ACJA), an organization established by the Communist Party of China, voiced its demand for Babu's immediate release in a message to the Federation of Progressive Trade Unions of Zanzibar. The ZNP supported the Federation of Progressive

Trade Unions, which comprised 4 unions totaling approximately 1,200 members; it also supported 4 other unions, adding another 500 members.[29] Compared with Chinese support to the ASP, the ACJA-supported ZNP demonstrated continued Chinese support for two divergent elements, widening "the cracks in Zanzibar society." "Ghana, China and Radio Cairo supported the Z.N.P. while Nyerere in Tanganyika supported the A.S.P." At the same time, China had shown support for the ASP in June 1960.[30] Thus, China was creating an ideal environment for future influence of political activities.

By the end of the year, China began direct in-person communications to the region by sending personnel to the mainland. Between 30 November and 14 December 1962, a Chinese cultural and friendship delegation toured Tanganyika. Led by Chu Kuang, vice chair of the CCRFC, the delegation stayed for two weeks.[31] The Chinese delegation attended the presidential inauguration of Julius Nyerere on 9 December. President Nyerere and Vice President Rashidi Kawawa received the head of the Chinese delegation; the Chinese representative signed a cultural cooperation agreement with a representative of the Republic of Tanganyika, covering the exchange of students, artists, publications, and other cultural materials.[32] China had quickly established a channel for social and political influence. On the occasion of the proclamation of the founding of the Republic of Tanganyika in December 1962, Premier Zhou also sent President Julius Nyerere a greeting.[33] This conferred official Chinese respect to the new government. On 14 December Ambassador Ho Ying presented his credentials to President Nyerere.[34] At the same time, the Chinese cultural and goodwill delegation headed by Chu Kuang ended its two-week visit to Tanganyika.

The following year brought continued Chinese activities to the region. In January 1963 a Chinese cultural and goodwill mission toured East Africa.[35] On 4 February 1963 Liu Ningyi, leader of the Chinese delegation, addressed the Third Afro-Asian People's Solidarity Conference in Moshi, Tanganyika. China took advantage of the international forum to communicate its political message. Reporting to the NPC regarding the event, Liu said simply, "We have always regarded the just struggle of other peoples of Asia and Africa as our own struggle and their victory as our own victory."[36] China was again creating a sense of shared backgrounds and interests—laying the political groundwork for the local environment. In February 1963 the *Washington Post* reported that Dar es Salaam had established "itself firmly as the most active nationalist center in Africa and the unofficial 'capital' of all the countries still under colonial rule."[37] Like Accra from 1957 to 1958, Dar es Salaam was haven to governments-in-exile, headquarters of banned political parties, and host to frequent African unity conferences. Therefore, China was in the midst of influential political groups representing not just Tanganyika but also aspiring nations across southern Africa. Headquarters of the Pan-African Freedom Movement for East, Central and Southern Africa (PAFMECSA) and the regional headquarters of the All-African Trade Union Federation (AATUF), Dar es Salaam more specifically was home to fourteen exiled or forbidden political parties from such countries as Mozambique, South Africa, and Southern Rhodesia (present-day Zimbabwe). By aligning with Tanganyika, China could use Dar es Salaam as a base for political activities across all of southern Africa.

China continued its operations by communicating to targeted, influential individuals who were invited to China. On 26 February 1963 three foreign journalists visited China. Among the group was W. M. Bhukoli, assistant propaganda secretary of TANU and editor of *Uhuru*, the Swahili language organ of TANU, who was received by Vice Premier Lu Ting-yi.[38] In May 1963 Chairman Mao also met with members of a Tanganyika women's delegation. Bibi Titi Mohamed, member of the Tanganyika parliament, member of the Central Committee of TANU, and chair of the National Union of Tanganyika Women, led the delegation to China.[39] Muslims, who were well organized, may also have been a target group. "In the postcolonial period (October 1963), a Muslim society known as Daawa al-Islamiyya was established to promote the unification and advancement of Muslims—for instance, by expanding the number of Muslim schools."[40] Thus, China was targeting and cultivating journalists and women, both of whom had political influence in Tanganyika and East Africa.

By the end of the year Chinese and Tanganyikan organizations were communicating the same messages. In November 1963 Chinese and Tanganyikan trade unions issued a joint statement in Beijing regarding the struggle against imperialism and colonialism and for national liberation. The Tanganyikan Federation of Labor and the ACFTU stated in part, "The two sides confirmed that imperialism, colonialism and the reactionaries of the various countries were common enemies of the workers and people of the various countries in Asia, Africa and Latin America."[41] In less than four years, Chinese activities had targeted groups in both Tanganyika and Zanzibar—identifying interest groups and preparing the environment for future operations.

Zanzibar achieved independence at the end of the year, and Chinese were present to congratulate in person. "A Chinese representative attended the independence celebrations of the Island State [of Zanzibar] and diplomatic relations were established on 12 December [1963]. This action took on a new dimension and significance when the Zanzibar revolution took place exactly a month after independence; [Communist] China simply transferred recognition to the new regime."[42] Ambassador to Tanganyika Ho Ying attended independence celebrations in Zanzibar.[43]

At about the same time, a joint communiqué issued by the Chinese and Tanganyikan governments announced that President Nyerere had accepted Chairman Liu's invitation to visit China in February 1964.[44] Chinese influence was expanding on both the mainland and the island. Of course, China's influence should be viewed strategically vis-à-vis its apprehension of U.S. expansion into the Indian Ocean region. For example, citing British, Indian, and U.S. open sources, the *Peking Review* noted with disdain the U.S. Seventh Fleet's expansion of operations into the Indian Ocean.[45] Before Nyerere traveled to Communist China, however, events in Zanzibar and Tanganyika occurred—to the long-term strategic benefit of China.

Ten

OPEN DOOR

By the mid-1960s China was dabbling in activities across the African continent, but particularly in East Africa. Tanganyika and Zanzibar were focal points of Chinese political interests. In Zanzibar a revolution changed the fabric of the society. The revolution restratified the economic structures and social systems and changed the ethnic composition of the island.[1] "In January 1964 the Zanzibar revolution exploded in East Africa, with vital consequences for the region as a whole. Among the immediate effects were the army mutinies of Tanganika, Uganda, and Kenya which happened later the same month."[2] But the relationship between the Zanzibar revolution and mainland mutinies was ambiguous, particularly as it pertained to African nationalism.[3]

The immediate spark behind the Zanzibar revolt appeared "to be the banning of a small, pro-Communist splinter party," the Umma Party.[4] Led by Babu, the Umma Party was formally outlawed on 5 January. Earlier, Babu had resigned as secretary general of the ZNP before the July 1962 election "because the Nationalist Party refused to accept a slate of pro-Communist candidates that he proposed."[5] Babu had been "a highly paid correspondent for the New China News Agency," a Chinese agent of influence.[6]

Another report indicated that the revolution had been planned clandestinely prior to Zanzibar's independence. "Every indication suggests that the revolution itself had been planned clandestinely before Zanzibar and its northern island of Pemba gained their independence from Britain Dec. 10."[7] According to this theory, John Okello was the main leader of the revolution and its primary instigator.[8] An interesting connection may have existed between Okello and Chinese-influenced Babu, dating back three years. In 1961 Okello and thirty young Zanzibaris went to Cuba for guerrilla training. That same year, the ZNP, of which Babu was secretary general, established a permanent political office in Havana.[9] Ganda reported that Okello was an "ardent Maoist" who was funded by China.[10] Whatever the cause, as a result of the revolution Abeid Karume became president of the newly created Zanzibar Revolutionary Council on 24 January.[11]

Chinese involvement in the revolution was questionable yet still plausible. Premier Zhou Enlai was in Ghana at the time of the Zanzibar revolution on 12 January 1964. The *New York Times* reported that U.S. officials did not see any direct connections between the events.[12] On the other hand, Secretary of State Dean Rusk testified before Congress that guerrillas trained in Communist China had taken part in the revolution.[13] Moreover, the new vice president of the Zanzibar revolutionary government, Abdullah Kassim Hanga, was quoted as stating, "Naturally, we support all African liberation movements."[14] Hanga's support for liberation movements coincided naturally with the long-held Chinese political position in Africa. Journalist Lawrence Fellows later observed, "China's big initial success in Africa was in helping to stage a revolution in Zanzibar in 1964."[15] Leaders from Kenya, Tanganyika, and Uganda suspected Communist China of involvement in the revolt as well.[16] The British also suspected Chinese influence: in the House of Lords, Lord Colyton, a respected former junior minister in the Colonial Office, suggested that Beijing had planned the whole revolution.[17] Whatever the implications of Lord Colyton's suggestion, there is no tangible evidence that Chinese agents carried out the revolution—although they may have helped inspire it. Regardless, China recognized the revolutionary government of the People's Republic of Zanzibar on 17 January 1964.[18]

The same month as the Zanzibar revolution, Tanganyikan soldiers on the mainland mutinied. In contrast to the Zanzibar revolution, "There appeared to be no direct evidence of Communist involvement in the East African troubles, as there was in Zanzibar."[19] But questions remained about the origins of the Tanganyika mutiny. "The mutiny resulted in the 'destruction' of the British arms with which the Tanganyikan army was equipped. . . . They had to be replaced."[20] Ambassador Ho Ying later argued that the newly developing state should not use scarce resources on arms and ammunition. "Ho's stint in East Africa, [moreover, had] been characterized by considerable mobility, a necessary quality in the fluid state of East African politics."[21] Instead, China offered to replace British arms with Chinese weapons free of charge, including tanks, mortars, rockets, and other weapons. China used propaganda to further the claim that the British were unwanted in Tanganyika. A Chinese article portrayed British intervention in the

East African army mutinies as a scheme "to stage a comeback" to the region. The *Peking Review* article stated, "In actions reminiscent of the days of the gunboat rule, the British colonialists used brute force to accomplish their 'civilizing mission.'"[22] After the mutiny, the CIA reported that President Nyerere became "highly suspicious of individual Westerners and especially of the UK and the US."[23] As a result, the mutiny created a conspiratorial mindset among Tanganyikan leaders and helped China begin supplying arms to Tanganyika. The mutiny became a means for furthering Chinese political and strategic influence in East Africa.

Meanwhile, China wasted no time in establishing a presence on the island of Zanzibar. In February 1964 Babu, the former correspondent of the NCNA who was at one point general secretary of the ZNP, became minister for external affairs. Babu worked with Chinese envoy Liu Kan to secure Chinese aid to Zanzibar, which included an announcement of a £185,000 grant as well as gifts of tractors, irrigation machinery, and technical assistance.[24] Babu made the announcement of Chinese aid (equivalent to $518,000 then) over Zanzibar radio.[25] On 15 February the Chinese embassy opened in Zanzibar. Notably, the Chinese ambassador had been selected prior to the revolution and arrived with some Swahili-speaking staff.[26] The revolution reinforced the U.S. government's assessment as well as the State Department report on the world situation that was submitted to the House Foreign Affairs Committee on 2 April 1964; this report listed Zanzibar as among the "critical points" subject to Communist influence.[27] Other countries the report listed included Algeria, Angola, Ghana, and Mali.

Chinese personnel were soon sent to Zanzibar to further Chinese influence on the island. In early April 1964 Ambassador Meng Ying and five diplomatic staff flew from Kenya to Zanzibar. Ambassador Meng presented his credentials on 7 April.[28] Around the same time, External Minister Babu said technical experts from China, Ghana, the Soviet Union, and Egypt would soon arrive in Zanzibar to help rebuild the country.[29] The presence of Ghanaian experts demonstrated a convergence of Chinese political interests in Africa.

Expanding Chinese influence on Zanzibar weakened the U.S. strategic position in the region. In April 1964 the new Zanzibari government ordered the closure of the U.S. tracking station, "to the advantage of the Chinese who secured some of the equipment."[30] Although not fully explained, this closure enhanced Chinese military technological capability through the acquisition of advanced satellite-tracking equipment. On 7 April President Karume summoned U.S. chargé d'affaires Frank Carlucci to tell him that the United States should dismantle and remove its bases in Zanzibar. On 9 and 11 April mass demonstrations were held opposing "U.S. imperialism." President Karume addressed one event and members of the Revolutionary Council and leaders of mass organizations participated in the other.[31] The public display of animosity toward the United States, if it was not actually organized by Chinese personnel, certainly served long-term Chinese political interests.

As China continued its activities, the union of Tanganyika and Zanzibar occurred on 26 April 1964, resulting in the United Republic of Tanganyika and Zanzibar. President Karume believed that union with Tanganyika was the most effective means of preserving Zanzibari autonomy.[32] There was reason to believe the United Republic of Tanganyika and Zanzanibar was to "protect African nationalism from Communist subversion."[33] According to anonymous sources, however,

> While China too did not relish the idea of Zanzibar being taken over by Mainland Tanganyika, the Chinese Ambassador, Ho Ying, moved adroitly to assure President Nyerere of China's support for the Union. China therefore began to work through the Union Government, and all her aid to Zanzibar was granted through President Nyerere while the Soviet Union and East Germany worked directly with Zanzibar. This gave President Nyerere reason to believe that China was totally in favour of the Union and Ho Ying was able to prepare the ground for increased Chinese activity.[34]

Notably, Ambassador Ho had previously been ambassador to Mongolia during the opening of the railway linking Mongolia to China.[35] Ambassador Ho was regarded as "Peking's key diplomat and trouble-shooter in Africa."[36] The creation of Tanzania was an example of China understanding the oft-changing political situation in the African political landscape, and using a capable individual to handle it. China had learned that the political environment in African nations was fluid, and that it was best to act with the changes than against them. The CIA assessed the situation along similar lines: "Instead of restraining the expansion of Communist influence, [the union between Tanganyika and Zanzibar was] probably facilitating the spread of this influence into Tanganyika."[37] Instead of hindering future activities, China understood the situation and exploited the union to its own benefit.

The Chinese continued to send personnel to the region as the political situation altered. According to British sources, in May 1964 twenty-four Chinese carrying diplomatic passports landed from a freighter moored off Zanzibar Harbor. Klein referred to the Chinese ship moored off the coast as the S.S. *Peace*.[38] "British official quarters were reported to be gravely concerned over recent moves by Peking that were believed to be designed to turn the island into a center of revolutionary subversion in the newly independent countries of Africa."[39] The possibility that China wanted to maintain a firm presence on the island after the union could not be discounted, particularly because the union was characterized as "hastily arranged."[40]

By the middle of the year, China had succeeded in establishing face-to-face ties with the new government. From 10 to 19 June 1964 a joint government delegation led by Tanzanian second vice president Rashidi Kawawa visited China and secured an interest-free loan of £5 million for Tanzania.[41] China gave another free grant of £1 million to Tanzania.[42] Vice President Kawawa also negotiated other undisclosed economic and military agreements. He returned greatly impressed and overwhelmed by Chinese capabilities and generosity. Serving as a guide for Vice President Kawawa was none other than Zanzibar's former minister for external affairs, and at this time a Tanzanian minister of state for economic planning, Babu.[43] Babu's familiarity with the Chinese was influential in the generosity of the financial assistance. In addition to economic considerations, the *New York Times* reported that Babu was engaged in other meetings while in Beijing. "Intelligence reports said he had concentrated on meetings with Chinese military leaders, notably with Marshal Ho Lung, a guerrilla warfare expert."[44] Later in the same year, the CIA finally concluded that Babu was a Communist. "He probably is a Communist—in any case his actions consistently serve the Communist interest."[45] Clayton also reported that this was "a visit during which construction of the [Tanzania-Zambia, or Tan-Zam] railway was officially discussed for the first time."[46] Before departing Beijing on 17 June, Vice President Kawawa said, "China is not only a great friend of the United Republic of Tanganyika and Zanzibar but also of the whole of Africa."[47] Kawawa's statement was confirmation of the success of China's political activities on the continent. China and Tanzania signed an agreement on economic and technical cooperation as well as a joint communiqué, which was published in full two days later.[48]

Prior to Kawawa's visit, China was active in maintaining political influence on Zanzibar. At the beginning of June, the *New York Times* reported that China had agreed to grant a long-term interest-free loan of $14 million to Zanzibar.[49] Notably, this economic aid package was directed to Zanzibar only, and not to the union between Tanganyika and Zanzibar.[50] Although China was engaged with the United Republic of Tanganyika and Zanzibar government, it was clearly maintaining separate and distinct relations with Zanzibar.

In June 1964 a Chinese economic and goodwill mission spent nine days in Tanzania. As the mission left Tanzania, China issued a statement hailing the "excellent revolutionary situation" prevailing in Africa.[51] The two countries eventually signed an economic and technical cooperation agreement. According to analysts, however, more developments that were significant were likely to have occurred behind the scenes. Delegations of Chinese women and youth visited Zanzibar as well, and Chinese technicians were working on the first twenty-five tractors to arrive as gifts from Beijing.[52]

China continued to expand its influence on both the mainland and the island in the mid-1960s. In public communications China and Zanzibar raised a unified voice. On 21 June 1964 youth organizations from China and Zanzibar signed a joint statement condemning the so-called new colonialism led by the United States. The Zanzibar and Pemba Afro-Shirazi Youth League and a visiting delegation of the All-China Youth Federation, at the end of their visit to Zanzibar, signed the joint statement.[53] As elsewhere, China was cultivating ties with the youth of the target country. On the mainland in Dar es Salaam a Chinese economic construction exhibition opened on 12 July 1964. At the opening ceremony, Vice President Kawawa and Ambassador Ho spoke of the close relations between the two countries.[54] Notably, the Chinese had held similar exhibitions in Algeria and Ghana to demonstrate Chinese development prowess. The previous day Beijing formally appointed Ho, Chinese ambassador in Dar es Salaam, to be ambassador in Tanzania and downgraded the Chinese embassy in Zanzibar to consulate. Wei Liang-Tsai noted further, "Though the change was a mere diplomatic formality, it did symbolize Peking's decision to use Dar es Salaam as a major base for intensified diplomatic operations in East Africa."[55]

Unlike in Ghana, China provided overt security assistance to Tanzania. In August 1964 the Tanzanian government invited a Chinese military mission of eleven instructors to teach in the use of Chinese weapons.[56] The military mission consisted of seven instructors and four interpreters and arrived some time before 9 September.[57] President Nyerere made reference to the Chinese instructors at a news conference and noted that the training period would not exceed six months. President Nyerere scoffed at suggestions that the Chinese would "transform Tanganyika to a colony."[58] On the island, China was already training about three hundred Zanzibaris as part of multinational training of two Zanzibar army battalions (along with Soviets and East Germans). In addition, China had sent twenty-one instructors to train the Tanzanian police force.[59] "Thus, in 1964, Tanzania became the first African country to have an official Chinese military mission to train its army, as distinguished from the clandestine training of guerrilla forces [in Ghana and other parts of sub-Saharan Africa]."[60] Simply, "This meant increased Chinese influence in the [national liberation] movements as well as increased adoption of Chinese tactics of guerrilla warfare."[61]

While training occurred in the southern region of Tanzania, Tanzanian authorities were supplying guerrillas with Chinese arms and weapons free of charge. Ogunsanwo reported that Pointe Noire in Congo-Brazzaville and Mtwara in Tanzania were entry points for Chinese arms for liberation movements in Mozambique and Angola.[62]

Testimony from an imprisoned black African fighter confirmed these reports: Sometime in late 1963, according to the testimony, Beijing selected an African named Peter Metchane and sent him for military training in China. Metchane went to Bechuanaland (present-day Botswana) and from there flew to Tanganyika, India, Burma, and finally to China. He was enrolled in the military academy at Nanjing and was trained in the use of antitank mines and other equipment. South Africa sentenced Metchane and another black African to ten years imprisonment for their involvement in armed liberation movements, which was the ultimate purpose of their foreign training. During the trial Metchane testified that "four other Africans" had enrolled at the same time in Nanjing.[63] Not only was Tanzania becoming a base of Chinese operations, therefore, but it was also serving as a transit point to China.

China continued its political activities by sending personnel to the mainland. At the end of August, a fourteen-person Chinese technical mission arrived in Dar es Salaam.[64] In June China had agreed to provide Tanzania approximately $92 million in the form of equipment, commodities, and technical aid personnel. This agreement, therefore, was a conduit for Chinese political influence. Keeping Zanzibar distinct from Tanzania, on 13 September 1964 Chairman Liu received members of the visiting Zanzibar and Pemba Afro-Shirazi Youth League delegation led by its president, Seif Bakari Omar.[65] Once again, China targeted Zanzibar's youth to influence and shape local attitudes and beliefs about China and the world.

The cumulative effect of Chinese influence in Tanzania was notable. The *New York Times* reported in 1964 that China had extended a total of $42 million in credits and grants to the United Republic of Tanganyika and Zanzibar for that year.[66] In October of that year the *New York Times* reported that Beijing created two new departments in the foreign affairs ministry to handle relations with Africa.[67] Chinese aid was directed to Tanzania as a whole as well as to Zanzibar specifically. The assistance was coupled with other Chinese-influenced activities. In October 1964 the Portuguese reported that five groups of guerrillas had penetrated Portugal's East African territory of Mozambique from Tanganyika. In operations against the guerrillas, the Portuguese captured guerrilla general Lucas Fernandes, who "was said to have received his military training in Peking." According to additional Portuguese reports, the Soviet Union and China were aiding Algerians, Cubans, and Tanzanians to subvert Portuguese Africa. The *New York Times* reported that arms and munitions were landing in Tanzania as well.[68] China had converted Tanzania into a political and security base of activities. Furthermore, at the end of 1964 Ali Mahfoudh, an Arab who was one of Babu's principal pro-Chinese lieutenants, headed to Mtwara on the mainland with men and equipment to assist one of the guerrilla movements in Mozambique.[69] This illustrated the diffusion of Chinese influence from its principal target (Babu) to others (Mahfoudh). China also exploited local organizations for operations. On 11 November 1964 the *Nationalist*, an organ of TANU, published photocopies of three "secret letters" in French that showed "beyond a doubt that the United States was scheming to subvert" the Tanzanian government.[70] Although not directly implicated, the Chinese had strong ties to TANU as well as to the NCNA mouthpiece on Zanzibar, *Zanews*.

The following year, China continued to cement its political relations with Tanzania through aid and agreements. Between December 1964 and January 1965, China offered to build two high-powered transmitters. On favorable terms, China would pay half the cost, £350,000, and provide the other half as an interest-free loan.[71] The Tanzanian government also made an agreement for the Chinese establishment of a state farm at Ruvu, costing approximately £450,000.[72] China agreed to provide equipment and training for the Ruvu state farm. In addition, as part of the £10 million loan to Tanzania, the Chinese agreed to build a fully integrated textile mill costing about £3 million, "the largest of its kind in East Africa." China and Tanzania signed a development agreement on 5 January 1965.[73] In U.S. figures the agreement allocated $7 million to build a textile mill—to be called the Mao Zedong mill—outside Dar es Salaam. In addition, Tanzania would use $3.08 million to establish the five-thousand-acre experimental farm and a farm implement factory, while the destination of the balance of funds was uncertain. In the same month, the CIA reported that southern African liberation forces were using Chinese trucks to transport weapons to the Congo and the

Mozambique border. In addition, the CIA reported twenty-seven Chinese military advisers were on the mainland and Zanzibar. They were originally sent to train Tanzanian troops, but the CIA believed that some were training African fighters.[74] This demonstrated that public aid and assistance could be used to expand Chinese political influence across the region.

Along Tanzania's border, an assassination occurred that hinted at Chinese covert activities in the region. China's diplomats were expelled from Burundi after Premier Pierre Ngendandumwe was shot and killed on 15 January 1965. Bujumbura had reappointed him in late 1964 purportedly to check rising Chinese political influence in Burundi. "From the Chinese Communists' large embassy in Bujumbura, Burundi's capital, Peking's agents [were] said to have supplied, financed and advised Congolese rebels as well as dissident elements in other new African countries."[75] Notably, Burundi lies east of the Congo on the northern shore of Lake Tanganyika. In May 1965 the CIA reported that "various liberation camps," including the Kigoma camp on Lake Tanganyika, were training approximately three thousand to four thousand Congolese.[76]

A related event occurred in 1964. Tung Chi-ping, a Chinese cultural attaché for the embassy in Burundi, defected to the United States on 26 May 1964. Two veteran diplomats, Ambassador Liu Yu-feng and Deputy Chief of Mission Chiang Yen, headed the Chinese embassy in Burundi. Within Burundi itself, according to the *Washington Post*, the embassy had "spread money liberally among various political factions, fanning the tribal rivalry that has plagued Burundi for centuries."[77] After his arrival in the United States, Tung stated that China was determined to take over the Congo as the first step in a conquest of Africa. Although Tung's statements may have been misinformation or disinformation, Tanzania's location east of the Congo was ideal to further Chinese political influence across Africa.[78]

While China was offering aid and assistance to mainland Tanzania, it also continued to engage in operations on Zanzibar. According to the CIA writing in May 1965, in January of that year Chinese on Zanzibar taped a conversation that led to the expulsion of two U.S. diplomats—counselor Robert Gordon of the embassy in Dar es Salaam and Frank Carlucci in Zanzibar—for "plotting the overthrow" of the Zanzibar regime.[79] In their phone conversation these diplomats reported that ammunition was used, tipping off Tanzanian officials; they used that word in the following context: "We have enough ammunition" to convince Washington of the need to send greetings to Karume on Zanzibar's first anniversary.[80] After hearing these tapes, President Nyerere ordered the two diplomats to leave the country within twenty-four hours.[81] China had been exerting political influence for some time on Zanzibar. The timing of the U.S. expulsions coincided directly with the killing of Ngendandumwe in Burundi, however. China, of course, offered its own perspective of the events in Zanzibar. Citing *Uhuru*, the *Peking Review* reported that Frank Carlucci was one of the advisers to Moise Tshombe and others in planning the 1961 assassination of Patrice Lumumba.[82] China intentionally created a sense of confusion surrounding political events in East and Central Africa. Despite such international intrigue, Sino-Tanzanian relations continued to flourish.

On the eve of President Nyerere's departure for an eight-day visit to China, Tanzania recalled its ambassador to the United States on 14 February 1965.[83] Tanzania made the recall in reaction to the expulsion of Tanzania's number two diplomat in Washington—which had been done in retaliation for the expulsion of two State Department personnel from Zanzibar. On 16 February President Nyerere and his party arrived in Shanghai on their way to Beijing for Nyerere's long-awaited visit to China.[84] He arrived in the Chinese capital the next day, accepting an invitation that Ambassador Ho had extended in 1964. In his welcoming speech to the Tanzanian president, Peng Chen, NPC Standing Committee vice chair and mayor of Beijing, declared, "In the fight against imperialism, colonialism and neo-colonialism, the Chinese people are for ever the reliable comrades-in-arms of the peoples of Tanzania and all Africa."[85] China and Tanzania signed a treaty of friendship in Beijing on 20 February and a joint communiqué on 23 February.[86] In the Sino-Tanzanian Joint Communiqué dated 23 February 1965, Tanzania voiced support for China on the world stage: "The Tanzanian side reaffirmed its support for the restoration of the legitimate rights of the People's Republic of China in the United Nations, its opposition to the imperialist plot for creating 'two Chinas,' and its support for the Chinese Government and people in their just struggle to safeguard state sovereignty and territorial integrity."[87]

At the same time, Beijing announced that representatives of the NPC would soon visit Africa. In Beijing the Chinese held a ten thousand–person rally in honor of President Nyerere, who returned home on 24 February.[88] On the same day, the Chinese press announced that Chairman Liu and Premier Zhou would visit Tanzania at a "convenient time."[89] The next day President Nyerere announced that China and Tanzania had signed a trade agreement worth over $14 million. Under the agreement, Tanzania exports to China would include 80,000 bales of cotton, 2 million pounds of tobacco, and 5,000 tons of copra.[90] Sino-Tanzanian relations were greatly enhanced as a result of Nyerere's first visit to China.

In addition to high-level political exchange visits, China engaged in activities to sustain Tanzania's political leadership. According to Alaba Ogunsanwo, "The Chinese first helped to train a field force unit which was meant to deter the army from staging [another] coup."[91] On 8 February 1965 battalion-level troops completed training in the use of Chinese arms. Troops then took part in a military parade on Monduli Plains near Arusha in northern Tanzania. On display were Chinese tank guns, heavy machine guns, mortars, and automatic rifles.[92] Toward the middle of the year, in May 1965, the CIA reported that twenty-seven Chinese military advisers were in Tanzania, including those on Zanzibar. After training the Chinese-equipped Tanzanian People's Defence Force (TPDF) battalion, Chinese advisers were giving a light weapons course to a six-hundred-person reserve group from the Mozambique border area. The CIA also reported that Chinese advisers had trained similar groups that had become a part of the ten thousand–person Volunteer Reserve Force, and that they would also train the Tanzanian police force, prison services, and National Youth Service.[93]

That same month, Kenyan authorities intercepted a shipment of Chinese arms after it had crossed the border from Tanzania. Uganda later claimed the weapons were for its army, and the Kenyans eventually released them.[94] While Tanzania acted as a base of operations as well as a transit point for Chinese arms deliveries, China continued to cultivate ties with nonmilitary sectors of Tanzania society. For example, "Already within [Tanzania] the Chinese were active in front organisations and trade unions." In addition, Tanzanian trade unions were known to have visited China, according to a labor leader who visited China.[95] Unlike its single-minded focus in Ghana, China diversified its activities in Tanzania, both political and security-related.

By this time, Chinese personnel and goods were arriving frequently in Tanzania. On 1 April 1965 the *New York Times* reported that in March a high-ranking Chinese foreign ministry delegation had toured Tanzania.[96] That same month, the CIA reported, ten Chinese economic advisers were brought into Zanzibar.[97] The most publicized visit occurred in June, when Premier Zhou Enlai made his first visit to Tanzania.[98] Premier Zhou visited several Chinese-built and -funded projects while in Tanzania, including the textile mill outside Dar es Salaam, a radio station at Kunduchi, a farm-training center at Mwanza, a food-processing plant at Arusha, and a rice-planting program in the south.[99] The *New York Times* reported that China funded many of its development projects by selling Chinese-made consumer goods in Tanzania.[100] During Zhou's visit President Nyerere spoke about the lessons of China's revolution. Ogunsanwo noted aptly, "Chinese-

Tanzanian relations in this period showed the quality and calibre of the Chinese diplomats, and what could be achieved with limited resources and the skilful use of opportunities."[101] Thus, Sino-Tanzanian relations were as strong as ever.

Chinese aid to Tanzania continued, itself becoming self-sustaining. "The Chinese [had] already begun to transport clothing, bicycles, sewing machines, canned goods, radios, toys and other items into Dar es Salaam for sale so as to raise funds to pay for development programs of Chinese [in Tanzania]."[102] One commentator noted in the *New York Times* the importance of Zhou's visit in June 1965: "The real significance of Chou's visit was undoubtedly to establish a 'presence' for Peking in East Africa."[103] Around the same time, the same paper reported that China had since September the previous year delivered 1,025 tons of arms and ammunition to Dar es Salaam, and that as many as 300 Chinese technicians were on the mainland. As recently as 8 May a shipment of 170 tons of Chinese small arms and ammunition had been unloaded in Dar es Salaam.[104] While on Zanzibar for the first time, Premier Zhou visited the Chinese training camp at Mtoni and spoke at a reception hosted by Vice President Karume, saying Zanzibar was "the nucleus of Tanzania."[105] (Karume assumed the position of Vice President after Zanzibar's union with Tanganyika.) Zhou understood the importance of Zanzibar to the United Republic of Tanzania and congratulated it on its revolution: "That was a marvelous achievement. The Chinese people sincerely admire the indomitable revolutionary and militant spirit of the fraternal Zanzibar people."[106] Before departing on 8 June Premier Zhou and President Nyerere signed a joint communiqué, in which China expressed "hearty joy [over the fact that Tanzania was] playing an increasingly important role in supporting the national-liberation movement in Africa."[107] Tanzania's role as a regional political leader was supported and facilitated by China. All the while, the two countries continued to express their shared common historical experiences.[108]

While China gave much attention to formal relations with the Tanzanian government, it maintained ties with targeted audiences within Tanzanian society as well. From 23 June to 4 July 1965, for example, members of a Tanzanian women's delegation visited China.[109] Madame Sophi Kawawa, wife of Vice President Kawawa, led the delegation. In her welcome speech, Teng Ying-chao of the hosting National Women's Federation pledged that the Chinese people would unite still more closely with the people and women of Tanzania and the rest of the world in the fight against the imperialist policies of war and aggression. Invited by the Chinese National Women's Federation, the Tanzanian delegation met with Chairman Mao and Chairman Liu, who conferred official respect to the women. During its stay, the Tanzanian delegation visited factories, a people's commune, the Children's Palace, and the Shanghai Industrial Exhibition. They also met with Shanghai women's representatives and saw a modern Chinese drama, "Battle-Drums on the Equator," which was based on an anti-imperialists theme and dramatized U.S. imperialism in the Congo. After the drama, Madame Kawawa said that the Asian and African peoples should unite to drive out the imperialists.[110]

In a similar visit, on 14 July 1965 a women's delegation from Zanzibar arrived in Beijing. Led by Madame Fatuma Karume, wife of Vice President Karume, the Tanzanian delegation attended a National Women's Federation banquet on 15 July and met with Chairman Liu on 20 July.[111] Chairman Mao met with a women's delegation from Tanzania on 24 July.[112] On 2 August the Tanzanian women's delegation attended a banquet, which Premier Zhou also attended. Madame Karume described Sino-Tanzanian friendship as a "tree of friendship."[113] These recurring women's visits to China were a part of the latter's overall political activities aiming to influence the Tanzanian public.

Chinese activities up to this point were diverse, small scale, and multifaceted, so its offer to build the Tanzania-Zambia (Tan-Zam) railway was therefore somewhat unexpected.[114] President Nyerere said on 22 September, "Communist China has offered to build a 1,000 mile railroad between the copper belt of Zambia and the Tanzania port of Dar Es Salaam."[115] A twelve-person team of Chinese surveyors arrived in August 1965 and began surveying.[116] However, Fellows reported, "The Chinese had no surveyors' tools and had never ordered any."[117] What the Chinese team was doing is therefore difficult to determine. To facilitate this massive project, Vice President Kawawa visited China at the invitation of Premier Zhou from 22 to 23 November.[118] (Formation of the Union of Tanganyika and Zanzibar created two vice presidential positions.) Accompanying Kawawa were Paul Bomani, minister for economic affairs and development planning, and Said A. Mtaki, junior minister for commerce and cooperatives. A few weeks prior to Kawawa's visit, the instruments of ratification for the Sino-Tanzanian Treaty of Friendship were exchanged in Dar es Salaam. By this point, the CIA considered Kawawa to be a "radical."[119] The revelation of the Tan-Zam railway was a significant indication of Chinese political priorities in Africa, with particular focus on Tanzania.

Meanwhile, Chinese aid and assistance continued to flow into Tanzania throughout the year. In October 1965 China purchased a surplus of £2 million of Tanzanian tobacco. By doing so, China saved Tanzania from financial woes and garnered Tanzanian goodwill to China. In 1965 twenty-two Chinese water engineers arrived in Zanzibar to advise on irrigation projects. At the same time, construction on a shoe factory began—which eventually was completed in 1967. The shoe factory experienced difficulties over leather supply, however.[120] On the personnel side, prior to 1966 China pressed Tanzania for the establishment of a Chinese economic mission. A large mission, headed by Chiang Ta, was eventually opened in Dar es Salaam to manage increasing economic activities. "This meant that closer co-operation and better working relationships could now develop between the government ministries and the Chinese economic mission on the spot."[121] Thus, China had established a local presence to facilitate its diverse activities in Tanzania.

Up until 1966 China was successful in establishing Tanzania as a base of political, economic, and security activities. Although the Great Proletarian Cultural Revolution (hereafter the Cultural Revolution) began the same year at home, China continued its multitude of operations in East Africa. In March 1966 the *Nationalist*, the organ of TANU, published an article pointing out that Africa's struggle had "entered a new phase, more determined and resolute, a struggle which must take us to final victory."[122] This was another example of Chinese-influenced propaganda because of the close relationship between TANU and China. By spring 1966 President Felix Houphouet-Boigny of the Ivory Coast was warning of the danger of China in the region: "The door is already open to the Chinese in East Africa."[123] President Houphouet-Boigny warned about long-term Chinese objectives in Africa, and he was correct. By this time, Western sources estimated that China had shipped approximately 11,000 tons of arms to Tanzania, and these same sources reported that Russia had shipped the same amount of arms. China, again according to Western sources, had approximately 250 to 300 technicians, trainers, and other personnel in Tanzania. For example, 22 Chinese instructors were at Tanzania's police training college. Thus, while in the midst of domestic upheaval, China nevertheless remained present and even active in East Africa.

Yet China continued to look for different channels to communicate its political message. From 20 to 24 April 1966, for example, the secretariat of the Afro-Asian Journalists' Association met in Beijing. Delegations from nineteen countries and areas attended, including Algeria and Tanzania. At the meeting, Peter Kagisa of the Tanzanian delegation pointed out that the CIA was engaged in subversive activities around the world. In Africa, Kagisa said, the CIA was trying to overthrow progressive governments, sabotage the OAU, and undermine influential progressive leaders.[124] With China as host, a Tanzanian delegation identified the United States as the enemy of African nations. At the same time, China continued to confer official and public respect to Tanzania. On 25 April Chairman Liu and Premier Zhou sent a joint message to President Nyerere congratulating him on Tanzania's National Day. The following day in Beijing, Tanzanian ambassador Waziri Juna hosted a reception to celebrate the occasion. Among the guests were Vice Premiers Chen Yi and Tan Chen-li, Vice Chairman Lin Peng of the Standing Committee of the NPC, and other leading members of government departments, the PLA, and Chinese people's organizations.[125] The diverse Chinese representation signified the all-around nature of China's relations with Tanzania, as well as the various means China used to conduct political activities in Africa. China's presence in Africa reached a point of maturity, as demonstrated in its relations with Tanzania.

Under a May 1966 cultural cooperation agreement, China provided aid and assistance to the Tanzanian government. Aid included printing works (such as the printing press used in the production of the *Nationalist*, the ruling TANU newspaper) and assistance to the headquarters of the TANU Youth League and the Economic Exhibition Pavilion at Nazi Moja in Dar es Salaam.[126] Later China expanded its economic assistance to Tanzania as well. On 4 June a Tanzanian economic delegation led by Paul Bomani, minister for economic affairs and development planning, arrived in Beijing. Madame Kunambi, executive member of the Central Committee of National Union of Tanzanian Women, arrived on the same plane as a guest of the Chinese National Women's Federation.[127] During their visits Vice Premier and Madame Li Hsien-nien, Chairman Liu, and Premier Zhou all received the Tanzanian delegations. On 7 June Minister Bomani hosted a banquet, stating, "We in Tanzania are grateful to the Government of the People's Republic of China for their assistance in our struggle against imperialism and neo-colonialism." In reply, Vice Premier Li Hsien-nien asked Bomani and his delegation to take the "militant friendship" of the Chinese people with them back to the Tanzanian people. Concluding the visit to Beijing, China and Tanzania signed an economic cooperation agreement on 8 June.[128] As a result China granted Tanzania a new interest-free loan of £3 million, designed to "initiate or bring to completion a number of development projects, most of which the British Government had promised to help build."[129] Thus, China had filled the role as chief provider of aid to Tanzania. This continued apace.

In the middle of the year, China and Tanzania signed an agreement to establish a joint shipping company. The company's initial capitalization, the *New York*

Times reported, would be the equivalent of $4.2 million and the line would operate two 10,000-ton vessels. "According to Tanzanian Government sources, the initial capital will be supplied entirely by China. Half of the initial capital will be an interest-free loan repayable from Tanzania's share of profits over the 10-year period from 1977."[130] The favorable conditions for Tanzania were an effective tool in advancing Chinese strategic influence. Ogunsanwo wrote the following astute statement: "It should also be pointed out that a joint shipping company would reduce the adverse publicity abroad accompanying any Chinese delivery of goods and weapons to Tanzania, something which was not always possible in the past."[131] China had arranged for the creation of a strategic line of communication across the Indian Ocean. In the midst of this profound accomplishment, on 30 July President Nyerere laid the foundation stone of the Chinese-built textile mill outside Dar es Salaam. Speaking at the ceremony, Ambassador Ho called the event "a highlight of long friendly relations" between the two countries.[132] Through economic development assistance, China was creating the atmosphere for future political activities in Tanzania.

China took full advantage of its broad relations with Tanzania. According to an anonymous source, a Tanzanian goodwill military delegation visited China in August 1966 and reached an understanding with the Chinese about future construction of a navy and air force for Tanzania.[133] In addition, the *New York Times* reported that naval officers were sent covertly to China to be trained. At the end of September 1966 a seven-person goodwill mission from TANU also embarked on a two-week visit of China.[134] The next month, in October 1966, the commissioner of Tanzania police, Hamza Aziz, also went on a study tour that included China. Notably, personnel from the Chinese embassy in Dar es Salaam saw Aziz off at the airport.[135]

As a result of Chinese influence, the *Peking Review* published an article in October describing young people in Morogoro, Tanzania, who destroyed pictures of Queen Elizabeth II and replaced them with pictures of President Nyerere: "Hence, an exceedingly important task for the new emerging Afro-Asian countries [was] to wipe out imperialist ideological influences in order to build up their new national cultures."[136] In the same month, three hundred college students protested in Dar es Salaam against Tanzania's national service plan. The *Peking Review* reported that an American professor was seen with the students. The next day, several thousand students and youth demonstrated in support of the plan. President Nyerere spoke at the rally saying the previous day's rally was "instigated by a certain foreign country."[137] Although China could not be directly implicated, its political activities targeting the Tanzanian youth influenced events in Morogoro and Dar es Salaam. The political nature of both was a hallmark of Chinese activity.[138]

By the end of the year, China had established another communication channel to the region. In early December 1966 President Nyerere opened a $560,000 shortwave radio transmitter built with aid from China. Marking the occasion, Ambassador Ho said, "This station will help in the liberation of Africa."[139] Based on a Dar es Salaam radio report on 7 December 1966, the station was completed three months ahead of schedule.[140] The transmitter could be used to send political messages and to direct agents for operations. For example, according to scholar Girish Mathur, on Chinese instructions "the UNITA [the Angolan guerrilla organization then headquartered in Zambia] blew up the railway line at several points towards the end of 1966 and the beginning of 1967," possibly to help convince Zambia of the need for the Tan-Zam railway.[141] Not coincidentally, at the time "Zambian officials still thought that the West could be goaded into backing the project for fear of a Chinese 'takeover.'"[142]

Chinese assistance to Tanzania flowed into the next year, extending nonrefundable aid to the Tanzanian Training School at Moshi in northern Tanzania.[143] Two months later, the *Peking Review* reported that a group of Chinese technicians arrived in Zanzibar to build a workshop to repair agricultural tools. There was also a Chinese medical team in Zanzibar.[144] Understanding East Africa's strategic importance, China knew the significance of maintaining influence on both the mainland and the island, and it worked diligently to do so.

Although relations with Tanzania were quite active, China looked continually to expand its political influence in southern Africa. As a result, from 21 to 25 June 1967 President Kenneth Kaunda led a Zambian delegation to China.[145] During its visit, the Zambian delegation visited a people's commune, factories, a university, and, significantly, a unit of the PLA. At the end of the visit, the two countries issued a joint communiqué on 25 June. "In August, 1967, according to *Current Scence*, published by the U.S. consulate general in Hong Kong, receptions were held by the Chinese embassies in Mali, the Congo (B[razzaville]), Tanzania, Guinea, Mauritania, Somalia, Morocco and Tunisia on the occasion of the 40th anniversary of the People's Liberation Army, blatantly emphasizing the relevance of Chairman Mao's guerrilla strategies."[146]

And, in a further effort to expand influence southward, from August to September 1967 a joint ministerial economic delegation from Tanzania and Zambia visited China.[147] In Beijing on 5 September, China, Tanzania, and Zambia signed an agreement on the construction of the long-discussed Tan-Zam railway. Vice Premier Li Hsien-nien signed for China, and Tanzanian minister of finance Amier Habib Jamal and Zambian minister of state A. J. Soko signed for their respective governments.[148] In a favorable gesture, China agreed to extend the interest-free loan given to both countries and Premier Zhou received all members of the Tanzania-Zambia economic delegation, which left Beijing on 6 September. Through patient and calculated efforts, therefore, China had embarked on its largest project to date in Africa.[149] This all occurred while China was in the domestic throes of the Cultural Revolution. While China may have retracted from many parts of the world, clearly it remained active and interested in East Africa.

Eleven

RAILWAY TO FRIENDSHIP

China's political influence in Africa reached its apex in Tanzania. Its activities in the country and region were a product of its intense interest and efforts. After Beijing secured the agreement to build the Tan-Zam railway, reports continued on the Chinese proposal to build a railway from Zambia's copper belt to the Tanzanian port city of Dar es Salaam. Although the proposal was symbolically important for the PRC, there were other material benefits for China as well. For example, Zambia exported 700,000 tons of copper per year, the non-Communist world's second-largest production. Also, by building the railway Tanzania could tap the agricultural potential of the Kilombero Valley and the mineral resources of the Mbeya area, both in southwest Tanzania and "both stymied by lack of transport."[1]

Zambia considered China's offer to build and finance the railway to Tanzania "a life-or-death proposition."[2] In addition to the material benefits, elements in Zambia were waging a guerrilla war against white rule throughout southern Africa, including anti-colonial wars in Angola, Southern Rhodesia (present-day Zimbabwe), as well as South Africa. And the Chinese were "training guerrillas in southern Tanzania to fight in Mozambique and other areas of southern Africa now run by whites.... Little [was] known about these Chinese."[3] Zambia needed a link through Tanzania to help support these efforts, and China offered the most viable opportunity. Zambia was no doubt aware of Chinese relations with Tanzania. According to the CIA, between 1954 and 1967 China extended $22.8 million in economic aid to Tanzania. The CIA reported that there were approximately 340 Chinese "economic technicians" in Tanzania in 1967. The CIA did not define "economic technicians" but estimated according to the number of persons present for a period of one month or more.[4] All of these interests served China's desire to become an integral part of African affairs.

Efforts to build the railway continued throughout the late 1960s. On 8 April 1968 China, Tanzania, and Zambia signed protocols providing for surveys and the design of the thousand-mile railway linking Tanzania and Zambia. At the time, construction was expected to begin in 1970.[5] The protocols covered forms of loans to be provided, the dispatch of technical personnel by China, treatment and working conditions of Chinese personnel, and physical survey and design work. The delegations held a week-long conference in Dar es Salaam before reaching an agreement on the protocols. Tanzanian finance minister A. H. Jamal, Zambian finance minister E. H. K. Mudenda, and chargé d'affaires ad interim Chou Po-ping signed on behalf of their countries.[6] The Tanzanian and Zambian delegations also hosted a reception in honor of the Chinese delegation, with Vice President Kawawa in attendance. By the end of April over 350 Chinese engineers and surveyors had arrived in Tanzania to work on the Tan-Zam railway. An article in the *Washington Post* distinguished between 150 engineers and surveyors who arrived earlier and 200 engineers who arrived at the time of printing. In November 1968 a Chinese inspection team surveyed the progress of the railway.[7] China continued to expand its presence in the region.

While China made intense effort to promote the Tan-Zam railway, it continued cultivating the political environment in Tanzania as well. On 26 April 1968 in Beijing, Tanzanian ambassador to China E. P. Mwaluko hosted a reception to celebrate the fourth anniversary of the founding of the United Republic of Tanzania. Premier Zhou, Vice Premier Chen Yi, Vice Chairman of the Standing Committee of the NPC Kuo Mo-jo, and other high-ranking officials were in attendance. Speaking at the reception, Ambassador Mwaluko pointed out that Chinese economic and technical aid was conducive to the African peoples' liberation from imperialist rule.[8] China nurtured the political relationship between Chinese aid and African political movements. Political relations remained at the forefront of Chinese interests, particularly in East Africa.

China's main effort continued to focus on the strategic value of Tanzania through construction of the Tan-Zam railway. In May 1968 another 150 Chinese engineers and technicians arrived in Dar es Salaam to conduct additional surveys for the thousand-mile Tan-Zam railway.[9] China finished building a textile mill at Ubungo, to be paid for by an interest-free loan. Friendship Textile Mill was commissioned in 1969.[10] One commentator observed the geopolitical importance of

Tanzania for the PRC: "The Tanzanians [were] receptive to the flow of Chinese weapons, for they can get them nowhere else as easily. A grip in Tanzania, whose vast area touches eight other countries, would give the Chinese a wide periphery in Africa and a base on the western littoral of the Indian Ocean." The same commentator mentioned Tanzania as a possible base of operations for guerrillas throughout Africa: "Of enormous potential importance [was] the military equipment and training that the Chinese provide for the dozen 'liberation' movements based in Tanzania."[11] While both observations may have been taken into account for building the Tan-Zam railway, the CIA's rationale for China's undertaking was more straightforward: "By undertaking the railroad projects [the Tan-Zam railway and also one between Guinea and Mali], Communist China apparently hope[d] to firmly establish itself in Africa, as well as to improve its image on the continent."[12] But the CIA may have overlooked Tanzania's strategic importance to China: both strategic and symbolic implications in Tanzania were crucial to China.

As an illustration of the close ties between the two countries, President Nyerere arrived in Beijing on 18 June 1968 for his second visit to China. Among Chinese guests welcoming him were Premier Zhou, Vice Premiers Chen Yi and Li Hsien-nien, and Chief of the General Staff of the PLA Huang Yang-sheng. Notable among President Nyerere's delegation were Ahmed Mahmud, member of the Zanzibar Revolutionary Council; Juma Almasi, National Executive Committee member of the ASP; Brigadier General Sarakikya of the TPDF; M. N. E. Shaidi, inspector general of the police; and Michael Indadha and J. Marusi, representatives of TANU.[13] While visiting China, President Nyerere secured £100,000 for agricultural projects, including irrigated farms, small-scale hydroelectric plants, and flood control measures. Thirteen Tanzanian delegations visited China in 1966, eight in 1967, and three in 1968.[14] China, while focused on the Tan-Zam railway, was also interested in sustaining diverse relations with Tanzania. By June 1968, there were more than a thousand Chinese in Tanzania—including those on Zanzibar. Chinese on the mainland were working on the proposed railway, ministering in hospitals, working on a government farm, surveying the possibility of building a dam, and constructing an extension to and serving as instructors in a police station.[15] Meanwhile, construction of the Tan-Zam railway continued.

In the fall of 1968 Chinese, Tanzanian, and Zambian representatives surveyed the Tanzanian section of the Tan-Zam railway. The section, totaling approximately 708 kilometers, began in May 1968 and was soon to be completed, the *Peking Review* reported. Addressing Tanzanian villagers and Chinese personnel in the Mlinba Mountains and on the Kihansi River, Tanzanian minister for communications, labor, and works J. M. Lusinde said, "The Tanzanian people are determined to see to it that the whole of Africa is liberated. And the construction of the railway is a contribution to the total liberation of Africa."[16] Representatives surveying the railway included Minister Lusinde, Zambian high commissioner to Tanzania W. J. Phiri, and chargé d'affaires ad interim Chou Po-ping. Chinese assistance in construction of the Tan-Zam railway was tangible and symbolic—furthering long-term Chinese political interests on the continent.

While the Tan-Zam railway became its centerpiece, China maintained diverse assistance programs on the mainland and Zanzibar. In November 1968, for example, a surprise joint military exercise on Zanzibar took place. According to the CIA, "Mainland Tanzania police quietly and efficiently seized control of the town of Zanzibar and were soon reinforced by Zanzibar Army units." Within the framework of technical assistance to Zanzibar, for example, China supplied twenty-five doctors and medical assistants, six technicians and instructors for a government printing facility and broadcasting station, as well as mechanics and engineers—in all totaling approximately four hundred on the island. The CIA also noted the following with some trepidation: "The Chinese have gradually become the dominant force [in terms of economic aid] because of their well-managed, relatively-inexpensive aid, their ability to live frugally and work hard, and their extensive and well-financed contacts—both overt and covert—with many influential Zanzibaris." In addition, China operated a training camp outside the town of Zanzibar, with seventeen advisers teaching small arms and guerrilla warfare. Chinese had also "taken over the former U.S. Project Mercury tracking station at Tungu, where they [were] training 800 new Zanzibari recruits."[17] To further its political and strategic interests, China denied the United States a strategic outpost (satellite tracking station in the Indian Ocean) and used the same facility for Chinese objectives (to train Zanzibaris).

While press reports and negotiations focused on the Tan-Zam railway, China continued to provide much aid to Zanzibar, including the training of Zanzibari youth in China (May 1966); a six-months' course sponsored by the Department of Works, Communications, and Power (May 1966); as well as the training of three hundred tractor drivers (February 1967).[18] China also helped to build a printing press at Saateni (October 1967); a leather and shoe factory (February 1968); a factory for the manufacture of small implements and tools requested by the Zanzibar minister of agriculture (February 1968); residential quarters for workers at Kisongoni (July 1966); and a tractor and farm implements repair plant (September 1968). In addition, a Chinese medical team built the island's first pharmaceutical workshop at the Lenin Hospital, which opened in August 1968; and China helped establish the Upenja State Farm. The first Chinese agrotechnicians arrived in 1965; they handed the farm over to the Zanzibar government in January 1969. Chinese activity in Zanzibar indicated a continuity of strategic importance placed on the island, since the onset of Chinese activities on the island in the late 1950s.[19]

In January 1969 Tanzania showed gratitude for consistent Chinese aid and assistance by reciprocating face-to-face diplomatic meetings. On 11 January 1969 in Beijing, Tanzanian ambassador E. P. Mwaluko hosted a reception to mark the fifth anniversary of the Zanzibar revolution. Vice Chairman Kuo Mo-jo, Vice Minister of Foreign Affairs Chi Peng-fei, and other government officials were present. Speaking of the Chinese at the reception, Ambassador Mwaluko said that the sincere aid provided by China to Tanzania had increased the two countries' courage and confidence.[20] Several months later in Beijing, on 26 April 1969 newly installed Tanzanian ambassador Salim Ahmad Salim hosted a reception to celebrate the fifth anniversary of the founding of the United Republic of Tanzania. In attendance were Premier Zhou, Vice Premiers Hsieh Fu-chih and Li Hsien-nien, and Vice Chairman Kuo Mo-jo. In his speech at the reception, Ambassador Salim said the African people had consistently enjoyed the firm support of the Chinese people and government in their struggles against imperialism and colonialism.[21] Sino-Tanzanian political relations were indeed close.

Tanzania had much to be thankful for because in March 1969, according to the *Washington Post*, there were 900 to 1,100 Chinese in Tanzania, approximately half on Zanzibar.[22] By June 1969 the second of five water projects in Zanzibar was completed, and aid was extended for enlarging the Dar es Salaam stadium.[23] That same month, Chung Hsi-tung was nominated as Chinese ambassador to Tanzania and Chin Li-chen, Chinese ambassador to Zambia.[24] These new diplomatic appointments signaled renewed focus on the Tan-Zam railway. Toward the end of the summer, in August, 280 technicians and surveyors from China arrived in Dar es Salaam to work on the railway.[25] Progress was made at the end of the year as well. On 14 November 1969, after five days of talks in Lusaka, railway delegations from China, Tanzania, and Zambia signed a supplementary agreement between the three governments. Chinese vice minister of railways Kuo Lu, Zambian minister of development and finance E. H. K. Mudenda, and Tanzanian minister of finance A. H. Jamal signed the document. The three delegations also signed minutes of talks relating to preconstruction preparatory work and a supplementary proposal on technical principles.[26] As the new decade approached, the Tan-Zam railway was gradually becoming a reality.

Because so much attention had been paid to Chinese-Tanzanian relations, and to the Tan-Zam railway in particular, there was public suspicion regarding both countries' intentions. In a rare interview granted in November 1969, President Nyerere added to the suspicion by sidestepping questions regarding Tanzanian acquisition of Chinese fighter jets. In July 1968 Vice President Kawawa said Tanzania would develop its own navy and air force.[27] But he did acknowledge that Tanzania had actively supported guerrilla movements against white minority governments in southern Africa "for years" without either an air force or a navy.[28] Nyerere's statements demonstrated Chinese strategic influence, particularly when viewed in light of the use of guerilla warfare here as well as elsewhere on the continent. China was an active supplier of security assistance to Tanzania.

In December 1969, for example, the Chinese-built military barracks in Nachingwea were handed over to the Tanzanian government, and Chinese military experts took over training of the Tanzanian armed forces the next month. Wei Liang-Tsai reported that a new Chinese-built stadium in Zanzibar was completed in early January as well.[29] At about this time, *Afrique Nouvelle* reported, China had 150 military instructors and 22 police instructors in Tanzania, and "Chinese military instructors [were] playing the role of political agents of Peking within the Tanzanian Army."[30] Clearly, then, China was engaged in diverse activities in Tanzania, both political and security-related. And during the Cultural Revolution China was not diplomatically isolated from the outside world. In fact, Chinese formal diplomatic relations increased from forty-one (pre–Cultural Revolution) to forty-five (post–Cultural Revolution).[31] Moreover, after 1970 "the PRC was the only country providing military equipment and training to the Tanzanian forces." From 1965 to 1969 Canadians established and trained the majority of the Tanzanian armed forces.[32]

A multitude of Chinese activities in Tanzania continued throughout the 1970s. For example, China began construction of a naval base in May 1970. The next month, a Chinese-aided farm implements factory opened in Ubungo, near Dar es Salaam.[33] By July a Chinese-built hospital in Mkoani on Pemba was operational and a vaccine plant at Mabibo, near Dar es Salaam, was completed. The vaccines were used against smallpox and tuberculosis.[34] China effectively combined security assistance with tangible development aid. Personal communications between the two countries continued as well.

At the invitation of the Chinese Ministry of National Defense, Colonel Ali Mahfudh, chief of operations and training of the TPDF, led a Tanzanian military delegation to China, from 28 September to 29 October 1970.[35] On 8 October the Tanzanian military delegation departed Beijing to visit Yenan, Xian, Changsha, Guangzhou, Shanghai, and Nanjing. This was the first well-publicized military-to-military exchange between the two countries, signifying an increased level of strategic cooperation.

Throughout the year, personal communications in the form of exchange visits continued with regularity. On 24 April the Tanzanian ambassador to China, Richard S. Wambura, hosted a reception marking the sixth anniversary of Tanzania's founding.[36] Premier Zhou, Vice Premier Li Hsien-nien, Vice Chairman Kuo Mo-jo, and other leading members of government departments were all in attendance. Three months later, in July 1970, two government delegations from Tanzania and Zambia visited China to discuss the Tan-Zam railway.[37] The delegations signed protocols and minutes of talks concerning construction of the Tan-Zam railway. Premier Zhou met with members of the delegations on 9 July.[38] Initial work on the Tan-Zam began the same month, with more than 150 miles of embankment prepared, hundreds of culverts and bridges put in place, and mountains of earth moved.[39] Furthermore, on 11 July 1970 Chairman Mao and Vice Chairman Lin Piao met members of the visiting Tanzanian and Zambian delegations—conferring overwhelming prestige on the railway project as well as relations with both countries. The Tanzanian delegation was led by Amier Habib Jamal, minister for finance; and the Zambian delegation was led by E. H. K. Mudenda, minister of development and finance.[40]

In a further sign of the railway's political importance to China, according to the *New York Times* the next month, Premier Zhou accepted invitations to visit several African countries, including Tanzania and Zambia: "A visit to Tanzania and Zambia would provide an opportunity for Premier Chou to focus world attention on the Tan-Zam railway, the largest single foreign aid enterprise entered into by Peking."[41] The official inauguration ceremony for the Tan-Zam railway took place on 26 October 1970. The cornerstone-laying ceremonies were held at the future terminal at Yombo.[42] Fang Yi, head of the Commission for Economic Relations with Foreign Countries, spoke at the ceremony.[43] According to the Tanzanian Ministry of Information, approximately 4,700 Chinese technicians and workers were in Tanzania, with the number expected to rise to 6,000 by December. Work on the railroad was scheduled to end by 1975. Local costs of the railway, estimated at 52 percent of the total, were to be met from proceeds of the sale of $16.8 million of Chinese consumer goods to be imported annually by Tanzania and Zambia. Once again, China provided favorable financial terms, an interest-free loan of £169 million ($412 million) repayable over thirty years beginning in

1983.[44] The large number of Chinese personnel demonstrated Chinese interests and capabilities in Africa. And President Nyerere, speaking at the inaugural ceremony at Kapiri Mposhi, expressed his country's "very warm gratitude" to Mao, the PRC, and the Chinese people.[45]

At the same time, China was firmly committed to strengthening political relations with Tanzania. On 5 November 1970 Vice Chairman of the PRC Tung Pi-wu and Premier Zhou sent a message of congratulations to President Nyerere after his reelection. The message read in part, "May the friendly relations and co-operation between our two countries constantly develop and grow in strength."[46] Chinese activities continued on the island as well. By the end of 1970, China had given Zanzibar a series of loans worth $12 million. "The schemes involved a large number of Chinese instructors and officials."[47] According to the *New York Times*, the number of Chinese personnel in Zanzibar ranged from one hundred to four hundred.[48] Thus, China was engaged—successfully and simultaneously—on the mainland as well as on the island. From 1954 to 1970 Tanzania was the leading recipient of Chinese economic credits and grants, totaling $252 million. Of that, though, $201 million was extended in 1970 alone, presumably for the Tan-Zam railway.[49]

The new decade brought no decline in Chinese activities in East Africa. On 12 January 1971 Tanzanian ambassador to China Wambura hosted a reception in Beijing to celebrate the ninth anniversary of Tanganyika's independence and the seventh anniversary of Zanzibar Revolution Day.[50] Vice Premier Li Hsien-nien, Vice Foreign Minister Chi Peng-fei, and other leading officials were in attendance. The following month Ambassador Wambura hosted a cocktail party to celebrate the sixth anniversary of the signing of the Treaty of Friendship between the PRC and Tanzania.[51] Attending the party were Vice Premier Li Hsien-nien, Vice Chairman Kuo Mo-jo, Vice Foreign Minister Chi Peng-fei, and others. At this time, according to the *New York Times*, approximately seven thousand Chinese were working on the railway in Tanzania and Zambia.[52] "According to the *Daily Telegraph* [2 March 1971] all the Chinese working on the Tan-Zam railway were army personnel. Some of them have stayed on in key positions even after the railway has begun operating because of recurring technical and mechanical problems."[53] The Tan-Zam railway "illustrat[ed] renewed aid potential" for China in Africa. Also in 1971, Chinese doctors in Zanzibar were working at the Lenin Hospital to fight disabling tropical diseases, and China was building radio towers in Zambia.[54] Thus, China carried on multiple activities in and around Tanzania.

China continued to communicate vocal political support for the Tanzanian regime. For example, on 25 April Premier Zhou sent greetings to President Nyerere for Tanzania's National Day.[55] The next day Tanzanian ambassador Wambura hosted a reception to celebrate Tanzania's National Day. Premier Zhou, Vice Premier Li Hsien-nien, and Vice Chairman Kuo Mo-jo all attended the reception on invitation. In his speech, Ambassador Wambura said that Tanzania supported Chinese entry into the UN and opposition to create two Chinas or one China–one Taiwan.[56] This demonstrated Tanzanian political support for China, after years of close bilateral relations. Along the same lines, seventeen countries sent a letter and memorandum to the UN secretary general dated 15 July 1971 requesting restoration of the lawful rights of China in the UN. Among the signatories were Algeria and Tanzania.[57] Internationally, China was benefiting from its political activities in Africa.

China had by this time become a close supplier of a multitude of services to Tanzania. "By June [1971], there will be 13,000 Chinese working on the 1,100-mile railroad, which is to link the Zambian copper mines to the Indian Ocean, bypassing white-ruled Rhodesia and Mozambique."[58] The CIA estimated in 1972 that there had been 14,700 Chinese economic technicians in Tanzania in 1971.[59] In addition, Chinese in Tanzania were "advising the army, planning a naval base and building a plant outside Dar es Salaam for the manufacture of smallpox vaccine." These efforts suggested that China was doing more than "concentrating on symbolic projects."[60] But the Tan-Zam railway was the most symbolic of its projects in Africa. The *Peking Review* reported that track-laying on the 502-kilometer Dar es Salaam–Murimba section was completed on 11 November 1971.[61] Work on the section began in October 1970 by two teams of Tanzanian, Zambian, and Chinese workers, engineers, and technical personnel. China's activities in East Africa were reaching their climax.

At the end of the year, Tanzanian, Zambian, and Chinese delegations held talks on the railway in Dar es Salaam. The 21–22 December talks resulted in the signing of the fifth round of talks on the Tan-Zam railway. Minister of Communications Yang Chieh led the Chinese delegation, signifying the symbolic importance of the project to China.[62] China, however, continued its other activities as well. In December 1971, for example, Premier Zhou sent a message to President Nyerere congratulating him on the tenth anniversary of Tanganyika's independence.[63] On 9 December Ambassador Wambura and his wife hosted a reception to mark the anniversary. That same day the Tanzanian national football team and the visiting Chinese national football team played a friendly match at Dar es Salaam's national stadium, with more than 70,000 spectators on hand.[64] In attendance at the reception were Premier Zhou, Vice Chairman of the Military Commission of the Central Committee of the Communist Party of China Yeh Chien-ying, Vice Chairman Kuo Mo-jo, and Acting Foreign Minister Chi Peng-fei. Chinese communications to Tanzania—in print and in person—reinforced the significant nature of Sino-Tanzanian political relations.

By this time, China was the sole provider of security assistance to Tanzania. In December 1971 the Chinese-built naval base was completed and handed over to the Tanzanian government.[65] As an example of growing military ties, between 1964 and 1972 Tanzania "received perhaps $40 million of Chinese military and commitments. The equipment delivered include[d] MIG jet fighters, light tanks, patrol boats, and various ground forces and support equipment. The Chinese [were] also constructing naval and air facilities in Tanzania."[66] From 20 to 25 August 1972 a Tanzanian goodwill delegation visited China. Minister of Foreign Affairs John S. Malecela led the delegation, and Lieutenant Colonel Hafidh Suleiman, member of the Zanzibar Revolutionary Council, was the deputy.[67] While in Beijing, the Tanzanian delegation met with Premier Zhou, Foreign Minister Chi Peng-fei, Minister of Economic Relations with Foreign Countries Fung Yi, Deputy Chief of the General Staff of the PLA Peng Shao-hui, and Vice Foreign Minister Ho Ying.[68] The inclusion of a PLA official was an indication of the strong security ties between the two countries. Tanzania was China's closest security partner in Africa.

The next year a Tanzanian official was assassinated. Lieutenant Hamoud, "recently returned from training in Eastern Europe," murdered Vice President Karume on 7 April 1972.[69] Although never fully explained, Hamoud's action may have been a simple personal vendetta: He was the son of Mohamed Hamoud Barwani, who had been the 1955 murderer of Ali Sultan Mugheiry, an Arab Association executive committee member on the Legislative Council who did not join the boycott against the British. The elder Hamoud was apparently killed in prison during the revolution. Nevertheless, China was suspected due to its history of activities on Zanzibar. Babu was allegedly involved in the assassination of Karume, but President Nyerere refused Zanzibar's request to extradite him and held him in prison until 1978.[70] Three days after the assassination, Acting Chairman Tung Pi-wu sent a message to President Nyerere expressing condolences for the death of Vice President Karume. The following day, Premier Zhou, Vice Chairman Yeh Chien-ying, Vice Premier Li Hsien-nien, and Foreign Minister Chi Peng-fei called at the Tanzanian embassy in Beijing to express condolences.[71]

Despite the assassination, three Tanzanian delegations visited China a month later.[72] The delegations included a military delegation led by Junior Minister of Defense and National Service Geoffrey Oscar Mhagama, a Home Affairs delegation led by Home Minister Saidi Ali Maswaya, and an education delegation of the University of Dar es Salaam. Between 5 and 20 May 1972 the Tanzanian military delegation visited China, but no details were made public.[73] The military and home delegations stayed for fifteen days. At a farewell banquet on 19 May, Junior Minister Mhagama said that under the leadership of Chairman Mao and President Nyerere the two countries and armies had established friendship on a solid basis.[74] In spite of Karume's assassination, therefore, overall Sino-Tanzanian relations continued to flourish. In all likelihood, China was not involved in Karume's assassination.

By 1972 Tanzania was "undoubtedly Peking's most important base in Africa and one of that country's best friends." This was particularly true with regard to Chinese security assistance to Tanzania. As an example: "Chinese merchant ships generally call[ed] at Dar es Salaam every 10 days and discharge[d] military supplies, construction equipment for [Tan-Zam] and general cargo—always under conditions of secrecy." In addition, Chinese technicians were building an air base for the Tanzanian air force, as well as advising and training Tanzanian personnel. The air base was in the vicinity of Ngerengere, west of Dar es Salaam. China also used Tanzania as a training base for African independence movements. Chinese instructors were "prominent in the training of terrorists in camps in Dar es Salaam, Bagomoya, Moshi, Mgulani, Songea, Kongwa, Morogoro and Nachingwea." Political indoctrination was an important part of the Chinese curriculum. In addition, Chinese instructors studied operational problems and acted as advisers to guerrillas and the ALC of the OAU.[75] China, thus, provided overt and covert security assistance.

China's strategic line of communication with Tanzania was well established by this time as well. On 18 November 1972, *Chamwino*, Sino-Tanzanian Joint Shipping Company's 10,000-ton-class ocean-going vessel, was commissioned as the company's third ocean-going ship.[76] The two others were the *Africa-Asia* and *Co-operation*. The time it took to develop this strategic communication line—1966 to 1972—was an indication of China's diplomatic approach, patient and long term. And on the financial front, in December 1972 a Chinese bank delegation returned from a visit to Albania, Romania, France, Algeria, Tanzania, Zambia, and Pakistan. Chiao Pei-hsin, acting chair of the board of directors and general manager of the Bank of China, led the delegation.[77]

The strategic nature of Sino-Tanzanian relations continued the next year. On 28 January 1973 Vice Minister of National Defense Wang Shu-sheng hosted a banquet for the visiting Tanzanian military delegation led by E. M. Sokoine, minister of defense and national service. Speaking at the banquet, Vice Minister Wang said the people of China and Tanzania had always united with and supported one another and were comrades-in-arms on the same front.[78] Their political unity and shared security concerns went hand in hand. "It [was] significant that one of China's leading strategists Lin Laing [was] in charge of indoctrination and motivation among terrorists in Dar es Salaam."[79] Identifying common interests, therefore, China was successful cultivating overall relations with Tanzania.

China's most publicized activity in Africa neared completion in 1973. Border ceremonies were held on 27 August 1973 for the Tan-Zam railway.[80] President Kuanda and President Nyerere were both on hand. By that time, 606 miles of track had been laid in Tanzania. Notably, 556 miles remained to be laid in Zambia. The next month, however, the *New York Times* reported that the Tan-Zam railway was "nearing completion more than a year ahead of the 1975 target date."[81] Off the mainland, Chinese activities continued as well. In December eighteen Chinese medical experts arrived in Zanzibar to work for two years. The following month, a new Chinese-built sugar factory was inaugurated in Zanzibar. At the opening ceremony, Aboud Jumbe, Tanzania's first vice president who succeeded Karume, expressed "hearty thanks" to the Chinese government.[82] Chinese activities in Tanzania remained diverse and multifaceted.

Keeping in mind the strategic position of Tanzania, local events took place that benefited China. On 4 February 1974 the Youth League of TANU held a demonstration in Dar es Salaam protesting the U.S. military presence in the Indian Ocean. P. S. Qorro, chair of the Youth League of TANU, led "thirty thousand" Tanzanian youth, students, and young workers through the capital to the U.S. embassy. The Youth League of the ASP held a similar demonstration outside the U.S. consulate on Zanzibar. Both youth leagues handed letters of protest to U.S. personnel.[83] These events demonstrated continued Chinese political influence on local politics, particularly activities targeting youth.

In the same year (1974), President Nyerere made his third visit to Communist China. "In [March] 1974, when Nyerere made an official visit, the PRC agreed to lend Tanzania more than £30 million [interest-free] by 1979 to develop coal and iron resources."[84] Beijing granted Dar es Salaam the interest-free loan (approximately $75 million over five years) "to complete existing projects, to exploit the coal mines in Tukuyu and iron ore in Chunya, and to build a 250-km railway to link the two points."[85] During the visit Chairman Mao met with President Nyerere for the third time—a symbolic gesture of the importance bestowed on relations with Tanzania.[86] They had met previously in Beijing in 1965 and 1968. At a welcoming banquet for President Nyerere, Premier Zhou said, "China and Tanzania are both developing countries belonging to the Third World."[87] The Tanzanian delegation later visited Beijing, Hebei, Heilongjiang, and Liaoning where delegates toured Beijing University, Beijing Iron Mine, Shashihyu Production Brigade, Daqing Oilfield, and Fushun Open-cut Coalmine.[88] Upon entering the community of international nations, China aligned itself with Tanzania and the rest of the developing world. The UN admitted the PRC in 1971, removing the representation of the Republic of China on Taiwan.

Tanzania, by this time, had become a firm base for Chinese activities in the region. In Guinea and Tanzania, the Communist Chinese were conducting guerrilla schools for liberation movements. Guinea may have been the replacement to Ghana, after relations soured with the latter. Beijing supplied graduates with arms and ammunition to conduct guerrilla operations in countries such as Angola, Mozambique, and South Africa. According to the U.S. Department of State, Southern Rhodesia (present-day Zimbabwe), in particular, had Communist Chinese–trained guerrillas operating from bases in Zambia and Mozambique.[89] In May 1974, however, Tanzania denied reports that it had offered China base construction rights and naval positioning rights along the Tanzanian coast.[90] Yet China's security assistance to Tanzania was apparent.

Between October 1975 and September 1976, China financed the construction of a military academy at Munduli in Arusha, providing Tanzania with an indigenous capability to train its military officers.[91] The academy may also have been intended for political training. Thus, between 1971 and 1975 China delivered $47 million in military aid to Tanzania. The CIA reported in early 1976 that in 1975, 700 Chinese military technicians had been in Tanzania, along with 4,100 economic technicians, as well as 10,000 economic technicians in Zambia.[92] Also, according to Legum, between 1955 and 1976 over 1,000 Tanzanian military personnel reportedly trained in China: 1,025, to be precise.[93] Sino-Tanzanian relations were clearly robust in the security domain.

In the meantime, completion of the Tan-Zam railway quickly approached. In September 1974 in Beijing, representatives of China, Tanzania, and Zambia signed minutes of the seventh rounds of Tan-Zam railway talks and three protocols on the railway. Minister A. C. Tandau led the Tanzanian delegation and N. S. Mulenga led the Zambian delegation, which arrived in Beijing on 15 September and departed on 19 September to visit other parts of China.[94] Track-laying for the Tan-Zam railway was completed in June 1975, and a trial run for the passenger and freight cars began on 23 October. Ceremonies were held for the trial run at the new Kapiri Mposhi Station in Zambia's Central Province. In attendance were President Kaunda, Vice President Kawawa, and various government and party officials. Representing China were ambassador to Tanzania Li Yao-wen, chargé d'affaires ad interim in Zambia Tang Yung, and acting head of the Chinese Railway Working Team Chin Hui. Ambassador Li congratulated Zambia and Tanzania at the ceremonies and stated, "This achievement of the Zambian and Tanzanian peoples has boosted the morale of the people and deflated the arrogance of the enemy."[95] Ambassador Li's statement emphasized the political importance of the railway, as it served as a symbol of the struggle against those who opposed Chinese interests—in Africa and elsewhere.

A year and a half later, Chinese personnel visited Tanzania once again. From 20 to 28 July 1976, Vice Premier Sun Chien led a Chinese delegation to Tanzania. During its stay, the delegation met with President Nyerere, Vice President and Chairman of the Zanzibar Revolutionary Council Jumbe, and Vice President and Prime Minister Kawawa. While touring Mbeya, Dar es Salaam, Arusha, Zanzibar, and the coastal regions, the Chinese delegation visited the Tan-Zam railway, numerous factories, an *ujamaa* (family or community) village, and the Ruvu National Service Camp.[96] The delegation also attended the Tan-Zam railway handover ceremony, a culmination of China's most ambitious project in Africa. Although construction of the railway was delayed at times, Leo Tansky was correct: "No country [could] implement project-type aid rapidly in the less developed countries."[97] Finally, on 9 September 1976 President Nyerere sent a message to Premier Hua Kuo-feng expressing "great sadness and solidarity" after Mao's death.[98]

From the onset, Chinese activities in Tanzania were multidimensional, covering the spectrum of activities—political, development, and security projects. Understanding the strategic importance of East Africa, China was more successful in Tanzania than anywhere else on the African continent during the Maoist era. Sino-Tanzanian relations were of prime importance to China, and it devoted substantial time and resources to achieve its aims. China learned from its activities across Africa and demonstrated, above all, pragmatism in its approach to Africa, even early on, in the 1950s, 1960s, and 1970s.

CONCLUSION
The Chinese Remain

China used Egypt as its entry point onto the African continent to begin influencing affairs in Africa—especially North, but later West and East. Today, China continues to exert influence in all three regions of the continent—indeed, across all of Africa. In a sense, Africa has become "the proving ground for a new activist China."[1] Today's current activities and influence owe much to China's initial operations during the Maoist era, from 1955 to 1976, which above all were pragmatic.

China began by supporting Algerian independence in the French-Algerian War, which created a divisive environment in the second-largest (by area) country in Africa—politically, socially, and economically.[2] After Algeria gained independence in 1962, these divisions subsided but remained latent. From their origins, the National Liberation Front and provisional government of the Algerian Republic offered China effective political partners with which to interact. And interact China did: Through a combination of exchange visits and public communications, China developed into a steadfast ally of the Algerian independence movement on the international scene. On the military front, the durable National Liberation Army enjoyed moral, financial, and material support from China, albeit the support was quantitatively minor. China also provided training to select officers of the army. Although its influence waned as Algeria became an independent nation-state, China was successful gaining an initial strategic foothold in this North African country, establishing social and political conditions favorable for future relations.

The former Gold Coast was socially and politically stable upon China's entrance. After becoming the country's dominant political figure, Nkrumah led a politically repressive regime in Ghana. China attempted to foster political and military relations with Nkrumah through publicized exchange visits, minor economic aid packages, and the training of foreign militants in Ghana. But without the support of effective domestic organizations, Nkrumah created divisions within his own regime and between his regime and the Ghanaian people. After Nkrumah was removed from power in 1966, China was expelled, but relations were later restored in 1972. Since Nkrumah never fully gained the loyalty of the Ghanaian military, police, or political establishment, there were no effective organizations to maintain his rule. China finally convinced Nkrumah to establish a people's militia, but Nkrumah's acquiescence was half-hearted (the militia was financed with minimal funds) and came at the eleventh hour (the same year he was ousted). China was unable to gain a revolutionary ally in this strategic West African country.

Due to its divergent colonial histories (with both German and British influences) and its ethnic make-up, Tanzania's environment was somewhat politically, socially, and economically divided. The 1964 union between Tanganyika and Zanzibar exacerbated latent political and ethnic differences between the mainland and the island. On Zanzibar in particular, social divisions were strained between the African and non-African (mostly Arab) peoples. For China, effective political organizations were present in Zanzibar (the ZNP) and on the mainland (the TANU). With the former, led by a Communist-trained agent, China used public communications and targeted development projects to penetrate through Zanzibar onto the mainland. From there, China helped fund, supply, and train the TPDF, police, paramilitary groups, and various armed national liberation movements based in Tanzania. Chinese economic aid and development projects abounded in Tanzania as well, the most notable being the Tan-Zam railway. While technologically unsophisticated, China used its personnel and material resources effectively. Through its interactions and operations, China exploited Tanzania for lasting benefit, establishing a strategic foothold and long-term influence in this East African nation.

During the Maoist era, it was unclear why China ventured onto the African continent, expending precious time, effort, and resources. According to a warning by former Côte d'Ivoire president Houphouet-Boigny, China's aim was "to obtain either open or covert control of governments and their economies rather than wholesale conversion of the African masses to Communism. . . . Africa, underpopulated Africa, is their long-term goal and we must be alive to the danger."[3] Scholar C. F. de Villiers' assessment of the Chinese in East and southern Africa explains another dimension of China's approach: "By becoming an important power in the whole of East and Southern Africa—even though this [was] in the long term—China could assure herself a key position. . . . This would not only facilitate China's scramble for Africa but would also assure her of a significant, new world status and would create many new problems for her opponents on the world scene. . . . Markets, minerals and other economic considerations are side attractions but in essence Africa, an extremely important pawn on the world chess-board, is at stake."[4] And similarly, Taylor explains Chinese objectives in the contemporary context: "Determined to be free of the overt influence of any one power, mindful of past domination by outsiders, and aiming to 'regain' its position of eminence in the international system, Beijing since the end of the Cold War has continuously courted Africa and the developing world as a means by which China may project its prestige and influence outside the narrow confines of East Asia and thus further its claims to the status of a 'great power.'"[5] Throughout its history, China has considered itself a world power—even a superior civilization without frontiers. Between 1955 and 1976, China sought to begin elevating itself to such a position, using actions to achieve strategic aims on the African continent.

Through its activities, China was able to expand ties to African countries and to establish conditions favorable to China, politically and strategically. Moreover, economic gains were added incentives for Chinese operations. China understood the future strategic value of the African continent, given its geographic size, scope, and diversity. From a long-term perspective, Chinese activities in Africa foreshadowed trade relations and access to natural resources, much of what is touted repeatedly today. Adjacent to Europe and the Middle East, "Africa with its bountiful economic resources has very important strategic value," wrote commentator Chang Ya-chun.[6] And journalist Richard Eder wrote cogently in 1965, "At the very least . . . the Chinese have established a firm presence in Africa from which they may be able to advance some longer-range goals."[7] Thus, China's central objective was to establish and expand influence on the African continent for long-term strategic benefit.[8]

To expand influence onto the African continent, China required an approach that took into account its capabilities at the time as well as the diverse contexts within each African region and nation. "Chinese attempts to penetrate Africa [were] not a haphazard affair. They follow[ed] carefully delineated lines of Communist ideology, as well as the demands of Chinese national interest."[9] Here, Professor William Zartman correctly analyzed China's approach on the African continent. Although overplaying the ideological influence of China's action, Zartman noted accurately that the Chinese followed their central objectives (their national interest) and were not the least bit haphazard about it. Furthermore,

Hutchison made clear that "China's African policy was pragmatic, somewhat cautious and depended for success, like all other nations' foreign policies, on good timing and on good luck."[10] This book would contend, however, that "good timing" was, sometimes, a result of Chinese actions rather than luck. As the three case studies demonstrate, China developed and implemented an approach to penetrate and influence Africa, ultimately, for its own strategic benefit.

China was meticulous in its operations, emphasizing the importance of image and timing. Colin Legum stated, "To achieve maximum impact [China] carefully timed the announcement of aid. . . . The Chinese [showed] great skill and psychological astuteness in the presentation of their aid policy." This demonstrated the Chinese penchant for using public pronouncements to influence perception and opinion. "Whenever possible, the Chinese [sought] Africans actively engaged in the mass media; their strongest preference [was] for key figures in ministries of information."[11] Chinese operations also demonstrated the use of exchange visits to communicate their messages in person. African visits to China and, conversely, Chinese visits and messages to Africa aimed to "confer dignity and prestige [and to create] Chinese-African unity. . . . Books, films, and radio broadcasts [were] a limited vehicle of Chinese activity, touching an imprecise audience, but they [added] to the background of fraternity and imagery on which Peking can build concrete acts of cooperation."[12] Chinese operations were deliberate not only in timing and presentation but also in targeting. "The Chinese propagandists and secret agents devote[d] special attention to poisoning the minds of young Africans."[13] Partly because of its Communist roots, China understood well the importance of the youth in any population, their influence as well as their potential future roles in society. Chinese operations were opportunistic: "The Chinese [did] not restrict their offer of support to revolutionary movements or revolutionary leaders. These the Chinese [sought] out and help[ed] whenever they [arose]."[14] Furthermore, writing in the context of diplomatic relations, Legum stated, China "appear[ed] to pick and choose in according degrees of support."[15] Thus, from a strategic perspective, Chinese operations revealed an emphasis on purposeful communications, proper timing, and opportunistic yet deliberate targeting.

Other significant characteristics of China's approach in Africa included flexibility and resourcefulness. Both characteristics were distinct in Chinese operations. For example, "Peking . . . recognized that influence of a purely ideological nature, aided only by Mao's precepts, [was] not very effective on African minds and hearts. The cumbersome apparatus of Maoist propaganda directed toward Africa operate[d] in an awkward and uneven fashion and yield[ed] minimal political gains."[16] As a result, China altered its operations from context to context—from Algeria to Ghana to Tanzania. The Chinese recognized the paramount importance of different contexts within each African nation. A Chinese ministry of foreign affairs directive from 1968, for example, noted the basic rule of knowing the target first before performing propaganda operations.[17] Over time, Chinese operations were tailored to suit the context as well as Chinese interests. "Peking's aid policies toward the African countries reflect[ed] changes in its political outlook, and the priority given to relations with the continent."[18] The varying character of operations demonstrated Chinese tactical and strategic flexibility. Around the world, China used different operations to achieve its objectives.[19] On the African continent, "the vast, heterogeneous environment of Africa [made] it difficult for any outside force to have a clear picture of the local situation and to arrive at any rational, effective policy."[20] Yet China chose intentionally the African continent as a targeted area of operations. Or, in the words of an assessment of the CIA in 1965, "In Peiping's view, Africa is the second [only to Asia] great area of opportunity."[21] The diverse African political, economic, and social environments lent themselves to the multitude of Chinese operations. "The People's Republic [showed] considerable skill in the application of its essentially limited funds and technicians."[22] For example, Chinese aid to African countries "enabled China to improve its political image among the Africans at relatively little expense."[23] Although downplaying Chinese influence, the CIA nonetheless revealed the resourcefulness of its operations: "Peiping [has] agents in positions to exert influence which may occasionally be of great importance in various African countries."[24] While these agents were by no means equivalent to the influence of military force, Chinese activities had disproportionate effect as "asymmetric equalizers."[25] Only after coming to a "complete awareness of China's very limited means and possibilities" could Beijing's leaders craft an approach to achieve maximum effectiveness.[26] Thus, flexibility and resourcefulness were part and parcel of the character of Chinese operations.

The Chinese approach comprised "well-managed, relatively-inexpensive aid, their ability to live frugally and work hard, and their extensive and well-financed contacts—both overt and covert."[27] China used limited resources to great effect, particularly by skillfully exploiting opportunities. Though it has many more resources at its disposal in the twenty-first century, China's fundamental approach on the African continent remains the same: self-interested, strategic, and pragmatic. What this bodes for the future of Africa is unclear, however. As the *Washington Post* published in 1960, the "more pessimistic observers, both in and out of [American] government, see China's increasing activity in Africa as the beginning of a vast flanking movement to turn all peoples of color against the white minority so long dominant in the world. While this may attribute too much design and calculated long-term planning to the ruthless men who have gained control over the Chinese giant, it is a potential that cannot be ignored."[28]

The history of China in Africa—its distant meddling—demonstrates that China was never exclusively revolutionary or ideological; rather, it exhibited long-term, pragmatic behavior from the very beginning on the continent. Today, the implications for China's past activities in Africa are significant. The United States and other interested nations in the world—in Europe as well as in Asia—have largely overlooked China's historical involvement in Africa, emphasizing instead current and fashionable trends.

The fact of the matter is that China's current official Africa policy is congruent with and reminiscent of its past Africa policies during the Maoist era.[29] Yet China continues to seek to exert its own influence in Africa, with greater resources and continued interference in the affairs of African nations. Certainly, China is not the poor nation it once was and claimed to be. But the shared historical past, especially common experiences of perceived exploitation and colonialism, remains alive in Africa and in China. It is a bond that the United States and the West can never create or use to their own benefit. China continues to use this shared history, as well as its past ways, to gain strategic benefit in Africa. Today China is actively seeking opportunities of influence on the continent by using the same general strategic approach as it did in the 1950s, 1960s, and 1970s.

In the final analysis, it is apparent that China's past activities in Africa served Chinese interests, and its activities now may serve the same in the future. It would be prudent for the United States to take China's historically pragmatic behavior on the continent into account fully as it develops its own Africa policies in the twenty-first century. Students, scholars, analysts, and policymakers ignore the historical realities of China in Africa at their own peril.

NOTES

INTRODUCTION

1. Herrlee G. Creel noted that Chinese–East African trade dates back to the tenth and eleventh centuries. Herrlee G. Creel, *The Origins of Statecraft in China: The Western Chou Empire*, vol. 1 (Chicago: University of Chicago Press, 1970), 11.
2. For discussion of Kenya, the most strategic country in greater Eastern Africa, see Donovan C. Chau, *Global Security Watch—Kenya* (Santa Barbara, CA: Praeger, 2010).
3. The following are some notable English-language works: John K. Cooley, *East Wind Over Africa: Red China's African Offensive* (New York: Walker and Company, 1965); G. P. Deshpande and H. K. Gupta, *United Front against Imperialism: China's Foreign Policy in Africa* (Bombay: Somaiya Publications, 1986); Emmanuel John Hevi, *The Dragon's Embrace: The Chinese Communists and Africa* (London: Pall Mall Press, 1967); Bruce D. Larkin, *China and Africa, 1949–1970: The Foreign Policy of the People's Republic of China* (Berkeley: University of California Press, 1971).
4. For example, contrast the following reports: Carter Dougherty, "China a Player in African Politics," *Washington Times*, 16 February 2004, A18; Karby Leggett, "China Flexes Economic Muscle Throughout Burgeoning Africa," *Wall Street Journal*, 29 March 2005, 1. Dougherty wrote, "China has emerged as a major player in African politics, with appeals for developing world solidarity increasingly overshadowed by the country's interest in securing access to vital raw materials." On the other hand, Leggett wrote, "In Africa, as in many other parts of the developing world, China is redrawing geopolitical alliances in ways that help propel China's rise as a global superpower."
5. See, for example, Liu Guijin, "China-Africa Relations: Equality, Cooperation and Mutual Development," speech to Institute for Security Studies, South Africa, 9 November 2004.
6. Princeton Lyman, "China's Rising Role in Africa," testimony before the U.S. Economic and Security Review Commission, hearing on "China's Global Influence: Objectives and Strategies," 21 July 2005; David H. Shinn, "China's Approach to East, North and the Horn Africa," testimony before the U.S. Economic and Security

Review Commission, hearing on "China's Global Influence: Objectives and Strategies," 21 July 2005; Michael E. Ranneberger, Hearing on "China's Influence in Africa," testimony before Subcommittee on Africa, Global Human Rights and International Operations, Committee on International Relations, U.S. House of Representatives, 28 July 2005. Lyman was former U.S. ambassador to South Africa and Nigeria; Shinn, former U.S. ambassador to Burkina Faso and Ethiopia; and Ranneberger, former deputy assistant secretary of state of African affairs.

7. Chris Alden, *China in Africa: Partner, Competitor or Hegemon?* (London: Zed Books, 2007); Deborah Brautigam, *The Dragon's Gift: The Real Story of China in Africa* (New York: Oxford University Press, 2011); Ian Taylor, *China and Africa: Engagement and Compromise* (London: Routledge, 2006); Ian Taylor, *China's New Role in Africa* (Boulder, CO: Lynne Rienner, 2010).

8. Robert I. Rotberg, ed., *China into Africa: Trade, Aid, and Influence* (Cambridge, MA: World Peace Foundation, 2008); Arthur Waldron, ed., *China in Africa* (Washington, DC: The Jamestown Foundation, 2008); Chris Alden, Daniel Large, and Ricardo Soares de Oliveira, eds., *China Returns to Africa: A Rising Power and a Continent Embrace* (New York: Columbia University Press, 2008).

9. David H. Shinn and Joshua Eisenman, *China and Africa: A Century of Engagement* (Philadelphia: University of Pennsylvania Press, 2012).

10. Shinn and Eisenman devote one chapter to historical Sino-African relations, "A Historical Overview of China-Africa Relations" (ibid., 17–55).

11. This book uses the year 1976 because it represents the end of Mao's rule of China. While 1990 could have also been used (representing the end of the Cold War), 1976 is a more defined year in Communist Chinese history. The book will use modern pinyin romanization of significant Chinese names, after established convention. Some names in the book will be romanized in the Wade-Giles format, as these names were so romanized in the context of the times.

12. Some have attempted to do so, for example, Alden, *China in Africa*; and Joshua Eisenman, Eric Heginbotham, and Derek Mitchell, eds., *China and the Developing World: Beijing's Strategy for the Twenty-First Century* (Armonk, NY: M. E. Sharpe, 2007).

13. Hevi, *The Dragon's Embrace*, 3.

14. Chang Ya-chun, *Chinese Communist Activities in Africa—Policies and Challenges* (Taipei, Republic of China: World Anti-Communist League and Asian Peoples' Anti-Communist League, 1981), 38.

15. See, for example, J. C. van Broekhuizen, "Moskau und Peking in Afrika," *Afrika Heute*, no. 21 (1 November 1966): 309–312; Ho Wei-Yang, "Die Politik der Chinesen in Afrika," *Aussenpolitik* 12, no. 3 (March 1961): 162–168; Werner Holzer, "Die überschätzte 'Gelbe Gefahr': Der sowjetisch-chinesische Konkurrenzkampf um Afrika," *Afrika Heute*, no. 22 (15 November 1966): 325–327; Fritz Schatten, *Afrika—Schwartz oder Rot?* (Munich: R. Piper, 1961); Christoph Stark, *Die Aussenpolitik der Volksrepublik China in Afrika von 1969 bis 1983, unter besonderer Berücksichtigung des südlichen Afrika* (Frankfurt: Peter Stark, 1990).

16. For my earlier strategic analysis of Chinese activities in Algeria and in Ghana, see Donovan C. Chau, "The French-Algerian War: Communist China's Support for Independence," in *Military Advising and Assistance, 1815–2007: From Mercenaries to Privatization*, ed. Donald Stoker (London: Routledge Press, 2008): 111–126; "Assistance of a Different Kind: Chinese Political Warfare in Ghana, 1958–1966," *Comparative Strategy* 26, no. 2 (April–June 2007): 141–161.

CHAPTER 1. OBJECTIVES

1. "The [skilled] researcher must develop an awareness that writing does not adequately express language and that language does not adequately convey thought, and he must, therefore, either possess or cultivate an educated skepticism of the printed word and, hopefully, the ability to penetrate vicariously to the level of reality which lies beneath the written label." Howard L. Boorman, "The Study of Contemporary Chinese Politics: Some Remarks on Retarded Development," *World Politics* 12, no. 4 (July 1960): 591.
2. Hevi, *The Dragon's Embrace*, 4.
3. Mao Tse-tung [Zedong], *On People's Democratic Dictatorship* (Beijing: Foreign Languages Press, 1950), 35. The People's Republic of China was inaugurated on 1 October 1949.
4. Chinese, and Asians in general, view politics and political acts in a highly symbolic fashion. "In Asia the masses of the people are more respectful of authority. Their leaders are concerned about questions of dignity, the need to uphold national pride, and other highly symbolic matters. Those in power want above all to be seen as protecting the prestige of the collectivity, which they are inclined to place above the goal of efficiency or of advancing specific interests in concrete ways." Lucian W. Pye, *Asian Power and Politics: The Cultural Dimensions of Authority* (Cambridge, MA: Harvard University Press, 1985), viii.
5. Boorman, "The Study of Contemporary Chinese Politics," 585.
6. Mao Tse-tung, *On People's Democratic Dictatorship*, 11.
7. Ibid., 15.
8. I will discuss the influence of China's Communist ideology as a secondary objective later in the chapter.
9. Mao Tse-tung, *On People's Democratic Dictatorship*, 11.
10. Interestingly, Lyman P. Van Slyke asserts that the Chinese People's Political Consultative Conference is the organization historically used for united front implementation and coordination. Lyman P. Van Slyke, *Enemies and Friends: The United Front in Chinese Communist History* (Stanford, CA: Stanford University Press, 1967), 237.
11. As Boorman notes, though, some caution should be taken in making such analogies: "Some subjects involved in the study of Western constitutional systems (political parties, parliamentary organization and procedure, and public opinion, for example) have no real counterpart in the Chinese Communist system." Boorman, "The Study of Contemporary Chinese Politics," 589.
12. "Common Program of the Chinese People's Political Consultative Conference, 29 September 1949," in *The People's Republic of China 1949–1979: A Documentary Survey*, ed. Harold C. Hinton (Wilmington, DE: Scholarly Resources, 1980), 55.
13. Alan Hutchison, *China's Africa Revolution* (Boulder, CO: Westview Press, 1976), 3.
14. Larkin, *China and Africa* ["The central end," "The CCP" (2)].
15. "Common Program of the Chinese People's Political Consultative Conference, 29 September 1949" ["The Central People's Government," "The People's Republic of China" (55), "Efforts shall be made" (54)].
16. Director of Central Intelligence, *Prospects for Communist China*, National Intelligence Estimate number 13–4–62, 2 May 1962, 6.
17. "China's National Defense," white paper issued by the Information Office of the State Council, the People's Republic of China, 27 July 1998, 1.
18. In the 1950s and 1960s U.S. media noted Chinese objectives to become a world power. See, for example, Felix Cotten, "Purported Peiping Blueprint of Red Conquest Shown Here," *Washington Post*, 31 May 1954, 2. (The *Washington Post* acquired

the *Washington Times-Herald* in 1954, and both names appeared in different ways until 1974. For simplicity, this book uses *Washington Post* for all references to that paper.) Stated explicitly a decade later, "China's long-run objective is to become the most important power on this planet to correspond with the fact that it has the largest population of any nation." Harry Schwartz, "China's Objective: Expansion of Power," *New York Times*, 2 February 1964, E6.

19. Liu Shao-chi [Shaoqi], *Internationalism and Nationalism* (Beijing: Foreign Languages Press, 1954), 49–50.
20. Liu Shao-chi [Shaoqi], "Report to the Trade Union Conference of the Asian and Australasian Countries, 16 November 1949," in Hinton, *The People's Republic of China 1949–1979* ["To fight for national independence" (121–122), "It is therefore necessary" (121)].
21. Analogously, legendary Prussian strategic theorist Carl von Clausewitz viewed the nature but not necessarily the character of war as permanent. Thus, "all wars are things of the same nature." Carl von Clausewitz, *On War*, trans. Michael Howard and Peter Paret (Princeton, NJ: Princeton University Press, 1976), 606.
22. George T. Yu, "China and the Third World," *Asian Survey* 17, no. 11 (November 1977): 1047.
23. Director of Central Intelligence, *Communist China*, National Intelligence Estimate Number 13–60, 20 December 1960, 19–20.
24. George T. Yu, "Peking versus Taipei in the World Arena: Chinese Competition in Africa," *Asian Survey* 3, no. 9 (September 1963): 441.
25. Mao Tse-tung [Zedong], *On New Democracy* (Beijing: Foreign Languages Press, 1960) ["[W]e want to change" (2), "All the imperialist powers" (29)].
26. Mao Tse-tung [Zedong], *On the Ten Major Relationships* (Beijing: Foreign Languages Press, 1977), 25.
27. Tang Tsou, "Mao Tse-tung and Peaceful Coexistence," *Orbis* 8, no. 1 (Spring 1964): 50.
28. Mao Tse-tung, *On New Democracy*, 75.
29. Mao Tse-tung, *On the Ten Major Relationships*, 2.
30. Ibid., 28.
31. A U.S. Department of Defense analysis of Chinese military power notes with apparent astonishment the Chinese desire to incorporate the information-led revolution in military affairs and foreign technologies (particularly, but not exclusively, Russian) to the People's Liberation Army (PLA) arsenal. Office of the Secretary of Defense, *Annual Report to Congress on the Military Power of the People's Republic of China* (Washington, DC), Report to Congress Pursuant to Fiscal Year 2000 National Defense Authorization Act, June 2000, 7. Clearly, the authors were *not* familiar with Mao's 1956 *On the Ten Major Relationships*.
32. Mao Tse-tung, *On the Ten Major Relationships* ["National defense" (6), "Only with the faster" (7), "We must strengthen" (8), "We must do our" (33)].
33. Mao Tse-tung [Zedong], "Opening Speech to the Eighth Party Congress, 15 September 1956," in Hinton, *The People's Republic of China 1949–1979* ["To achieve a lasting peace," "We must endeavor," "We must give" (359)].
34. Central Intelligence Agency (CIA), *Chinese Communist Ministry of Foreign Affairs Foreign Policy Report*, Information Report, 3 July 1961, 8.
35. Mao Tse-tung, "Opening Speech to the Eighth Party Congress, 15 September 1956," 359.
36. Liu Shao-chi [Shaoqi], "Report on the Work of the Central Committee," in Hinton, *The People's Republic of China 1949–1979*, 381.

37. "From the late 1920s until at least 1930, Chinese Communist Party (CCP) [CPC] intelligence was directed by Chou En-lai." Jeffrey T. Richelson, *Foreign Intelligence Organizations* (Cambridge, MA: Ballinger Publishing Company, 1988), 273. With this knowledge of Zhou, one may consider the 1955 Bandung Conference an intelligence operation.
38. According to the New China News Agency (NCNA), Zhou stated at a reception marking the seventh anniversary of Burma's independence, "[T]hey [the PRC] are willing, together with the Union of Burma and other Asian and African countries, to fight against colonialism, to extend the peace area and to maintain peace in Asia, Africa and the world." "Red China Wants Asian-African Bloc to Fight 'Colonialism,' Premier Says," *Washington Post*, 5 January 1955, 1.
39. According to Kahin, the important foreign policy objectives of the Bandung Conference organizers (Burma, Ceylon, India, Indonesia, and Pakistan), included the following: "(1) avoidance of war, most immediately between China and the United States; (2) development of China's diplomatic independence of Soviet Russia; (3) containment of Chinese and Vietminh military power and political influence at the southern border of China and the eastern boundaries of Cambodia and Laos, and the combating of illegal and subversive Communist activities in all non-Communist Asia, particularly in their own countries." George McTurnan Kahin, *The Asian-African Conference: Bandung, Indonesia, April 1955* (Ithaca, NY: Cornell University Press, 1956), 5.
40. Cited in "Supplementary Speech by Premier Chou En-lai at the Asian-African Conference, April 19, 1955," in ibid., 52. After listening to the other delegates at the conference express fear and anxiety at Communist China's international actions, Zhou purportedly wrote this speech spontaneously.
41. Cited in "Speech by Premier Chou En-lai to the Political Committee of the Asian-African Conference, April 23, 1955," in ibid., 56. By discarding all these "differences," Zhou aimed at two goals: (1) bring the delegates to a common PRC position, and (2) circumvent the PRC's strategic objectives.
42. Chou En-lai [Zhou Enlai], "Report to National People's Congress on the International Situation, 30 July 1955," in Hinton, *The People's Republic of China 1949–1979* ["We all recognize" (180), "We sympathize with," "Their victory will strengthen" (297)].
43. Larkin, *China and Africa*, 3.
44. Cooley, *East Wind over Africa*, 7.
45. Herbert Passin, *China's Cultural Diplomacy* (New York: Praeger, 1963), 10.
46. George T. Yu, "China's Failure in Africa," *Asian Survey* 6, no. 8 (August 1966): 462.
47. *Afro-Asian Solidarity against Imperialism: A Collection of Documents, Speeches and Press Interviews from the Visits of Chinese Leaders to Thirteen African and Asian Countries* (Beijing: Foreign Languages Press, 1964), 144.
48. George T. Yu, "Africa in Chinese Foreign Policy," *Asian Survey* 28, no. 8 (August 1988): 851.
49. Ibid.; Yu, "China's Failure in Africa," 462.
50. Wei Liang-Tsai, *Peking versus Taipei in Africa 1960–1978* (Taipei, ROC: Asia and World Institute, 1982), 21.
51. Yu, "Africa in Chinese Foreign Policy," 850–851.
52. See, for example, James C. Curran, *Communist China in Black Africa: The Tan-Zam Railway, 1965–1970* (Carlisle, PA: U.S. Army War College, 26 April 1971), 13; A. M. Halpern, "The Foreign Policy Uses of the Chinese Revolutionary Model," *China Quarterly*, no. 7 (July–September 1961); Colin Legum, "The Soviet Union,

China and the West in Southern Africa," *Foreign Affairs* 54, no. 4 (July 1976); Gerald Segal, "China's Strategic Posture and the Great-Power Triangle," *Pacific Affairs* 53, no. 4 (Winter 1980–1981); Thomas Perry Thornton, "Peking, Moscow, and the Underdeveloped Areas," *World Politics* 13, no. 4 (July 1961).
53. But for a pragmatic analysis of Mao, see Lucian W. Pye, "Mao Tse-tung's Leadership Style," *Political Science Quarterly* 91, no. 2 (Summer 1976): 219–235.
54. Wei Liang-Tsai, *Peking Versus Taipei in Africa*, 21.
55. For a strategic understanding of the Soviet nuclear intent, see Richard Pipes' groundbreaking work, "Why the Soviet Union Thinks It Could Fight and Win a Nuclear War," *Commentary* 64, no. 1 (July 1977): 21–34.
56. Herbert Passin was not confused when he wrote, "The long-range [objective] is certainly revolutionary subversion, the overthrow of existing governments, and the establishment of Communist governments linked to the Communist *bloc*." Passin, *China's Cultural Diplomacy*, 10. Rather, Passin did not take the next analytical step necessary to see that the PRC desired to restructure the international order and become a global power—and the Communist ideology was a *means* to this end.
57. Cooley, *East Wind over Africa*, 217.
58. Ian Taylor, "China's Foreign Policy towards Africa in the 1990s," *Journal of Modern African Studies* 36, no. 3 (September 1998): 459.
59. Joseph P. Smaldone, "Soviet and Chinese Military Aid and Arms Transfers to Africa: A Contextual Analysis," in *Soviet and Chinese Aid to African Nations*, ed. Warren Weinstein and Thomas H. Henriksen (New York: Praeger, 1980), 102.
60. Chang Ya-chun, *Chinese Communist Activities in Africa*, 31.
61. Melvin Gurtov, "Communist China's Foreign Aid Program," *Current History* 49, no. 289 (September 1965): 153. It still does so today.
62. Ibid., 154.

CHAPTER 2. ORGANIZATIONS
1. "However, the importance of subversive activities should not be underestimated. There [was] constant consultation between the Chinese and Communist and front organisation leaders from all over Asia. We know, too, that the Chinese [supplied] military training as well as general revolutionary training in special schools." Passin, *China's Cultural Diplomacy*, 11.
2. This examination of Chinese organizations in Africa is not meant to be exhaustive; rather, it is meant to provide the reader with a general understanding of the types of organizations that further China's objectives on the continent.
3. Richelson, *Foreign Intelligence Organizations*, 293. However, Wise and Ross date the Red China News Agency to 1932. David Wise and Thomas B. Ross, *The Espionage Establishment* (New York: Random House, 1967), 191.
4. Wise and Ross, *The Espionage Establishment*, 191.
5. Ibid.
6. Richelson, *Foreign Intelligence Organizations*, 293.
7. Alan P. L. Liu, "Ideology and Information: Correspondents of the New China News Agency and Chinese Foreign Policy Making," *Journal of International Affairs* 26, no. 2 (1972): 132.
8. Richelson, *Foreign Intelligence Organizations*, 293.
9. Maochun Yu, "Ch—y in China," *Wall Street Journal*, 27 April 2004, A18.
10. "The New China News Agency: Mao's Messengers around the World," *Current Scene* 4, no. 7 (1 April 1966): 5.
11. Richelson, *Foreign Intelligence Organizations*, 293.

12. "The New China News Agency: Mao's Messengers around the World," 5; Wang Chia-yu, "Peiping's 'New China News Agency' (NCNA)," *Issues and Studies* 2, no. 3 (December 1965): 12.
13. Wang Chia-yu, "Peiping's 'New China News Agency' (NCNA)," 12.
14. "The New China News Agency: Mao's Messengers around the World" ["Extremely close cooperation" (5), "As part of the government" (6)].
15. Notably, NCNA offices sent dispatches directly to the Ministry of Foreign Affairs (MFA). Howard H. S. Chao, *Story without End: A Chinese Diplomat Escapes* (Hong Kong: Phoenix Press, 1965), 30. The interoperability of NCNA and the MFA no doubt facilitated this information exchange.
16. Wise and Ross, *The Espionage Establishment*, 192.
17. Liu, "Ideology and Information," 143.
18. "The New China News Agency: Mao's Messengers around the World," 5.
19. Chao, *Story without End*, 30.
20. Liu, "Ideology and Information," 142.
21. Ibid., 144. Similarly, when analyzing British propaganda efforts in the former Gold Coast (modern-day Ghana) during the Second World War, Professor Wendell Holbrook wrote, "Radio was valuable to the propaganda campaign, but rallying a war effort still required the co-operation and direct intercession of traditional leaders." Wendell P. Holbrook, "British Propaganda and the Mobilization of the Gold Coast War Effort, 1939–1945," *Journal of African History* 26, no. 4 (1985): 355.
22. Liu, "Ideology and Information," 144.
23. Wang Chia-yu, "Peiping's 'New China News Agency' (NCNA)" ["NCNA personnel stationed" (14), "NCNA correspondents overseas" (8), "NCNA personnel maintain[ed]," "NCNA personnel transmit[ted]" (14)].
24. Information from "Chiang Kwei-lin, Hsn-hua-she Shih-erh nien [Twelve years with the New China News Agency]" (Taipei, ROC: Chen Shen Broadcasting Co., 1962). Cited in Liu, "Ideology and Information," 134–135.
25. Wang Chia-yu, "Peiping's 'New China News Agency' (NCNA)," 8.
26. Liu, "Ideology and Information," 134.
27. Ibid.
28. "Externally, it [was] a principal organization for political struggles." Wang Chia-yu, "Peiping's 'New China News Agency' (NCNA)," 8. Moreover, the most scholarship and materials are available for the NCNA vis-à-vis other organizations.
29. Richelson, *Foreign Intelligence Organizations*, 276.
30. Fritz Schatten, *Communism in Africa* (New York: Praeger, 1966), 219. The Commission for Cultural Relations with Foreign Countries also supervised overseas friendship and cultural organizations.
31. Richelson, *Foreign Intelligence Organizations*, 278.
32. Harvey W. Nelsen, *The Chinese Military System: An Organizational Study of the Chinese People's Liberation Army* (Boulder, CO: Westview Press, 1981), 57.
33. "Making More Friends for Better Mutual Understanding," *Beijing Review* 37, no. 8 (21 Feburary 1994): 18.
34. Richelson, *Foreign Intelligence Organizations*, 278.
35. "Making More Friends for Better Mutual Understanding," 19.
36. Richelson believes the foreign ministry; Schattan believes the state council. Richelson, *Foreign Intelligence Organizations*, 277; Schatten, *Communism in Africa*, 219.
37. Wise and Ross, *The Espionage Establishment*, 182.
38. Schatten, *Communism in Africa*, 219–220.
39. Ibid.

40. Ibid.
41. Paraphrased from ibid.
42. Schatten, *Communism in Africa*, 220. According to Passin, it was "modeled after the Soviet VOKS (Society for Cultural Advancement)" as well. Passin, *China's Cultural Diplomacy*, 132.
43. Schatten, *Communism in Africa*, 220.
44. The phrase "world-wide galaxy," is taken from Allen Dulles: "The first element of the Kremlin's nonmilitary apparatus of subversion is the galaxy of world-wide Communist parties." Allen Dulles, *The Craft of Intelligence* (Westport, CT: Greenwood Press, 1977), 225 ["for reaching specialized" (228)].
45. Robert H. Bass, "Communist Fronts: Their History and Function," *Problems of Communism* 9, no. 5 (September–October 1960): 15.
46. William R. Kintner, *The Front Is Everywhere: Militant Communism in Action* (Norman: University of Oklahoma Press, 1950), 197.
47. David Williams, "Front Organisations," in *"We Will Bury You": Studies in Left-Wing Subversion Today*, ed. Brian Crozier (London: Tom Stacey, 1970), 85.
48. Otto Kuusinen, a veteran Finnish Communist aptly described front organizations at a meeting of the Comintern Executive Committee in March 1926: He advocated the creation of "a whole solar system of organizations and smaller committees around the Communist Party . . . actually working under the influence of the party, but not under its mechanical control." Kuusinen quoted in Crozier, *"We Will Bury You,"* 87.
49. Alaba Ogunsanwo, *China's Policy in Africa 1958–71* (London: Cambridge University Press, 1974), 97.
50. Jan S. Prybyla, "Communist China's Economic Relations with Africa 1960–1964," *Asian Survey* 4, no. 11 (November 1964): 1139.
51. Milton Sacks, "The Strategy of Communism in Southeast Asia," *Pacific Affairs* 23, no. 3 (September 1950): 246.
52. Hutchison, *China's Africa Revolution*, 37 ["AAPSO was formed" (p. 37)]; Schatten, *Communism in Africa*, 269.
53. Schatten also contended that the AAPSO was founded to represent peoples of two Eastern contingents—embracing bourgeois as well as pro-Communists—and to recognize the Soviet Union as an Asian country. Schatten, *Communism in Africa*, 271–272.
54. Charles Neuhauser, *Third World Politics: China and the Afro-Asia People's Solidarity Organization, 1957–1967* (Cambridge, MA: Harvard University Press, 1968), 11.
55. This organizational description of the AAPSO is based on the reorganization after the second conference in Conakry, Guinea, in 1960. Prior to 1960 the AAPSO's organizational structure included the conference and the council.
56. Neuhauser, *Third World Politics*, 25.
57. Ibid.
58. Hutchison, *China's Africa Revolution*, 40.
59. For more on Mao and guerrilla warfare, see Mao Tse-tung [Zedong], *Guerrilla Warfare*, trans. Samuel B. Griffith (London: Cassell & Company, 1962); and Mao Tse-tung [Zedong], "On Protracted War," in *Selected Works of Mao Tse-tung* (Beijing: Foreign Languages Press, 1975).
60. Larkin, *China and Africa*, 33.
61. Steven F. Jackson, "China's Third World Foreign Policy: The Case of Angola and Mozambique, 1961–93," *China Quarterly*, no. 142 (June 1995): 393.
62. Ibid.
63. Gordon Harris, *Organization of African Unity*, vol. 7 (New Brunswick, NJ: Transaction Publishers, 1994), xv.

64. John Markakis, "The Organisation of African Unity: A Progress Report," *Journal of Modern African Studies* 4, no. 2 (October 1966): 135–153. After the 1966 Summit, the specialized commissions were reduced to three: (1) Defense; (2) Economic, Social, and Transport; and (3) Scientific, Technical, and Research. A. F. Addona, *The Organization of African Unity* (Cleveland, OH: World Publishing, 1969), 129.
65. The ALC had its roots in the "not too effectual organization," the Pan-African Movement for East, Central, and South Africa (PAFMECSA). Addona, *The Organization of African Unity*, 136.
66. Richard Gibson, *African Liberation Movements: Contemporary Struggles against White Minority Rule* (New York: Oxford University Press, 1972), 8; Markakis, "The Organisation of African Unity," 141.
67. Gibson, *African Liberation Movements*, 8.
68. Markakis, "The Organisation of African Unity," 141–142.
69. Ogunsanwo, *China's Policy in Africa*, 171.
70. Milton Viorst, "Continental Freedom Struggle: Blackening Africa," *New Republic* 172, no. 15 (14 April 1975) ["For a decade" (9), "Most of the money" (10)].
71. "The Committee's operations are financed by a special fund which is not part of the regular O.A.U. budget, and is provided for through special assessments and contributions." Markakis, "The Organisation of African Unity," 142.
72. Viorst, "Continental Freedom Struggle," 10.
73. Markakis, "The Organisation of African Unity," 142.
74. Emmannuel M. Dube, "Relations between Liberation Movements and the O.A.U.," in *Essays on the Liberation of Southern Africa*, ed. N. M. Shamuyarira (Dar es Salaam: Tanzania Publishing House, 1971), 62.
75. Notably, "The African Liberation Committee grant[ed] its assistance to a number of organizations that . . . never so far raised a gun." Gibson, *African Liberation Movements*, 11.

CHAPTER 3. INITIAL ENTRY

1. Alf Andrew Heggoy, *Insurgency and Counterinsurgency in Algeria* (Bloomington, IN: Indiana University Press, 1972), 22. But Heggoy also cites 1925 as the founding year of ENA. See Heggoy, 51.
2. Ibid., 22–23. And according to Favrod, Hadj always advocated programs that combined the Islamic concepts he learned in traditional Algerian schools with egalitarian social theories he developed through contacts with the Communist Party. Charles-Henri Favrod, *Le F.L.N. et l'Algérie* (Paris: Plon, 1962), 89.
3. Heggoy noted, "All of Algerian revolutionary organizations inherited Communist methodology from the ENA and its successors, but they also inherited the strong anti-Communism first introduced into the Algerian proletarian party by Messali Hadj." Heggoy, *Insurgency and Counterinsurgency in Algeria*, 41.
4. John Ruedy, *Modern Algeria: The Origins and Development of a Nation* (Bloomington, IN: Indiana University Press, 1992) ["divided and demoralized" (144), "Algerian leaders drew" (145)]. For a succinct explanation of the Algerian nationalist movement, see Ruedy, 129–144.
5. Alistair Horne, *A Savage War of Peace: Algeria 1954–1962* (New York: Viking Press, 1977), 41.
6. "During World War I, about 173,000 Algerians conscripted into service with the French army fought with valor against the Germans; 25,000 of the Algerians were killed in combat." Jean R. Tartter, "National Security," in *Algeria: A Country Study*, ed. Helen Chapin Metz (Washington, DC: Federal Research Division, Library of Congress, 1994), 250.

7. John Talbott, *The War without a Name: France in Algeria, 1954–1962* (New York: Alfred A. Knopf, 1980), 23.
8. Horne, *A Savage War of Peace*, 38.
9. Heggoy, *Insurgency and Counterinsurgency in Algeria*, 30.
10. Ruedy, *Modern Algeria*, 153.
11. Heggoy, *Insurgency and Counterinsurgency in Algeria*, 36–38.
12. Ruedy, *Modern Algeria*, 153.
13. Anthony Toth, "Historical Setting," in Metz, *Algeria: A Country Study*, 43.
14. Talbott, *The War without a Name*, 25.
15. Ruedy, *Modern Algeria*, 153.
16. Ruedy, *Modern Algeria*, 153 ["Its most notable exploit" (153)]; Heggoy, *Insurgency and Counterinsurgency in Algeria*, 33; Talbott, *The War without a Name*, 25.
17. Heggoy, *Insurgency and Counterinsurgency in Algeria*, 34. Heggoy posited that the OS was similar to the underground PPA organization.
18. Ibid., 35.
19. William B. Quandt, *Revolution and Political Leadership: Algeria, 1954–1968* (Cambridge, MA: Massachusetts Institute of Technology Press, 1969), 66–86; Talbott, *The War without a Name*, 27.
20. Talbott, *The War without a Name*, 27.
21. Horne, *A Savage War of Peace*, 130–131.
22. Kahin, *The Asian-African Conference*, 17. For another, more personal, account of the conferences, see Richard Wright, *The Color Curtain: A Report on the Bandung Conference* (New York: World Publishing, 1956).
23. Horne, *A Savage War of Peace*, 131.
24. "Asian-African Conference Closes," *Survey of China Mainland Press*, no. 1033 (23–25 April 1955): 10. Translated by the American consulate general in Hong Kong and originally published in *NCNA*, 24 April 1955.
25. W. A. C. Adie, "Chinese Policy towards Africa," in *The Soviet Bloc, China and Africa*, ed. Sven Hamrell and Carl Gösta Widstrand (Uppsala: Scandinavian Institute of African Studies, 1964), 50.
26. Wei Liang-Tsai, *Peking versus Taipei in Africa*, 104.
27. Ogunsanwo, *China's Policy in Africa*, 9.
28. Adie, "Chinese Policy towards Africa," 50–51.
29. Ogunsanwo, *China's Policy in Africa*, 9.
30. Adie called China's activities "people's diplomacy." W. A. C. Adie, "China and the Bandung Genie," *Current Scene* 3, no. 19 (15 May 1965): 5–15.
31. Ogunsanwo, *China's Policy in Africa*, 37.
32. Adie, "Chinese Policy towards Africa," 51.
33. Richard Lowenthal, "China," in *Africa and the Communist World*, ed. Zbigniew Brzezinski (Stanford, CA: Stanford University Press, 1963), 152.
34. Chang Ya-chun, *Chinese Communist Activities in Africa*, 5.
35. Donald W. Klein, "Peking's Diplomats in Africa," *Current Scene* 2, no. 36 (1 July 1964): 4.
36. "China and the World: In Brief," *Peking Review* 1, no. 18 (1 July 1958): 19.
37. Harris, *Organization of African Unity*, 369.
38. Archibald Cary Coolidge, "The European Reconquest of North Africa," *American Historical Review* 17, no. 4 (July 1912): 731.
39. *Communist China in Africa* (Taipei, ROC: Asian Peoples' Anti-Communist League, 1961), 32; Wei Liang-Tsai, *Peking versus Taipei in Africa*, 106. In November 1957

a National Day of Solidarity with the Algerian People was celebrated in Beijing. Adie, "Chinese Policy towards Africa," 51. See also "China and the World: China-Morocco Diplomatic Relations," *Peking Review* 1, no. 36 (4 November 1958): 22; "Foreign Trade New: Sino-Morocco Trade Agreement," *Peking Review* 1, no. 36 (4 November 1958): 22.
40. Lowenthal, "China," 165; Wei Liang-Tsai, *Peking versus Taipei in Africa*, 106.
41. Adie, "China and the Bandung Genie," 6.
42. Schatten, *Communism in Africa* ["China was more," "the only State," "diplomatic activity" (198)].
43. "China and the World: Briefs," *Peking Review* 1, no. 35 (23 October 1958): 21.
44. Lowenthal, "China," 165; Ogunsanwo, *China's Policy in Africa*, 30; Wei Liang-Tsai, *Peking versus Taipei in Africa*, 106.
45. Lowenthal, "China," 165.
46. Ogunsanwo, *China's Policy in Africa*, 30.

CHAPTER 4. SUPPORTING INDEPENDENCE
1. Tartter, "National Security," 238.
2. For a theoretical discussion on the French perspective of *la guerre révolutionnaire*, see George A. Kelly, "Revolutionary Warfare and Psychological Action," in *Modern Guerrilla Warfare: Fighting Communist Guerilla Movements, 1941–1961*, ed. Franklin Mark Osanka (New York: Free Press, 1962).
3. Horne, *A Savage War of Peace*, 79.
4. Toth, "Historical Setting," 44.
5. Heggoy, *Insurgency and Counterinsurgency in Algeria*, 86.
6. Note also the following Algerian command organizations that were established on 20 August 1956: National Council of the Algerian Revolution (Conseil National de la Révolution Algérienne, CNRA), Algeria's first sovereign parliament, and its executive board, Committee of Coordination and Enforcement (Comité de Coordination et d'Exécution). Ruedy makes the following commentary on the CNRA: "Although with its initial personnel the first CNRA never formally met as a whole, its creation marked a major step in defining political institutions and in broadening the revolutionary leadership." Ruedy, *Modern Algeria*, 166.
7. Heggoy, *Insurgency and Counterinsurgency in Algeria* ["the backbone" (102), "to undermine the French" (120)].
8. "'Our 600 Million Back Up Algerian People,'" *Peking Review* 1, no. 6 (8 April 1958): 21.
9. Schatten, *Communism in Africa*, 198.
10. Georges Beuchard, *L'Equivoque algérienne* (Paris: Nourvelles Editions Debresse, 1949), 34.
11. Horne, *A Savage War of Peace*, 78–79.
12. Adie, "China and the Bandung Genie," 6.
13. *Communist China in Africa*, 2–3. Twenty-seven African states and regions attended the conference, including delegates from Algeria and Zanzibar. Tung Feng, "The Bandung Spirit Thrives," *Peking Review* 1, no. 9 (29 April 1958): 7.
14. "Our 600 Million Back Up Algerian People," 21.
15. Ogunsanwo, *China's Policy in Africa*, 48.
16. "Our 600 Million Back Up Algerian People," 21.
17. Ibid.
18. Throughout this manuscript, the author will cite different currencies based on the sources used. All values are historical.

19. Adie, "Chinese Policy towards Africa," 51; "China and the World: Friendly Aid to Algeria," *Peking Review* 1, no. 7 (15 April 1958): 18; Ogunsanwo, *China's Policy in Africa*, 43.
20. Tung Feng, "Bandung Spirit," 7.
21. Wei Liang-Tsai, *Peking versus Taipei in Africa*, 105. Heggoy dates the establishment of GPRA to 18 September. Heggoy, *Insurgency and Counterinsurgency in Algeria*, 117.
22. "China and the World: China Recognizes Algeria," *Peking Review* 1, no. 31 (30 September 1958): 25.
23. *Communist China in Africa*, 32; Ogunsanwo, *China's Policy in Africa*, 51. Ben Khedda was minister of social affairs at the time. The delegation also went to North Korea and North Vietnam in 1958.
24. An article in the *Peking Review* reported Shahidi to be vice chair of the Chinese Committee for Afro-Asian Solidarity. "China Welcomes Algerian Delegation," *Peking Review* 1, no. 41 (9 December 1958): 15.
25. "China and the World: Algerian Delegation in China," *Peking Review* 1, no. 42 (16 December 1958): 20.
26. Lawrence Fellows, "Algerians Seek Aid from Peiping," *New York Times*, 1 December 1958, 8. Communist Chinese sources also mention the trip: "China and the World: Algerian Delegation to China," *Peking Review* 1, no. 39 (25 November 1958): 19.
27. "China and the World: Algerian Delegation to China," 19, 20.
28. Fellows, "Algerians Seek Aid from Peiping," 8.
29. "Mission Accomplished!," *Peking Review* 1, no. 44 (30 December 1958): 22.
30. "Sino-Algerian Communique," *Peking Review* 1, no. 43 (23 December 1958): 24.
31. "Sportsmen Patriots," *Peking Review* 1, no. 4 (30 December 1958): 23.
32. "To the Victory of the Algerian People!," *Peking Review* 1, no. 43 (23 December 1958): 24.
33. Cooley, *East Wind over Africa*, 155.
34. Wei Liang-Tsai, *Peking versus Taipei in Africa*, 105.
35. Lowenthal, "China," 162–163.
36. Adie, "Chinese Policy towards Africa," 52.
37. Ogunsanwo, *China's Policy in Africa*, 53.
38. "China and the World: Afro-Asian Youth Conference," *Peking Review* 2, no. 6 (10 February 1959): 18.
39. "China and the World: Briefs," *Peking Review* 2, no. 13 (31 March 1959): 23.
40. "China and the World: Solidarity with Fighting Algeria," *Peking Review* 2, no. 39 (1 October 1959): 28.
41. Ogunsanwo, *China's Policy in Africa*, 52.
42. Adie, "Chinese Policy towards Africa," 51.
43. Cited in ibid., 52.
44. Heggoy, *Insurgency and Counterinsurgency in Algeria*, 138.
45. Adie, "Chinese Policy towards Africa," 52.
46. "National Support for Algerian Independence," *Peking Review* 2, no. 14 (7 April 1959): 16–17.
47. "China and the World: Algerians' Visit Ends," *Peking Review* 2, no. 19 (12 May 1959): 25.
48. Reuters, cited in *Communist China in Africa*, 41–42. Zartman cited the PRC giving $10 million worth in arms shipments to Algeria in 1959. William Zartman, "Tiger in the Jungle," *Current Scene* 2, no. 2 (6 August 1962): 2. A November 1959 Reuters report from Tunis said that the PRC was training Algerian units and had granted the GPRA credits worth £1.75 million for arms, propaganda and administrative equipment. Adie, "Chinese Policy towards Africa," 52. Similarly, the British Broad-

casting Corporation (BBC) reported that China had granted a $10 million credit for the purchase of military equipment and the financing of administration and propaganda, and had also agreed to supply large quantities of U.S. weapons seized during the Korean War. Cited in Ogunsanwo, *China's Policy in Africa*, 53.

49. Schatten, *Communism in Africa*, 198.
50. "China and the World: Ties with North Africa," *Peking Review* 2, no. 47 (24 November 1959): 21.
51. *Communist China in Africa*, 33–34.
52. Ogunsanwo, *China's Policy in Africa*, 45.
53. "China and the World: 'Algeria Day,'" *Peking Review* 3, no. 14 (5 April 1960): 32.
54. Adie, "Chinese Policy towards Africa," 52.
55. Ibid., 53. The delegation of the GPRA visited China from 30 April to 3 May, from 7 to 9 May, and from 13 to 20 May 1960.
56. Ogunsanwo, *China's Policy in Africa*, 100. The following provides another perspective on the visiting delegation: "Welcome to Algeria's Delegates," *Peking Review* 3, no. 18 (3 May 1960): 5.
57. "China Hails Fighting Algeria," *Peking Review* 3, no. 19 (10 May 1960): 13.
58. Thomas F. Brady, "North Africans Turning to East," *New York Times*, 5 May 1960, 9. The following supports the previous source: "Chinese Penetration of Africa," *Afrique Nouvelle* (Dakar), 10–16 June 1965, 34. The latter found in Joint Publications Research Service (31368), *Translations on Africa*, no. 230, 2 August 1965, 33–39.
59. "Sino-Algerian Joint Communique," *Peking Review* 3, no. 21 (24 May 1960) ["full support," "The two parties" (16–17)].
60. Adie, "Chinese Policy towards Africa," 53.
61. "Africa Hears Red Chinese Propaganda," *Washington Post*, 31 May 1960, A7.
62. Adie, "Chinese Policy towards Africa," 53.
63. Feng Chih-tan, "The Awakening of Africa," *Peking Review* 3, no. 27 (5 July 1960): 13.
64. Marquis Childs, "The New Entry in Africa: China," *Washington Post*, 10 August 1960, A14.
65. Ibid. Note again the Chinese emphasis on youth.
66. "China and the World: Sino-Algerian Friendship," *Peking Review* 3, no. 39 (27 September 1960): 27.
67. "Cairo Visit Implies Peking Aid to Algeria," *Washington Post*, 25 September 1960, A4.
68. *Communist China in Africa*, 34.
69. "Premier Chou En-lai's Speech at Banquet in Honor of Premier Abbas Ferhat," *Peking Review* 3, no. 40 (4 October 1960): 41–42.
70. "Speech by Premier Abbas Ferhat at Peking Banquet," *Peking Review* 3, no. 40 (4 October 1960): 44.
71. "Premier Abbas Ferhat in Peking," *Peking Review* 3, no. 40 (4 October 1960): 40.
72. "Sino-Algerian Joint Communique," *Peking Review* 3, no. 41 (11 October 1960): 16–17.
73. "Premier Abbas Concludes Visit in China," *Peking Review* 3, no. 41 (11 October 1960): 18.
74. Abbas also suggested that the Soviet Union would provide material assistance to the FLN. Arnaldo Cortesi, "Algerian Implies Reds Offer Arms," *New York Times*, 31 October 1960, 8.
75. "China and the World: Chinese Show at Tunis Fair," *Peking Review* 3, no. 43 (25 October 1960): 21.
76. "China Firmly Supports Algerian People's Just Struggle," *Peking Review* 3, no. 45 (8 November 1960): 26.

77. Thomas S. Brady, "Lag in Peiping Aid to Algeria Likely," *New York Times*, 5 November 1960, 2.
78. Adie, "Chinese Policy towards Africa," 53.
79. *Communist China in Africa*, 42.
80. "China and the World: No Carve-up of Algeria," *Peking Review* 4, no. 28 (14 July 1961): 22.
81. "China and the World: Algerian Anniversary," *Peking Review* 4, no. 38 (22 September 1961): 22.
82. Mao Sun, "A Righteous Cause Will Triumph," *Peking Review* 4, no. 45 (10 November 1961): 10.
83. "China Reiterates Support for Algeria," *Peking Review* 4, no. 45 (10 November 1961): 11.
84. Central Intelligence Agency, *Chinese Communist Activities in Africa*, Memorandum, 30 April 1965, 8. Memorandum found in *CIA Research Reports Africa, 1946–1976* (Frederick, MD: University Publications of America, 1982).

CHAPTER 5. CLOSE AND MILITANT

1. "Premier Chou En-lai Greets the Algerian People's Victory," *Peking Review* 5, no. 12 (23 March 1962): 5.
2. "The Algerian People's Great Victory," *Peking Review* 5, no. 12 (23 March 1962): 6 ["The conclusion of," "the revolutionary double" (6)].
3. "Premier Chou En-Lai Greets the Algerian People's Victory," *Peking Review*, 5.
4. "China Recognizes the Republic of Algeria," *Peking Review* 5, no. 27 (6 July 1962): 9; "Algeria Becomes Independent," *Peking Review* 5, no. 28 (13 July 1962): 8.
5. For the Algerians, the postindependence environment was not entirely smooth, as leaders jockeyed for positions of superiority. Without delving too deeply into the situation, "The three major contenders for political predominance were the provisional government established by the FLN in 1958, the military officials, and the *wilaya* commands (administrative district councils established by the military in the pre-independence period)." John P. Entelis and Lisa Arone, "Government and Politics," in Metz, *Algeria: A Country Study*, 177.
6. Ogunsanwo, *China's Policy in Africa*, 154.
7. "China and the World: Donations to Algerians," *Peking Review* 5, no. 25 (22 June 1962): 20.
8. Wang Wei and Lu Ming-chu, "Algerian Algeria," *Peking Review* 5, no. 25 (22 June 1962): 9.
9. "China and the World: Sino-Algerian Relations," *Peking Review* 5, no. 37 (14 September 1962): 22.
10. Ogunsanwo, *China's Policy in Africa*, 92.
11. Adie, "Chinese Policy towards Africa," 54; "Algeria's First National Day," *Peking Review* 5, no. 25 (9 November 1962): 22.
12. "Algeria Backing U.N. Entry of the Chinese Communists," *New York Times*, 1 October 1962, 10.
13. Waverley Root, "Peking Hits Snags in Africa Trade Promotion," *Washington Post*, 8 November 1962, C18.
14. "News in Brief," *Peking Review* 6, no. 12 (22 March 1963): 18.
15. "News in Brief," *Peking Review* 6, no. 20 (17 May 1963): 20.
16. "The Week: Guests from Africa," *Peking Review* 6, no. 36 (6 September 1963): 4.
17. "Chinese Exhibitions Abroad," *Peking Review* 6, no. 41 (11 October 1963): 5.
18. "Algeria and Peking Sign Cultural Pact," *New York Times*, 12 September 1963, 8.

19. Ogunsanwo, *China's Policy in Africa*, 154; "Red China Offers Algeria a Credit of $50 million," *New York Times*, 10 October 1963, 13.
20. "The Week: Sino-Algerian Friendship," *Peking Review* 6, no. 42 (18 October 1963): 3.
21. "Red China Offers Algeria a Loan," *Washington Post*, 10 October 1963; "The Week," *Peking Review* 6, no. 41 (11 October 1963): 3.
22. "The Week: Sino-Algerian Friendship," 3–4.
23. Hsiao Ming, "China Hails Independent Algeria," *Peking Review* 6, no. 45 (8 November 1963): 18.
24. Ibid., 17.
25. Schatten, *Communism in Africa*, 202 ["described how," "He also recalled" (202)].
26. The significant works in the area include Mao Tse-tung, *Guerrilla Warfare*; Mao Tse-tung, "On Protracted War"; Mao Tse-tung [Zedong], "Problems of Strategy in China's Revolutionary War," in *Selected Works of Mao Tse-tung* (Beijing: Foreign Languages Press, 1975).
27. Tartter, "National Security," 239.
28. Peter Braestrup, "Algerians Decry Criticism by U.S.," *New York Times*, 3 April 1964, 6.
29. Cooley, *East Wind over Africa*, 157 ["Colonel Hu Pin-fu" (157)].
30. "Round the World: Algeria: F.L.N. Congress," *Peking Review* 7, no. 18 (1 May 1964): 31.
31. "Mao Sends a Message," *New York Times*, 13 January 1964, 4. During the visit, on 11 January 1964, China established diplomatic relations with Tunisia. Peter Braestrup, "Tunis Recognizes Communist China," *New York Times*, 11 January 1964, 7.
32. "The Week: Premier Chou En-lai in Algiers," *Peking Review* 6, no. 52 (27 December 1963): 4.
33. Peter Braestrup, "Chou Sees 'Grand Success,'" *New York Times*, 12 January 1964 ["President Ahmed Ben Bella of Algeria," "the country most susceptible" (21)].
34. Director of Central Intelligence, *Chou En-Lai's African Tour* (Washington, DC), *Current Intelligence Weekly Review* (17 January 1964), 5.
35. "The strange friendship of the Chinese and Albanian [Communist] Parties is based not only on ideological sympathies but on the memory of a similar experience at the hands of the Soviet Union." David A. Charles, "The Dismissal of Marshal P'eng Teh-huai," *China Quarterly*, no. 8 (October–December 1961): 76. China and Albania had had negative experiences with the Soviet Union, sharing the same ill will.
36. Lowenthal, "China," 163.
37. Prybyla, "Communist China's Economic Relations with Africa," 1139.
38. "The Week: Algerian Guests in Peking," *Peking Review* 7, no. 6 (7 February 1964): 32.
39. Peter Braestrup, "Algeria May Ship Oil to Red China," *New York Times*, 26 January 1964, 5.
40. "The Week: Chairman Mao Receives Algerian Guests," *Peking Review* 7, no. 17 (24 April 1964): 3.
41. "The Week: Sino-Algerian Trade Co-operation," *Peking Review* 7, no. 39 (25 September 1964): 3.
42. "Tenth Anniversary of Algerian Revolution Marked in China," *Peking Review* 7, no. 45 (6 November 1964): 9.
43. "Chinese Held Countering the Russians in Algeria," *New York Times*, 1 November 1964, 14.

44. "Algeria and China Renew Pact," *New York Times*, 4 June 1965, 10.
45. "The Week: Militia Delegation from Algeria," *Peking Review* 8, no. 1 (1 January 1965): 4.
46. "The Week: Algerian Special Envoy Visits Peking," *Peking Review* 7, no. 52 (25 December 1964): 3.
47. "The Week: Militia Delegation from Algeria," 4.
48. "Algeria Signs Pact for Red China Arms," *New York Times*, 12 February 1965, 13 ["the supplying of," "common struggle against" (13)].
49. "Chou in Algiers to See Ben Bella," *New York Times*, 31 March 1965, 2.
50. The transport planes were received four days before the coup on 19 June 1965. Ogunsanwo, *China's Policy in Africa*, 155–156.
51. "China-Algeria Joint Communique," *Peking Review* 8, no. 15 (9 April 1965): 10.
52. Tad Szulc, "Peking Steps Up Drive for Allies," *New York Times*, 1 April 1965, 3.
53. "The Week: Algerian Delegation in Peking," *Peking Review* 8, no. 24 (11 June 1965): 4.
54. Cited in the BBC weekly supplement dated 18 June 1956 in Ogunsanwo, *China's Policy in Africa*.
55. Tartter, "National Security," 239.
56. "The Week: Algeria's Independence Day Greeted," *Peking Review* 8, no. 28 (9 July 1965): 4.
57. "The Week: Algerian Government Delegation Arrives in Peking," *Peking Review* 8, no. 35 (27 August 1965): 5.
58. "China-Algeria Joint Communique," *Peking Review* 8, no. 36 (3 September 1965): 7.
59. "The Week: Chinese Leaders Meet Algerian Delegation," *Peking Review* 8, no. 36 (3 September 1965): 7.
60. "The Week: Chen Yi Visits Algeria and Mali," *Peking Review* 8, no. 38 (17 September 1965): 4.
61. Ogunsanwo, *China's Policy in Africa*, 223.
62. "Chinese to Build Hall," *Washington Post*, 4 December 1966, A30. Reportedly, actual work on the project did not begin until November 1968.
63. "The Week: Algerian Revolution Anniversary," *Peking Review* 8, no. 45 (5 November 1965), 3 ["There is a deep" (14)].
64. "Peking Buying French Trucks," *New York Times*, 20 November 1965, 14.
65. Ogunsanwo, *China's Policy in Africa*, 155.
66. "Round the World: African Opinion: Origins of Anti-China Slanders," *Peking Review* 9, no. 4 (21 January 1966): 29.
67. "A.A.J.A. Secretariat Meets in Peking," *Peking Review* 9, no. 18 (29 April 1966): 13, 14.
68. Ibid.
69. Cited from BBC summary of world broadcasts in Ogunsanwo, *China's Policy in Africa*, 224.
70. Ibid.
71. Leo Tansky, "China's Foreign Aid: The Record," *Current Scene* 10, no. 9 (September 1972): 10, Table IV.
72. Ibid.
73. Ibid.
74. Louis B. Fleming, "China Gets U.N. Ally in Algeria," *Washington Post*, 24 February 1968, A12. The following discussion is based on Fleming's report.
75. Ogunsanwo, *China's Policy in Africa*, 224.

76. "Friendship Log: Teaching and Learning from Each Other," *Peking Review* 15, no. 10 (10 March 1972): 19.
77. "Heal the Wounded, Rescue the Dying, Practise [*sic*] Revolutionary Humanitarianism—Chinese Medical Team in Algeria," *Peking Review* 12, no. 31 (1 August 1969): 23.
78. "The Week: Chinese Government and Military Delegation Leaves for Algeria to Attend National Day Celebrations," *Peking Review* 12, no. 45 (7 November 1969): 3.
79. "The Week: Algerian Embassy Gives Reception Marking 15th Anniversary of Revolution," *Peking Review* 12, no. 45 (7 November 1969): 3.
80. "The Week: Premier Chou Greets Algeria's National Day," *Peking Review* 13, no. 45 (6 November 1970): 29.
81. "The Week: Algerian Government Delegation Visits China," *Peking Review* 14, no. 31 (30 July 1971): 3, 28.
82. "The Week: News Briefs," *Peking Review* 14, no. 34 (20 August 1971): 23.
83. "Joint Communique of Government Delegation of People's Republic of China and Government Delegation of Democratic People's Republic of Algeria," *Peking Review* 14, no. 32 (6 August 1971): 24, 25 ["places of interest" (24)].
84. Philip Snow, *The Star Raft: China's Encounter with Africa* (Ithaca, NY: Cornell University Press, 1988), 115.
85. "Albania, Algeria and 16 Other Countries Table Draft Resolution at U.N.," *Peking Review* 14, no. 35 (27 August 1971): 6.
86. Tad Szulc, "Peking Reported in Drive to Play Key Role in Mideast and Africa," *New York Times*, 17 October 1971, 3.
87. "The Week: Algeria National Day Greeted," *Peking Review* 14, no. 35 (5 November 1971): 4.
88. "The Week: 10th Anniversary of Algeria's Independence Greeted," *Peking Review* 15, no. 28 (14 July 1972): 6 ["The independence of Algeria" (6)].
89. "Round the World: Algeria: Bouteflika's Statement on Mediterranean Situation," *Peking Review* 15, no. 41 (13 October 1972): 21–22.
90. "The Week: China–Algeria," *Peking Review* 15, no. 46 (17 November 1972): 17.
91. "The Week: News Briefs," *Peking Review* 15, no. 51 (22 December 1972): 23.
92. "The Week: News Briefs," *Peking Review* 15, no. 52 (29 December 1972): 4. The delegation returned from a visit to Albania, Romania, France, Algeria, Tanzania, Zambia, and Pakistan.
93. "The Week: Algeria Delegation Ends Visit," *Peking Review* 16, no. 20 (18 May 1973): 3, 6. On 10 May the delegation left Beijing.
94. "The Week: Foreign Minister Chi Replies to His Algerian Counterpart," *Peking Review* 17, no. 8 (22 February 1974): 3.
95. "At Banquet Welcoming President Boumediene: Premier Chou's Speech," *Peking Review* 17, no. 10 (8 March 1974): 7.
96. "The Week: President Boumediene Visits China," *Peking Review* 17, no. 10 (8 March 1974): 4.
97. "Joint Communique," *Peking Review* 17, no. 10 (8 March 1974): 10.
98. Jack Anderson, "Secret Agent Diplomacy," *Washington Post*, 24 March 1974, C7.
99. "The Week: 20th Anniversary of Algerian Armed Revolution," *Peking Review* 17, no. 45 (8 November 1974): 4–5.
100. "Profound Mourning for Passing of the Chinese People's Great Leader Chairman Mao Tsetung," *Peking Review* 19, no. 40 (30 September 1976): 58.
101. Central Intelligence Agency, *Communist Economic and Military Aid to Africa*, Memorandum, 18 February 1976, 3.

102. Bruce D. Larkin, "Chinese Aid in Political Context: 1971–1973," in *Chinese and Soviet Aid to Africa*, ed. Warren Weinstein (New York: Praeger, 1975), 14.
103. Colin Legum, ed., *Africa Contemporary Record: Annual Survey and Documents, 1977–78* (New York: African Publishing Company, 1979), C189.

CHAPTER 6. RIPE FOR REVOLUTION?
1. John H. Dalton, "Colony and Metropolis: Some Aspects of British Rule in Gold Coast and Their Implications for an Understanding of Ghana Today," *Journal of Economic History* 21, no. 4 (December 1961) ["There was practically," "[t]here was no feudal aristocracy," "Economically the peoples" (552), "The effects of" (561)].
2. Lloyd Garrison, "Portrait of Nkrumah as Dictator," *New York Times*, 3 May 1964, 15.
3. Kenneth W. Grundy, "Nkrumah's Theory of Underdevelopment: An Analysis of Recurrent Themes," *World Politics* 15, no. 3 (April 1963): 439.
4. Garrison, "Portrait of Nkrumah as Dictator," 15, 108 ["study their tactics" (108)].
5. J. D. Fage, *A History of West Africa: An Introductory Survey* (Cambridge: Cambridge University Press, 1969), 208–209; James L. McLaughlin and David Owusu-Ansah, "Historical Setting," in *Ghana: A Country Study*, ed. LaVerle Berry (Washington, DC: Federal Research Division, Library of Congress, 1995), 27.
6. Director of Central Intelligence, *The Outlook for Ghana*, National Intelligence Estimate Number 74-57, 27 December 1957, 3.
7. W. Scott Thompson, *Ghana's Foreign Policy 1957–1966* (Princeton, NJ: Princeton University Press, 1969), 7.
8. Kwame Nkrumah, "The Movement for Colonial Freedom," *Phylon* 16 (4th quarter 1955): 398.
9. Nkrumah quoted in Director of Central Intelligence, *The Outlook for Ghana*, 4.
10. Colin Legum, "Socialism in Ghana: A Political Interpretation," in *African Socialism*, ed. William H. Friedland and Carl Rosberg (Stanford, CA: Stanford University Press, 1964), 139.
11. Robert C. Good, "Changing Patterns of African International Relations," *American Political Science Review* 58, no. 3 (September 1964): 634.
12. For more in-depth treatment on the conference, see Kahin, *The Asian-African Conference*.
13. Grundy, "Nkrumah's Theory of Underdevelopment" ["Freedom thus becomes" (442), "mobilized for" (445)].
14. Kwame Nkrumah, *Ghana: The Autobiography of Kwame Nkrumah* (New York: Nelson, 1957), 11 ["positive action," "as a last resort" (11)].
15. Grundy, "Nkrumah's Theory of Underdevelopment," 443.
16. See Kwame Nkrumah, *Handbook on Revolutionary Warfare: A Guide to the Armed Phase of the African Revolution* (New York: International Publishers, 1969).
17. Grundy noted the important relationship between nonviolence as advocated by Gandhi and the use of force: "[I]t must be remembered that the threat of violence was always present and tended to temper the British response to nationalist demands." Grundy, "Nkrumah's Theory of Underdevelopment," 443.
18. Director of Central Intelligence, *The Outlook for Ghana*, 3.
19. Kwame Nkrumah, *I Speak of Freedom: A Statement of African Ideology* (New York: Praeger, 1961), 218.
20. Dalton, "Colony and Metropolis," 564.
21. Director of Central Intelligence, *The Outlook for Ghana*, 3.
22. Jack Goody, "Consensus and Dissent in Ghana," *Political Science Quarterly* 83, no. 3 (September 1968) ["controlled virtually all," "[b]oth administratively" (337)].

23. Director of Central Intelligence, *The Outlook for Ghana* ["Much of the Northern Region" (2), "deep-rooted," "unruly" (5), "a large percentage" (6)].
24. Grundy, "Nkrumah's Theory of Underdevelopment," 444.
25. Ogunsanwo, *China's Policy in Africa*, 73.
26. Thompson, *Ghana's Foreign Policy*, 46.
27. Ogunsanwo, *China's Policy in Africa*, 54.
28. Kwame Nkrumah, *Ghana's Policy at Home and Abroad* (Washington, DC: Information Office, Embassy of Ghana, 1957), 3. This is a reprint of Nkrumah's speech to the Ghanaian Parliament on 29 August 1957.
29. "China and the World: Cultural News," *Peking Review* 1, no. 3 (18 March 1958): 20.
30. Ganda (pseudonym), "Report on Maoist Subversion in Africa," *ABC* (Madrid), 22 August 1971, 2. Article in Joint Publications Research Service (54615), *Translations on Africa*, no. 1088, 3 December 1971, 1–33.
31. "China and the World: Cultural News," *Peking Review* 1, no. 8 (22 April 1958): 22.
32. Ogunsanwo, *China's Policy in Africa*, 28.
33. Fage, *A History of West Africa*, 218.
34. Maxwell Owusu, "Government and Politics," in Berry, *Ghana: A Country Study*, 243. The two states, Ghana and Guinea, believed the union created a nucleus for a Union of West African States. Thompson, *Ghana's Foreign Policy*, 57.
35. Adie, "Chinese Policy towards Africa," 55.
36. Fage, *A History of West Africa*, 47.
37. Kwame Nkrumah, *Speech on Foreign Policy* (Accra: Ghana Information Services, 1959), 11. This was Nkrumah's foreign policy speech given to the National Assembly on 16 December 1959.
38. Good, "Changing Patterns of African International Relations" ["The radicals," "The radical view" (633)].
39. Schatten, *Communism in Africa*, 197.
40. "Peiping Campaign in Africa Grows," *New York Times*, 10 September 1960, 3.
41. David Anderson, "Small Countries Fear Taiwan War," *New York Times*, 25 September 1958, 6.
42. Ogunsanwo, *China's Policy in Africa*, 54.
43. "China and the World: Briefs," *Peking Review* 2, no. 10 (10 March 1959): 18.
44. "China and the World: Ghana's Anniversary Greeted," *Peking Review* 3, no. 11 (15 March 1960): 25.
45. *Nkrumah's Subversion in Africa: Documentary Evidence of Nkrumah's Interference in the Affairs of Other African States* (Accra-Tema: Ghana Ministry of Information, November 1966), 3 ["furthering the activities" (3)].
46. Thompson, *Ghana's Foreign Policy*, xxiii.
47. "Chinese Government Leaders Greet New African States," *Peking Review* 3, no. 27 (5 July 1960): 11.

CHAPTER 7. TOWARD REVOLUTIONARY FRIENDSHIP

1. "China and the World: China–Ghana Diplomatic Ties," *Peking Review* 3, no. 28 (12 July 1960): 26.
2. "Ghana, China Exchange Envoys," *Washington Post*, 6 July 1960, A1
3. Thompson, *Ghana's Foreign Policy*, 297.
4. "Red China Envoy in Ghana," *New York Times*, 6 September 1960, 20.
5. "China and the World: First Chinese Ambassador to Ghana," *Peking Review* 3, no. 37 (14 September 1960): 41.

6. "Red China Replaces Ambassador to Cairo," *Washington Post*, 21 January 1966, A17.
7. "Reds to Open Embassy," *Washington Post*, 5 August 1960, A11.
8. For his complete speech, see *Osagyefo at the United Nations* (Accra: Ghana Information Services, 1960).
9. Dana Adams Schmidt, "Nkrumah Speaks," *New York Times*, 24 September 1960, 1.
10. "Ghana Names Peiping Envoy," *New York Times*, 23 October 1960, 24.
11. Ernest W. Lefever, *Spear and Scepter: Army, Police, and Politics in Tropical Africa* (Washington, DC: Brookings Institution), 1970, 54. Note that earlier in the year five officials joined two Chinese diplomats in the newly created embassy in Accra.
12. Feng Chih-tan, "From Dark Night to Dawn," *Peking Review* 4, no. 34 (25 August 1961): 7–9.
13. Feng Chih-tan, *Glimpses of West Africa* (Beijing: Foreign Languages Press, 1963) ["green gold" (37), "Ghana is a country" (41)]; see also pp. 37–39.
14. "Kenyan Backs Red Aid," *New York Times*, 28 June 1961, 6.
15. "China and the World: Ghanaian National Day," *Peking Review* 4, no. 28 (14 July 1961) ["conveyed the Chinese," "acclaimed the continuous," "The Vice-Premier reaffirmed" (22)].
16. Nkrumah arrived in Communist China via Albania and the Soviet Union. "Nkrumah Arrives in Soviet Capital," *Washington Post*, 13 August 1961, A1.
17. China repeatedly insisted on the latter. The *Peking Review* also referred to the recent CAPFA visit to Ghana. "Rousing Welcoming for President Nkrumah," *Peking Review* 4, no. 3 (18 August 1961): 5–6.
18. "New Stage in Sino-Ghanaian Relations," *Peking Review* 4, no. 34 (25 August 1961): 5; "Peiping and Ghana Set Up Closer Ties," *New York Times*, 19 August 1961, 6.
19. "China Lends Ghana Nearly 20 Million," *New York Times*, 22 August 1961, 13.
20. Ogunsanwo, *China's Policy in Africa*, 91.
21. "Joint Communique," *Peking Review* 4, no. 34 (25 August 1961): 5–6.
22. Clare McDermott, "China, Ghana Sign Amity, Trade Pacts," *Washington Post*, 19 August 1961, A9.
23. "Nkrumah in Peiping," *New York Times*, 15 August 1961, 2; "Treaty of Friendship," *Peking Review* 4, no. 34 (25 August 1961): 7.
24. "China and the World: China and Africa," *Peking Review* 4, no. 38 (22 September 1961): 22.
25. "China and the World: Chinese Exhibition in Accra," *Peking Review* 4, no. 33 (18 August 1961): 23.
26. "China and the World: Ghana Likes Chinese Exhibition," *Peking Review* 4, no. 38 (22 September 1961): 22.
27. "China and the World: Between China and Ghana," *Peking Review* 4, no. 45 (10 November 1961) ["aroused tremendous," "expressed deep," "sold out," "Seeds of friendship" (19)].
28. Ibid.
29. "China and the World: Chinese-African Friendship," *Peking Review* 5, no. 3 (19 January 1962): 23.
30. "China and the World: Briefs," *Peking Review* 5, no. 14 (6 April 1962): 21.
31. "China and World: Sports," *Peking Review* 5, no. 26 (29 June 1962): 21.
32. "Ghana, China Sign Economic Accord," *Washington Post*, 20 October 1962, A14.
33. "China and the World: Sino-Ghanaian Co-operation Protocol," *Peking Review* 5, no. 43 (26 October 1962): 23.

34. Cited from *Jeune Afrique* (Tunis), 15 and 21 April 1962, in Adie, "Chinese Policy towards Africa," 58.
35. Thomas P. Ofcansky, "National Security," in Berry, *Ghana: A Country Study*, 288.
36. "China and the World: Ghanaian Goodwill Delegation," *Peking Review* 6, no. 4 (25 January 1963): 19.
37. "News in Brief," *Peking Review* 6, no. 10–11 (15 March 1963): 79.
38. "Guineans Leave China," *Washington Post*, 19 June 1963, A17.
39. "The Week: Sino-Ghanaian Friendship," *Peking Review* 6, no. 34 (23 August 1963): 4.
40. "Text of Joint Statement of Chinese and Ghanaian Trade Unions," *Survey of China Mainland Press*, no. 3091 (30 October 1963): 31. Translated by the American consulate general in Hong Kong, and originally published in *New China News Agency*, 27 October 1963.
41. "Round the World: Africa: Militant Journalism," *Peking Review* 6, no. 47 (22 November 1963): 25.
42. "Chairman Mao Tse-tung's Message to President Nkrumah," *Peking Review* 7, no. 3 (17 January 1964): 4.
43. Lloyd Garrison, "Ghana Punishes Security Police," *New York Times*, 18 January 1964, 8.
44. Thompson, *Ghana's Foreign Policy*, 293.
45. "Chou Is Welcomed On Visit to Ghana," *New York Times*, 12 January 1964, 21.
46. Lloyd Garrison, "Nkrumah Praises Chou as a Leader," *New York Times*, 15 January 1964, 7.
47. Lloyd Garrison, "Chou Greeted Unofficially by Ghana," *New York Times*, 13 January 1964, 4.
48. Garrison, "Nkrumah Praises Chou as a Leader," 7.
49. "Nkrumah Continuing His Drive for a One-Party Socialist State," *New York Times*, 20 January 1964, 64.
50. For Nkrumah's speeches at the state dinners on 13 and 15 January as well as the complete text of the joint communiqué, see *Chou En-Lai in Ghana* (Accra: Ministry of Information and Broadcasting, 1964).
51. "Mao Sends a Message," 4.
52. "Ghana Joins Chou in Pleas for Talks," *New York Times*, 17 January 1964, 2.
53. Snow, *The Star Raft*, 94. Snow referenced an interview with Yaw Turkson, a former Ghanaian diplomat.
54. Cited from Ghana Radio, 13 February 1964, in Ogunsanwo, *China's Policy in Africa*, 144.
55. Max Frankel, "U.S. Aides Unconvinced Pro-Reds Run Zanzibar," *New York Times*, 24 January 1964, 1.
56. "Round the World: Ghana Hits Back: U.S. Imperialism Exposed," *Peking Review* 7, no. 7 (14 February 1964): 26.
57. "Round the World: Zanzibar: On Guard against Intervention," *Peking Review* 7, no. 7 (14 February 1964): 28.
58. Braestrup, "Algerians Decry Criticism by U.S.," 6.
59. "Apartheid Must Go," *Peking Review* 7, no. 16 (17 April 1964): 11–12.
60. "The Week: Ghana's National Day," *Peking Review* 7, no. 28 (10 July 1964): 4.
61. "Ghana to Get Red China Loan," *New York Times*, 16 July 1964, 9.
62. Tansky, "China's Foreign Aid," 10, Table IV.
63. "The Week: Sino-Ghanaian Anniversary," *Peking Review* 7, no. 35 (28 August 1964): 3-4.

64. Ofcansky, "National Security," 288.
65. Thompson, *Ghana's Foreign Policy* ["Most of the men," "humiliation" (360)].
66. Ofcansky, "National Security," 288; Ogunsanwo, *China's Policy in Africa*, 147; Wei Liang-Tsai, *Peking versus Taipei in Africa*, 118. Coincidentally (or not), Half Assini was near the birthplace of Nkrumah. Thompson, *Ghana's Foreign Policy*, 148.
67. *Nkrumah's Subversion in Africa*, 8.
68. Ofcansky, "National Security," 288.
69. Ogunsanwo, *China's Policy in Africa*, 147.
70. "Communist Chinese Propaganda and Africa," *Afrique Nouvelle* (Dakar), 6–12 November 1969, 9. Article found in Joint Publications Research Service (49369), *Translations on Africa*, no. 840, 3 December 1969, 1–29.
71. Ogunsanwo, *China's Policy in Africa*, 172–173.
72. "Ghana Adds Backing for Peking," *New York Times*, 11 December 1964, 5.
73. *Nkrumah's Subversion in Africa*, 18; Wei Liang-Tsai, *Peking versus Taipei in Africa 1960–1978*, 119.
74. Wei Liang-Tsai, *Peking versus Taipei in Africa*, 119n40.
75. Central Intelligence Agency, *Chinese Communist Activities in Africa*, Memorandum, 30 April 1965, 7. Memorandum found in CIA Research Reports Africa, 1946–1976 (Frederick, MD: University Publications of America, 1982).
76. *Nkrumah's Subversion in Africa*, 18 ["a 90-day course" (39)].
77. "Peking Accused in Subversion," *Washington Post*, 14 March 1965, A16.
78. "Peking Assures Ghana," *Washington Post*, 4 May 1965, 10.
79. "Peking Accused in Subversion."
80. "African Assails China's Actions," *Washington Post*, 5 August 1965, A25.
81. Ibid.
82. Ofcansky, "National Security," 289.
83. Central Intelligence Agency, *Chinese Communist Activities in Africa*, 7 ["At least part of this shipment may be intended for the Congolese rebels" (7).]
84. "The Week: Ghana's National Day," *Peking Review* 8, no. 11 (12 March 1965) ["On the occasion," "He pointed out" (5)].
85. Szulc, "Peking Steps Up Drive for Allies." Congo-Brazzaville was also mentioned as a stopover visit of the NPC delegation.
86. Ogunsanwo, *China's Policy in Africa*, 128.
87. "Peking Assures Ghana," C4.
88. Wei Liang-Tsai, *Peking versus Taipei in Africa*, 120.
89. Ogunsanwo, *China's Policy in Africa*, 128.
90. Liu Ning-i [Ningyi], "Report on Visit to Five African Countries," *Peking Review* 8, no. 21 (21 May 1965): 20 ["dealt imperialism" (22)].
91. Thompson, *Ghana's Foreign Policy*, 401.
92. The protocol was retroactive to 30 September 1964, when China first dispatched an advisory team in country. Wei Liang-Tsai, *Peking versus Taipei in Africa*, 119.
93. *Nkrumah's Subversion in Africa*, 3, 4 ["It was the duty" (4)].
94. Thompson, *Ghana's Foreign Policy*, 398.
95. *Nkrumah's Subversion in Africa*, 47.
96. "Round the World: Africa: Spark of Armed Revolt," *Peking Review* 9, no. 9 (25 February 1966): 29. Geographically, Equatorial Guinea is southeast across the Gulf of Guinea from Ghana.

CHAPTER 8. REVOLUTION DERAILED
1. Edward Feit, "Military Coups and Political Development: Some Lessons from Ghana and Nigeria," *World Politics* 20, no. 2 (January 1968): 180.

2. "Ankrah Calls Nkrumah Africa's No. 1 Tyrant," *Washington Post*, 1 March 1966, A10.
3. Lloyd Garrison, "Coup in Ghana: Elaborately Organized Upheaval," *New York Times*, 5 March 1966, 2.
4. Feit, "Military Coups and Political Development," 192.
5. Lefever, *Spear and Scepter*, 29.
6. There was only a single copy found; the work was never published.
7. *Nkrumah's Subversion in Africa*, 42, 47.
8. Ibid., 48.
9. Central Intelligence Agency, *China Plans to Restore Nkrumah to Power in Ghana*, Intelligence Information Cable, 7 March 1966, 1. Cable found in *CIA Research Reports Africa, 1946–1976* (Frederick, MD: University Publications of America, 1982).
10. "Africa's Revolutionary Tide Cannot Be Stemmed," *Peking Review* 9, no. 11 (11 March 1966): 9.
11. "Protests to Ghanaian Authorities," *Peking Review* 9, no. 11 (11 March 1966): 7.
12. Sidney Taylor, "Ghana Says Nkrumah, Peking Plot," *Washington Post*, 7 April 1966, A22.
13. Ofcansky, "National Security," 289.
14. "Peking Charges Beating," *New York Times*, 5 March 1966, 2.
15. "China Strongly Protests against Worsening of Sino-Ghanaian Relations by Ghanaian Authorities," *Peking Review* 9, no. 13 (25 March 1966): 8–9 ["worsen relations" (9)].
16. Snow, *The Star Raft*, 103. Once again, Snow referenced an interview with former Ghanaian diplomat Turkson.
17. "Nkrumah's Status Explained," *New York Times*, 5 March 1966 ["entrusted with the leadership," "instruments of," "all the rights" (2)].
18. Drew Middleton, "Ivory Coast Head Calls China Peril," *New York Times*, 10 April 1966, 17.
19. Thompson, *Ghana's Foreign Policy*, 12–13.
20. Houphouet-Boigny quoted in Middleton, "Ivory Coast Head Calls China Peril," 17 ["to obtain either," "Africa, underpopulated Africa" (17)].
21. "Ghana Accuses Chinese of Arming Foes in Guinea," *New York Times*, 7 April 1966, 5.
22. "Communique of the Afro-Asian Emergency Writers' Meeting," *Peking Review* 9, no. 29 (15 July 1966): 8.
23. "Resolution on the Ghana Coup," *Peking Review* 9, no. 29 (15 July 1966): 41.
24. "Chairman Mao Receives Delegates and Observers to Afro-Asian Writers' Emergency Meeting," *Peking Review* 9, no. 30 (22 July 1966): 3.
25. "Ghana Acts to Revise Accords with Reds," *Washington Post*, 7 September 1966, D5.
26. "The Week: Protest against Ghanaian Authorities' Anti-Chinese Provocations," *Peking Review* 9, no. 41 (7 October 1966): 38.
27. "The Week: Protest against Ghanaian Authorities' Unilateral Suspension of Relations between China and Ghana," *Peking Review* 9, no. 45 (4 November 1966): 5.
28. "Peking Ending Ghana Ties," *New York Times*, 30 October 1966, 4.
29. "Peking Starts Withdrawing Embassy Force from Ghana," *Washington Post*, 30 October 1966, A24.
30. According to news reports cited in Wei Liang-Tsai, *Peking versus Taipei in Africa*, 121.
31. The following discussion is based on "Ghana Charges Plot to Return Nkrumah," *New York Times*, 23 February 1967, 28.
32. Lefever, *Spear and Scepter*, 57.

33. See also *Nkrumah's Deception of Africa* (Accra: Ghana Ministry of Information, 1967), especially chaps. 10 and 11.
34. Central Intelligence Agency, *Drawings on Communist Economic Aid Extended to Less Developed Countries 1954–1967*, 1 May 1968, 1.
35. Central Intelligence Agency, "Unclassified Table on Communist Economic Credits and Grants Extended to Less Developed Countries of the Free World, 1954–1970 and Years 1969 and 1970." Memorandum for the Department of State, 4 March 1971, 1.
36. "China Supports Africa's Struggle against Imperialism and Colonialism," *Peking Review* 15, no. 6 (11 February 1972): 15.
37. "The Week: Resumption of Diplomatic Relations between China and Ghana," *Peking Review* 15, no. 9 (3 March 1972): 3.
38. "Supporting African National-Liberation Movement," *Peking Review* 15, no. 11 (17 March 1972): 11.
39. "West African Crops Drought-Stricken," *New York Times*, 27 January 1974, 220.
40. He died of skin cancer in Bucharest, Romania.
41. "The Week: Ghanaian Guests Welcomed," *Peking Review* 15, no. 37 (15 September 1972): 22.
42. Based on local African sources cited in Wei Liang-Tsai, *Peking versus Taipei in Africa*, 121.
43. "China's Aid to Africa," in *Chinese and Soviet Aid to Africa*, ed. Warren Weinstein (New York: Praeger, 1975), 280.

CHAPTER 9. INDEPENDENCE AND REVOLUTION

1. Kenneth Ingham, *A History of East Africa* (New York: Praeger, 1965), 375, 397 ["One of the most important" (375)].
2. Anthony Clayton, *The Zanzibar Revolution and Its Aftermath* (Hamden, CT: Archon Books, 1981), 21–22.
3. Abdin Chande, "Radicalism and Reform in East Africa," in *The History of Islam in Africa*, ed. Nehemia Levtzion and Randall L. Pouwels (Athens, OH: Ohio University Press, 2000), 359.
4. Judith Listowel, *The Making of Tanganyika* (New York: London House and Maxwell, 1965), 82.
5. Chande, "Radicalism and Reform in East Africa," 259.
6. Clayton, *The Zanzibar Revolution*, 16–17.
7. Chande, "Radicalism and Reform in East Africa," 360.
8. Listowel, *The Making of Tanganyika*, 121.
9. Chande, "Radicalism and Reform in East Africa," 360.
10. J. D. Fage and Roland Oliver, eds. *The Cambridge History of Africa*, vol. 7 (Cambridge: Cambridge University Press, 1986), 217.
11. Clayton, *The Zanzibar Revolution*, 38–39 ["a land of" (38)].
12. Chande, "Radicalism and Reform in East Africa," 360.
13. Milton Bracker, "Peiping's Signal Strong in Africa," *New York Times*, 27 June 1959 ["bombarding East," "Everyone who has heard," "Listeners in Zanzibar" (2)].
14. "China and the World: Zanzibar Leader in China," *Peking Review* 3, no. 2 (12 January 1960): 23.
15. "China and the World: Chinese Leaders Receive Latin American and African Guests," *Peking Review* 3, no. 31 (2 August 1960): 26.
16. "China and the World: Support for African Peoples," *Peking Review* 3, no. 26 (28 June 1960): 32.

17. Leonard Ingalls, "Peiping Presses Gains in Africa; Foothold Is Sought in Zanzibar," *New York Times*, 4 September 1960, 2 ["Chinese Communist influence," "The Communist Chinese" (2)].
18. "Reds' Use of Zanzibar Feared," *New York Times*, 30 December 1960, 5. The mention of the UAR is notable because of the Arab connection, particularly to Zanzibar.
19. Clayton, *The Zanzibar Revolution*, 60.
20. For instance, Ogunsanwo, *China's Policy in Africa*, 74; Wei Liang-Tsai, *Peking versus Taipei in Africa*, 202.
21. Shen Su, "Political Map of Africa Changes Fast," *Peking Review* 5, no. 1 (5 January 1962): 14.
22. Seaghan Maynes, "Philip Arrives to Raise Flag of Free Tanganyika," *Washington Post*, 9 December 1961, 8; "Red China Replaces Ambassador to Cairo," A17.
23. "China and the World: Greetings to Tanganyika," *Peking Review* 4, no. 50 (15 December 1961): 30 ["after years," "extending warm," "The people of China," "the Tanganyikan people," "[T]here is only" (30)].
24. Adie, "Chinese Policy towards Africa," 58. Adie also wrote that China established an embassy at the same time. Adie, "China and the Bandung Genie," 9. In the previous year the *Washington Post* reported that a "private exchange of preliminary documents" had taken place to allow China to set up its embassy in Dar es Salaam. Richard C. Wald, "Tanganyika and Red China Agree on Diplomatic Ties," *Washington Post*, 12 December 1961, A8.
25. "China and the World: Release Zanzibar Journalist!," *Peking Review* 5, no. 28 (13 July 1962): 20.
26. Schatten, *Communism in Africa*, 213.
27. Clayton, *The Zanzibar Revolution*, 46.
28. Robert Conley, "Leftists Strengthen Hold Over Zanzibar," *New York Times*, 20 January 1964, 6.
29. Clayton, *The Zanzibar Revolution*, "As General Secretary of the Z.N.P." (45n44); see also p. 42.
30. Ibid. ["the cracks in" (43), "Ghana, China and Radio Cairo" (48)]. Clayton also explained that the "depth of local ethnic and class divisions" helped create the domestic environment that emerged in 1963 (Clayton, *The Zanzibar Revolution*, 48).
31. Wei Liang-Tsai, *Peking versus Taipei in Africa*, 202.
32. Chen Kung-chi, "Tanganyika Impressions," *Peking Review* 6, no. 17 (26 April 1963): 20–21; Wei Liang-Tsai, *Peking versus Taipei in Africa*, 202.
33. "China and the World: Founding of Tanganyikan Republic," *Peking Review* 5, no. 50 (14 December 1962): 27.
34. "China and the World: Sino-Tanganyikan Ties," *Peking Review* 5, no. 51 (21 December 1962): 22.
35. Adie, "Chinese Policy towards Africa," 58.
36. Liu Ning-i [Ningyi], "Unite to Fight against Imperialism," *Peking Review* 6, no. 7 (15 February 1963): 9.
37. Russell Howe, "Tanganyika Capital Is Haven for African Revolutionaries," *Washington Post*, 17 February 1963, E4.
38. "News in Brief," *Peking Review* 6, no. 10–11 (15 March 1963): 79.
39. "The Week: Chairman Mao Receives Tanganyika Women's Delegation," *Peking Review* 6, no. 22 (31 May 1963): 4.
40. Chande, "Radicalism and Reform in East Africa," 360.
41. "Joint Statement of Chinese and Tanganyikan Trade Unions," *Survey of China Mainland Press*, no. 3111 (3 December 1963): 36. Translated by the American con-

sulate general in Hong Kong, and originally published in *New China News Agency*, 28 November 1963.
42. Ogunsanwo, *China's Policy in Africa*, 116.
43. "The Week: Zanzibar's Independence Day," *Peking Review* 6, no. 50 (13 December 1963): 4
44. "The Week: Tanganyika President to Visit China," *Peking Review* 6, no. 49 (6 December 1963): 4.
45. "Round the World: Indian Ocean: 7th Fleet on the Prowl," *Peking Review* 6, no. 51 (20 December 1963): 24.

CHAPTER 10. OPEN DOOR
1. Clayton, *The Zanzibar Revolution*, xvi.
2. Ali A. Mazrui, "Thoughts on Assassination in Africa," *Political Science Quarterly* 83, no. 1 (March 1968): 41.
3. One report cited "Spanish-speaking soldiers wearing Cuban-type uniforms." "Cuban-Type Uniforms Seen," *New York Times*, 15 January 1964, 5. Conley reported, "By most responsible accounts, African nationalists had little to do with it [the revolution]. They were used as camouflage, it is understood, behind which the guerrillas could operate." Robert Conley, "Nationalism Is Viewed as Camouflage for Reds—Toll 2,000 to 4,000," *New York Times*, 19 January 1964, 1.
4. "Roots of Zanzibar Upheaval Reach Back Ten Centuries," *Washington Post*, 13 January 1964, A13.
5. Alastair Matheson, "China Steps Up Africa Program," *Washington Post*, 30 August 1963, B6.
6. Ibid. For an interesting work with a memoir and essays in honor of Babu, see Haroub Othman, ed., *Babu: I Saw the Future and It Works* (Dar es Salaam, Tanzania: E & D Limited, 2001).
7. Conley, "Leftists Strengthen Hold Over Zanzibar," 6.
8. Clayton, *The Zanzibar Revolution*, 50–116. However, Clayton relies on Okello's own autobiographical account, which was written while he was in prison. John Okello, *Revolution in Zanzibar* (Nairobi: East African Institute Press, 1967).
9. Tad Szulc, "Okello, Cuba-Trained Zanzibari, Called Key Man in Power Fight," *New York Times*, 31 January 1964, 3.
10. Ganda (pseudonym), "Reports on Maoist Subversion in Africa" ["ardent Maoist" (28)].
11. After assuming the presidency, Karume requested all foreign states not to meddle in his country's internal affairs. He specifically asked that foreign ships remain outside Zanzibar territorial waters. However, the British frigate *Rhyl* reportedly sailed to Zanzibar to evacuate British subjects and a dhow with a U.S. chargé d'affaires and four journalists entered Zanzibar illegally. "Round the World: Zanzibar: New Government," *Peking Review* 7, no. 4 (24 January 1964): 20.
12. "[U.S.] Officials say they see no direct connection between last week's revolt in Zanzibar and the more recent uprisings in Tanganyika and Uganda." Paul Grimes, "Unrest in Africa Is Worrying U.S.," *New York Times*, 25 January 1964, 2.
13. Conley, "Nationalism Is Viewed as Camouflage for Reds," 3.
14. Frankel, "U.S. Aides Unconvinced," 11. See also "New Zanzibar Chief Vows Ties with All," *New York Times*, 15 January 1964, 1. Hanga had been educated in the Soviet Union and married to a Russian woman. Ogunsanwo, *China's Policy in Africa*, 136.
15. Lawrence Fellows, "Chinese Communist Presence in East African Nations Grows," *New York Times*, 25 May 1968, 2.

16. Director of Central Intelligence, *Chou En-Lai's African Tour*, 9.
17. Clayton, *The Zanzibar Revolution*, 104n117.
18. Ogunsanwo, *China's Policy in Africa*, 136.
19. "African Unrest," *New York Times*, 26 January 1964, E1.
20. Ogunsanwo, *China's Policy in Africa*, 138. The call to replace British weapons was based on an anonymous source.
21. Klein, "Peking's Diplomats in Africa," 6.
22. "Round the World: East Africa: Operation Return," *Peking Review* 7, no. 6 (7 February 1964): 33–34 ["to stage a comeback," "In actions reminiscent" (33)].
23. Central Intelligence Agency, *A Reassessment of Julius Nyerere*, Special Memoradum No. 17-65, 10 June 1965, 4. Memorandum found in *CIA Research Reports Africa, 1946–1976* (Frederick, MD: University Publications of America, 1982).
24. Cited from Zanzibar Radio, 4 and 19 February 1964, in Clayton, *The Zanzibar Revolution*, 135; Ogunsanwo, *China's Policy in Africa*, 136.
25. Robert Conley, "U.S. Fails to Stop Zanzibar's Diplomatic Break," *New York Times*, 21 February 1964, 5; "Zanzibar Expels Top British Aide," *Washington Post*, 21 February 1964, A30.
26. Clayton, *The Zanzibar Revolution*, 108.
27. Braestrup, "Algerians Decry Criticism by U.S.," 6.
28. Beijing recalled Meng on 30 July after the union of Tanganyika and Zanzibar. "Shuffles Mark Year in Peking Diplomacy," *Washington Post*, 9 January 1965, A7.
29. "Soviet Arms Cargo in Zanzibar Denied," *New York Times*, 6 April 1964, 6.
30. Clayton, *The Zanzibar Revolution*, 107. Clayton did not believe the station had any military application, but does not provide any documentary evidence except for stating that Babu "misrepresented" the station as a "rocket base."
31. "Round the World: Zanzibar Demands Removal of U.S. Bases," *Peking Review* 7, no. 16 (17 April 1964): 20.
32. Clayton, *The Zanzibar Revolution*, 112.
33. Robert Conley, "Tanganyika Vote Complete Union," *New York Times*, 26 April 1964, 17.
34. Anonymous sources are reported in Ogunsanwo, *China's Policy in Africa*, 137.
35. Klein, "Peking's Diplomats in Africa," 5.
36. "Shuffles Mark Year in Peking Diplomacy," A7.
37. Central Intelligence Agency, *Implications of Growing Communist Influence in URTZ*, Special Memorandum No. 12-64, 29 September 1964, 3. Memorandum found in *CIA Research Reports Africa, 1946–1976* (Frederick, MD: University Publications of America, 1982).
38. Klein, "Peking's Diplomats in Africa," 7n12.
39. "China Said to Seek Base in Zanzibar for Subversion," *New York Times*, 28 May 1964, 18.
40. Ibid.
41. The *New York Times* reported it was a "10-man goodwill mission." "Tanganyikans to Visit Peking," *New York Times*, 8 June 1964, 32. Wei reported an interest-free loan of £10 million ($28 million). Wei Liang-Tsai, *Peking versus Taipei in Africa*, 206.
42. Cited from *Sunday Times* [London], 21 June 1964, in Ogunsanwo, *China's Policy in Africa*, 137. Wei reported a gift of £1 million. Wei Liang-Tsai, *Peking versus Taipei in Africa*, 206.
43. Director of Central Intelligence, *Tanzania Taking the Left Turn*, Special Report, 21 May 1965, 5. As of May 1964, Babu was minister for commerce and cooperatives.

But at the time Babu was also one of three ministers of state in the Directorate of Development and Planning. Sydney Gruson, "Tanganyika-Zanzibar Union Is Reported Shaky," *New York Times*, 3 June 1964, 9.
44. Tad Szulc, "Zanzibar Chiefs Tighten Red Ties," *New York Times*, 21 June 1964, 13. Szulc does not reveal the details of the "intelligence reports."
45. Central Intelligence Agency, *Implications of Growing Communist Influence in URTZ*, 6.
46. Clayton, *The Zanzibar Revolution*, 115.
47. "Tanganyika-Zanzibar Guests Visit China," *Peking Review* 7, no. 25 (19 June 1964): 6.
48. For the text, see "Joint Communique of China and Tanganyika-Zanzibar," *Peking Review* 7, no. 25 (19 June 1964): 12–13.
49. The loan was announced prior to Kawawa's visit. "Zanzibar Promised Big Loan by Peking," *New York Times*, 9 June 1964, 16.
50. Point made in Peter Vanderwicken, "Red Threat to Africa Is Eased by Zanzibar's Link with Tanganyika," *Wall Street Journal*, 13 July 1964, 1.
51. "China Hails African Outlook," *New York Times*, 21 June 1964, 13.
52. Robert Conley, "Stakes High in Zanzibar," *New York Times*, 28 June 1964, E5.
53. "The Week: Chinese and Zanzibar Youth Stand Together," *Peking Review* 7, no. 27 (3 July 1964): 4.
54. "The Week: Ghana's National Day" (10 July 1964), 4.
55. Wei Liang-Tsai, *Peking versus Taipei in Africa*, 207.
56. Cited from Colin Legum, "Observer, 30 August 1964," in Colin Legum, "Africa and China: Symbolism and Substance," in *Policies toward China: Views from Six Continents*, ed. A. M. Halpern (New York: Council on Foreign Relations, 1965), 425; Ogunsanwo, *China's Policy in Africa*, 138.
57. Wei Liang-Tsai, *Peking versus Taipei in Africa*, 207n68.
58. "Round the World: Tanzam Republic: President Nyerere Protests," *Peking Review* 7, no. 37 (11 September 1964): 30.
59. Wei Liang-Tsai, *Peking versus Taipei in Africa*, 207n68.
60. Ibid.
61. Ogunsanwo, *China's Policy in Africa*, 172.
62. Ibid., 232.
63. "South Africa Jails 2 Men for Arms Training in China," *New York Times*, 8 September 1965, 22.
64. "Mission from China Reaches Tanganyika," *Washington Post*, 27 August 1964, C17.
65. "The Week: Chairman Liu Receives Zanzibar Guests," *Peking Review* 7, no. 38 (18 September 1964): 4.
66. Seymour Topping, "Gains Reported for China," *New York Times*, 9 October 1964, 3.
67. "Chinese Reds Set Up 2 Bureaus on Africa," *New York Times*, 27 October 1964, 2.
68. "Lisbon Confirms Move by Africans," *New York Times*, 11 October 1964, 15 ["was said to have received" (15)].
69. Specifically, to assist the Mozambique Liberation Front, Frente de Libertação de Moçambique (FRELIMO). Clayton, *The Zanzibar Revolution*, 112, 119.
70. "U.S. Plot against Tanzania Exposed," *Peking Review* 7, no. 47 (20 November 1964): 15.
71. Cited from Dar Es Salaam Radio, 28 December 1964, in Ogunsanwo, *China's Policy in Africa*, 139.
72. Cited from Dar Es Salaam Radio, 11 January 1965, in Ogunsanwo, *China's Policy in Africa*, 139.

73. Kampala Radio, 6 January 1965, in Ogunsanwo, *China's Policy in Africa* ["the largest" (40)]. "China to Aid Tanzania," *New York Times*, 6 January 1965, 11.
74. Central Intelligence Agency, *Chinese Communist Activities in Africa*, 9.
75. "Burundi Repulse to Peking Noted," *New York Times*, 31 January 1965, 5.
76. Director of Central Intelligence, *Tanzania Taking the Left Turn*, 3.
77. Donald H. Louchheim, "Burundi Gives Peking First Setback in Africa," *Washington Post*, 31 January 1965, A18.
78. China was active in Congo-Brazzaville, west of the Congo, as well; evaluation of these operations would require a separate in-depth analysis.
79. Director of Central Intelligence, *Tanzania Taking the Left Turn*, 4.
80. Robert Conley, "Tanzania Recalls Envoy from U.S. in Protest over Expulsion of a Diplomat," *New York Times*, 15 February 1965, 12.
81. "Tanzania Expels 2 U.S. Diplomats," *New York Times*, 16 January 1965, 1.
82. "Round the World: Tanzania: U.S. Spies Expelled," *Peking Review* 8, no. 6 (5 February 1965): 28.
83. "Ambassador to U.S. Recalled by Tanzania," *Washington Post*, 15 February 1965, A9.
84. "Nyerere in Shanghai," *Washington Post*, 17 February 1965, A19.
85. "China Hails President Nyerere's State Visit," *Peking Review* 8, no. 9 (26 February 1965): 7.
86. "China Signs Pact with Tanzanians," *New York Times*, 21 February 1965, 21; "Sino-Tanzanian Treaty of Friendship," *Peking Review* 8, no. 9 (26 February 1965): 9.
87. "Sino-Tanzanian Joint Communique," *Peking Review* 8, no. 9 (26 February 1965): 10.
88. For the full text of Nyrerere's speech at the rally, see Julius K. Nyerere, *Freedom and Unity: A Selection from Writings and Speeches, 1952–65* (Dar es Salaam, Tanzania: Oxford University Press, 1966), 323–325.
89. "Tanzania President Back from Red China," *Washington Post*, 25 February 1965, A15.
90. "China, Tanzania Sign Trade Pact," *Washington Post*, 26 February 1965, A1.
91. Ogunsanwo, *China's Policy in Africa*, 139.
92. Cited from Dar Es Salaam Radio, 8 February 1965, and *The Times* [London], 2 September 1964, in Ogunsanwo, *China's Policy in Africa*, 139.
93. Director of Central Intelligence, *Tanzania Taking the Left Turn*, 3.
94. Lawrence Fellows, "China Denounced By Kenya Official," *New York Times*, 13 June 1965, 21.
95. Ogunsanwo, *China's Policy in Africa*, 135 ["Already within" (135)].
96. Szulc, "Peking Steps Up Drive for Allies."
97. Director of Central Intelligence, *Tanzania Taking the Left Turn*, 8.
98. "Premier Chou Visits Tanzania," *Peking Review* 8, no. 24 (11 June 1965): 5–6.
99. Lawrence Fellows, "Tanzania to Greet Chou Today; Her Capital Is in Festive Array," *New York Times*, 4 June 1965, 4.
100. Lawrence Fellows, "Monetary Union in Africa to End," *New York Times*, 11 June 1965, 8.
101. Ogunsanwo, *China's Policy in Africa*, 141.
102. Lawrence Fellows, "Chou Visit Perils East Africa Unity," *New York Times*, 8 June 1965, 11.
103. "Chou in Africa," *New York Times*, 10 June 1965, 34.

104. Lawrence Fellows, "Nyerere Tempers Welcome to Chou," *New York Times*, 5 June 1965, 7.
105. Lawrence Fellows, "Chou, in Zanzibar, Attacks U.S. after Welcome by Large Crowd," *New York Times*, 7 June 1965, 2.
106. "Premier Chou Visits Tanzania," 6.
107. "China-Tanzania Joint Communique," *Peking Review* 8, no. 24 (11 June 1965): 7.
108. For example, Nyerere paid tribute to the Long March during a state banquet honoring visiting Zhou on 4 June 1965. For an extract of his speech, see Julius K. Nyerere, *Freedom and Socialism: A Selection from Writings and Speeches, 1965–67* (Dar es Salaam, Tanzania: Oxford University Press, 1968), 33–34.
109. "The Week: Chairman Mao Receives Tanzania Women's Delegation," *Peking Review* 8, no. 27 (2 July 1965): 3.
110. "The Week: Tanzanian Women's Delegation Leaves for Home," *Peking Review* 8, no. 28 (9 July 1965): 4.
111. "The Week: Tanzanian Women's Delegation from Zanzibar," *Peking Review* 8, no. 30 (23 July 1965): 16.
112. "The Week: Chairman Mao Meets Women's Delegation from Zanzibar," *Peking Review* 8, no. 31 (30 July 1965): 3.
113. "The Week: Madame Karume Leaves Peking," *Peking Review* 8, no. 32 (6 August 1965): 4. On 3 August the delegation left Beijing for Shanghai.
114. In this book, the term Tan-Zam railway is used in lieu of the more contemporary TAZARA, as the latter refers to the Tanzania-Zambia Railway Authority, a specific administrative entity that was not present in the 1960s or 1970s.
115. Lawrence Fellows, "China May Build Africa Railroad," *New York Times*, 22 September 1965, 1.
116. Donald H. Louchheim, "Zambia Wants New Railway as Lifeline," *Washington Post*, 7 September 1965, A14.
117. Fellows, "China May Build Africa Railroad," 2.
118. "Welcome to Vice President Kawawa," *Peking Review* 8, no. 48 (26 November 1965): 13.
119. Central Intelligence Agency, *A Reassessment of Julius Nyerere*, 3.
120. Clayton, *The Zanzibar Revolution*, 135.
121. Ogunsanwo, *China's Policy in Africa*, 197.
122. The *Nationalist* cited in "The Week: Imperialist-Instigated Coups Strengthen African Solidarity," *Peking Review* 9, no. 12 (18 March 1966): 3–4.
123. Drew Middleton, "Ivory Coast Head Calls China Peril," 17.
124. "A.A.J.A. Secretariat Meets in Peking," 13, 15.
125. "The Week: Tanzania's National Day," *Peking Review* 9, no. 18 (29 April 1966): 4.
126. Cited from NCNA, 22 May 1966, in Ogunsanwo, *China's Policy in Africa*, 202–203.
127. "The Week: Tanzanian Economic Delegation Visits Peking," *Peking Review* 9, no. 24 (10 June 1966): 31.
128. "The Week: Tanzanian Minister Ends Visit," *Peking Review* 9, no. 25 (17 June 1966) ["We in Tanzania" (4)]. The delegation also spent three days in Shanghai before departing China on 12 June.
129. Cited from NCNA, 18 June 1966, in Ogunsanwo, *China's Policy in Africa*, 198. Wei described the event in this manner: "Peking came to the rescue in June, 1966, offering an interest-free loan of two million pounds ($5.6 million) and a grant of 1 million pounds ($2.8 million)." Wei Liang-Tsai, *Peking versus Taipei in Africa*, 212.
130. "Tanzania and China to Start Ship Line," *New York Times*, 8 July 1966, 17.

131. Ogunsanwo, *China's Policy in Africa*, 199. Blake referred to the shipping line as "largely symbolic." Alex Blake, "Peking's African Adventures," *Current Scene 5*, no. 15 (15 September 1967): 6.
132. "Textile Mill Stone Laid," *Washington Post*, 31 July 1966, A10.
133. Ogunsanwo, *China's Policy in Africa*, 212–213.
134. "Tanganyikans to Visit Peking," *New York Times*, 26 September 1966, 3.
135. "Police Chief on Tour," *Washington Post*, 12 October 1966, A6.
136. "Round the World: Youth in Tanzania: A Clean Sweep!," *Peking Review* 9, no. 44 (28 October 1966): 39.
137. "Round the World: Tanzania: Answering Imperialist Provocation," *Peking Review* 9, no. 46 (11 November 1966): 39.
138. Along the same lines, from 2 to 6 December 1966 the Congress of the AATUF was held in Dar es Salaam. Trade unionists from approximately thirty African countries attended. Due to the military coup in Ghana, the AATUF's headquarters was moved from Accra to Dar es Salaam. At a press conference on 8 December, the general secretary of the AATUF declared that the AATUF would stand firm in the struggle against imperialism and colonialism and would give unstinted support to all revolutionary forces in order to speed up the African revolution—which was certainly in Chinese interests. "Round the World: A.A.T.U.F. Congress: U.S. Imperialist Aggression Condemned," *Peking Review* 9, no. 51 (16 December 1966): 38–39.
139. "Tanzania Radio Station," *Washington Post*, 10 December 1966, A2.
140. Ogunsanwo, *China's Policy in Africa*, 202.
141. Girish Mathur, *China in Africa* (New Delhi: Kalamkar Prakashan, 1978), 23 "the UNITA" (23).
142. Ogunsanwo, *China's Policy in Africa*, 206.
143. Ibid., 204.
144. "An Unusual Gift," *Peking Review* 11, no. 11 (15 March 1968): 36.
145. "Joint Communique of the People's Republic of China and the Republic of Zambia," *Peking Review* 10, no. 17 (30 June 1967): 12.
146. Blake, "Peking's African Adventures," 4.
147. According to BBC summary of week broadcasts cited in Ogunsanwo, *China's Policy in Africa*, 207.
148. "The Week: Agreement on Construction of Tanzania-Zambia Railway Signed in Peking," *Peking Review* 10, no. 38 (15 September 1967): 39.
149. A human interest story involving Chinese-Tanzanian relations: In August 1966 a Chinese hydraulic engineer named Chang Min-tsai arrived in Tanzania. He was part of a Chinese group of experts working on the Kidunda water conservancy project on the Ruvu River. As he was surveying the river's lower reaches, in October 1967, he was stung and poisoned by wasps, and he subsequently died. He was buried in a cemetery in Dar es Salaam. "Wholeheartedly Serving the People Of the World—Chinese Aid Personnel Abroad," *Peking Review* 11, no. 11 (15 March 1968): 35. Chang was stung on 4 October and died on 8 October. "'The Best Friends of the African People'—Chinese Foreign Aid Personnel in Tanzania," *Peking Review* 11, no. 27 (5 July 1968): 27.

CHAPTER 11. RAILWAY TO FRIENDSHIP

1. Anthony Astrachan, "Proposed Tanzam Railway Becomes an African Issue," *Washington Post*, 16 November 1967, F1.
2. Anthony Astrachan, "Zambia Threatened at 5 Border Points," *Washington Post*, 5 November 1967, A22.

3. Stanley Meisler, "China's Foothold in Tanzania," *Washington Post*, 23 June 1968, H12.
4. CIA, *Drawings on Communist Economic Aid*, 1, 3–4 ["economic technicians" (1)].
5. "Red China to Aid Rail Project," *New York Times*, 9 April 1968, 5.
6. "The Week: China, Tanzania and Zambia Sign Three Protocols for Construction of Tanzania–Zambia Railway," *Peking Review* 11, no. 16 (19 April 1968): 26.
7. "China Aid to Tanzania," *Washington Post*, 29 April 1968, A3.
8. "Tanzanian Ambassador Gives National Day Reception," *Peking Review* 11, no. 18 (3 May 1968): 8, 29.
9. Fellows, "Chinese Communist Presence in East African Nations Grows," 2. The 150 additional Chinese engineers that arrived in Dar es Salaam were the final team to survey the railroad. The survey was expected to take fifteen months and construction seven or eight years. From May 1968 on, Chinese engineers and technical personnel in charge of survey and design arrived in Tanzania and Zambia in groups. "Friendship Fostered in Hard Struggle," *Peking Review* 12, no. 43 (24 October 1969): 33.
10. "African Newsletter: Tanzania Develops Its Own Industry," *Peking Review* 16, no. 2 (12 January 1973): 23.
11. Fellows, "Chinese Communist Presence in East African Nations Grows" ["The Tanzanians," "Of enormous imporance" (2)].
12. Central Intelligence Agency, *The New Look in Chinese Communist Aid to Sub-Saharan Africa*, Intelligence Memorandum, September 1968, 3.
13. "President Nyerere Arrives in Peking," *Peking Review* 11, no. 25 (21 June 1968): 3–4.
14. Ogunsanwo, *China's Policy in Africa*, 204. President Nyerere was scheduled to be in China from 18 to 21 June. "Tanzanian to Visit Red China," *New York Times*, 3 June 1968, 11. On 22 June, President Nyerere's delegation left Beijing for North Korea. "President Nyerere's Visit to China," *Peking Review* 11, no. 26 (28 June 1968): 5.
15. Meisler, "China's Foothold in Tanzania," H12.
16. "Tanzanian, Zambian, Chinese Government Representatives Inspect Survey Work on Tanzanian Section of Tanzania–Zambia Railway," *Peking Review* 11, no. 45 (8 November 1968): 27.
17. The civilian side of the project was known as Project Courier. Central Intelligence Agency, *The Current Disarray in Zanzibar*, Intelligence Memorandum, 2 December 1968, 7 ["Mainland Tanzania" (1), "The Chinese" (6)].
18. The following is based on radio reports in Zanzibar and Beijing, as well as BBC weekly supplement reports. Ogunsanwo, *China's Policy in Africa*, 203.
19. All Chinese ambassadors in Africa were recalled except for one during the Cultural Revolution. The one exception was Huang Hua in Cairo. In 1968 the PRC was also back in Africa to support the Biafra movement in Nigeria. China reportedly transferred arms to Biafra from arms depots in Dar es Salaam via Luanda. "Communist Chinese Propaganda and Africa." Snow perceived a different Chinese approach in Africa after the Cultural Revolution: "Fresh waves of Chinese diplomats were hurried back to the continent to spread the new message. A particular effort was made to concentrate them in the region most troubling to Peking's strategists, the western Indian Ocean and the East African coast. Forty to fifty envoys were assigned to the single island of Mauritius: in the Comoro islands, between Mozambique and Madagascar, Chinese diplomats maintained in the mid-seventies the only embassy of any major power." Snow, *The Star Raft*, 122. In fact, Mauritius is east of Madagascar. The Cultural Revolution did not substantially alter China's approach in Africa, though the number of its personnel may have diminished.
20. "The Week: 5th Anniversary of Zanzibar Revolution Celebrated," *Peking Review* 12, no. 3 (17 January 1969): 3.

21. "The Week: Tanzania Ambassador Gives National Day Reception," *Peking Review* 12, no. 19 (5 May 1969): 49.
22. Anthony Astrachan, "Tanzania's Socialist 'Revolution' Is Blend of Many Cultures," *Washington Post*, 10 March 1969, A9.
23. According to BBC and Chinese sources cited in Ogunsanwo, *China's Policy in Africa*, 251.
24. "Peking Aide Seen in Interim Role," *New York Times*, 15 June 1969, 4.
25. "Chinese Arrive in Tanzania," *New York Times*, 18 August 1969, 2.
26. "The Week: Chinese, Tanzanian, Zambian Governments Sign Supplementary Agreement on Tanzanian—Zambian Railway," *Peking Review* 12, no. 48 (28 November 1969): 4.
27. "Tanzanian Defense Chinese Rail Aid," *New York Times*, 23 November 1969, 23.
28. C. C. Miniclier, "Dealings with Peking Defended by Nyerere," *Washington Post*, 19 November 1969, A24.
29. Wei Liang-Tsai, *Peking versus Taipei in Africa*, 213.
30. "Communist Chinese Propaganda and Africa," 18.
31. Thus, the following report is misleading: Tillman Durdin, "Cultural Revolution Led to Diplomatic Isolation," *New York Times*, 14 October 1970, 20.
32. Eugene K. Keefe, "National Security," in *Tanzania: A Country Study*, ed. Irving Kaplan, 237–269 (Washington, DC: Foreign Area Studies, American University, 1978), 256 ["the PRC was" (256)].
33. "African Newsletter: Tanzania Develops Its Own Industry," 23; Wei Liang-Tsai, *Peking versus Taipei in Africa*, 213.
34. Wei Liang-Tsai, *Peking versus Taipei in Africa*, 213–214.
35. "The Week: Tanzanian Military Delegation Visits China," *Peking Review* 13, no. 45 (6 November 1970): 29.
36. "The Week: Tanzanian Ambassador to China Gives National Day Reception," *Peking Review* 13, no. 18 (30 April 1970): 30.
37. "2 African Teams in Peking," *New York Times* 6 July 1970, 4; Ogunsanwo, *China's Policy in Africa*, 252.
38. "Tanzanian Government Delegation and Zambian Government Delegation Visit China," *Peking Review* 13, no. 29 (17 July 1970): 16.
39. Charles Mohr, "Kaunda Leads Tanzam Rail Ceremonies," *New York Times*, 27 October 1970, 2.
40. "Chairman Mao and Vice-Chairman Lin Meet Tanzanian and Zambian Government Delegation," *Peking Review* 13, no. 29 (17 July 1970): 4.
41. "Long Foreign Trip by Chou Expected," *New York Times*, 18 August 1970, 5.
42. "Tanzania–Zambia Railway: A Bridge to China?," *New York Times*, 29 January 1971, 65.
43. Mohr, "Kaunda Leads Tanzam Rail Ceremonies," 2.
44. "Tanzania–Zambia Railway: A Bridge to China?," 65.
45. Julius K. Nyerere, *Freedom and Development: A Selection from Writings and Speeches, 1968–73* (London: Oxford University Press, 1974), 239.
46. "The Week: Vice-Chairman Tung and Premier Chou Congratulate President Nyerere of Tanzania on His Re-election," *Peking Review* 13, no. 46 (13 November 1970): 4.
47. Cited from the *Africa Record*, December 1970 in Clayton, *The Zanzibar Revolution*, 149.
48. Ibid., 149n76. Howe reported the figure to be between four hundred and five hundred Chinese in Zanzibar. Marvin Howe, "Zanzibar, Though Heavily Dependent

on Chinese Communist Aid, Maintains Independent Policies," *New York Times*, 23 September 1970, 10.
49. Ibid.
50. "The Week: Tanzanian Ambassador to China Gives Reception," *Peking Review* 14, no. 4 (22 January 1971): 3.
51. "The Week: 6th Anniversary of Sino-Tanzanian Friendship Treaty Celebrated," *Peking Review* 14, no. 9 (26 February 1971): 17.
52. "Tanzania–Zambia Railway: A Bridge to China?," 65.
53. Mathur, *China in Africa*, 24.
54. William Borders, "China Quietly Renewing an Active Role in Africa," *New York Times*, 9 April 1971, 1.
55. "The Week: 6th Anniversary of Sino-Tanzanian Friendship Treaty Celebrated," 17.
56. "The Week: Tanzanian Ambassador Gives Reception," *Peking Review* 14, no. 18 (30 April 1971): 3.
57. "Albania, Algeria and 16 Other Countries," 6.
58. Borders, "China Quietly Renewing an Active Role," 15.
59. Central Intelligence Agency, *Communist Economic Aid Extensions and Technical Assistance to Selected African Countries*, Memorandum for the Defense Intelligence Agency, 20 January 1972, 2.
60. Borders, "China Quietly Renewing an Active Role" ["advising the army," "concentrating" (15)].
61. "Friendship Log: Tanzania–Zambia Railway," *Peking Review* 15, no. 1 (7 January 1972): 21; Ogunsanwo, *China's Policy in Africa*, 252. Curiously, Mathur also mentioned the following: "Once again Savimbi [of UNITA] received the signal from Peking, and the explosions on the railway line from Zambia to Angolan port of Lobito were resumed. Zambia was faced with the choice of either allowing its copper exports to dry up or agreeing to the continuance of Chinese workers." Mathur, *China in Africa*, 24.
62. "Friendship Log: Tanzania–Zambia Railway," 21.
63. "The Week: Tanganyika's Independence Anniversary Saluted," *Peking Review* 14, no. 51 (17 December 1971): 3.
64. "The Week: News Briefs," *Peking Review* 14, no. 52 (24 December 1971): 18.
65. Wei Liang-Tsai, *Peking versus Taipei in Africa*, 214.
66. Ibid.
67. "The Week: Tanzania Goodwill Delegation in Peking," *Peking Review* 15, no. 35 (1 September 1972): 4, 22.
68. The delegation also visited Shijiazhuang and Shanghai. Ibid., 22.
69. Clayton, *The Zanzibar Revolution*, 152.
70. Wei Liang-Tsai, *Peking versus Taipei in Africa*, 205n63.
71. "The Week: Condolence on Karume's Death," *Peking Review* 15, no. 15 (14 April 1972): 3.
72. "The Week: Guests from Tanzania," *Peking Review* 15, no. 22 (2 June 1972): 3.
73. Wei Liang-Tsai, *Peking versus Taipei in Africa*, 214.
74. "The Week: Guests from Tanzania," 4.
75. "Red Onslaught on Southern Africa," *Bulletin of the Africa Institute of South Africa* 10, no. 9 (October 1972): 358–359 ["undoubtedly Peking's," "Chinese merchant ships" (358), "prominent in the training" (359)].
76. "Friendship Log: Friendly Co-operation," *Peking Review* 15, no. 50 (15 December 1972): 21. Chamwino was the Swahili name of a village in the Dodoma region of central Tanzania.

77. "The Week: News Briefs," *Peking Review* 15, no. 52 (29 December 1972): 4.
78. "The Week: Tanzanian Visitors," *Peking Review* 16, no. 5 (2 February 1973): 5, 13.
79. C. F. de Villiers, "China's Decade in Africa," *Bulletin of the Africa Institute of South Africa* 11, no. 8 (September 1973): 300.
80. Larkin, "Chinese Aid in Political Context," 18.
81. "Zambia Seeks More Control of Copper," *New York Times*, 1 September 1973, 33.
82. Wei Liang-Tsai, *Peking versus Taipei in Africa*, 214.
83. "Round the World: Tanzania: U.S. Fleet in Indian Ocean Protested," *Peking Review* 17, no. 7 (15 February 1974): 20 ["thirty thousand" (20)].
84. H. Mark Roth, "The Political System," in Iving Kaplan, ed., *Tanzania: A Country Study* (Washington, DC: Foreign Area Studies, American University, 1978), 122.
85. Wei Liang-Tsai, *Peking versus Taipei in Africa*, 215.
86. "The Week: Chairman Mao Meets President Nyerere," *Peking Review* 17, no. 13 (29 March 1974): 3.
87. "At Banquet Welcoming President Nyerere: Premier Chou's Speech," *Peking Review* 17, no. 13 (29 March 1974): 8.
88. "The Week: President Nyerere Ends Visit to China," *Peking Review* 17, no. 14 (5 April 1974): 7.
89. Anderson, "Secret Agent Diplomacy." The Soviet Union was also cited as a supporter of guerrilla movements.
90. Wei cited a BBC news source. Wei Liang-Tsai, *Peking versus Taipei in Africa*, 215.
91. Ibid.
92. Central Intelligence Agency, *Communist Economic and Military Aid to Africa*, Memorandum, 18 February 1976, 1–2, 5.
93. Legum, *Africa Contemporary Record*, C189.
94. "The Week: Talks on Tanzania–Zambia Railway," *Peking Review* 18, no. 39 (26 September 1974): 9.
95. "Tanzania–Zambia Railway: Tracklaying Completed and Trial Run Starts," *Peking Review* 18, no. 44 (31 October 1974): 19 ["This achievement" (20)].
96. "The Week: Vice Premier Sun Chien Returns from Zambia and Tanzania," *Peking Review* 19, no. 32–33 (9 August 1976): 4.
97. Tansky, "China's Foreign Aid," 2n2.
98. "Profound Mourning for Passing," 57.

CONCLUSION
1. Chris Alden, Daniel Large, and Ricardo Soares de Oliveira, "Introduction: China Returns to Africa," in Alden et al., *China Returns to Africa*, 24.
2. Algeria was the third largest until the split of Sudan and creation of South Sudan in July 2011.
3. Houphoet-Boigny quoted in Drew Middleton, "Tanzanian Denies Peking Influence," *New York Times*, 17 March 1966, 17.
4. Villiers viewed Africa in a realist perspective. C. F. de Villiers, "China's Decade in Africa," 302.
5. Taylor, "China's Foreign Policy towards Africa in the 1990s," 460.
6. Chang Ya-chun, *Chinese Communist Activities in Africa*, 12.
7. Richard Eder, "Peking's Frustration," *New York Times*, 16 August 1965, 8.
8. Tansky wrote the following about objectives of Chinese aid: "Chinese aid to the Third World countries has been dispensed in order to establish and expand Peking's influence, to purvey Communist ideology and support radical regimes, and to under-

mine Western and, in recent years, Soviet influence." Tansky, "China's Foreign Aid," 1. In the author's view, Tansky's first objective subsumes the latter objectives.
9. Zartman, "Tiger in the Jungle," 1.
10. Hutchison, *China's Africa Revolution*, 106.
11. Legum, "Africa and China: Symbolism and Substance" ["To achieve maximum" (416), "Whenever possible" (413)].
12. Zartman, "Tiger in the Jungle," 5.
13. "Communist Chinese Propaganda and Africa," 16.
14. Legum, "Africa and China: Symbolism and Substance," 412.
15. Ibid.
16. "Communist Chinese Propaganda and Africa," 28.
17. Central Intelligence Agency, *Ministry of Foreign Affairs Directive Citing Mistakes Committed by Embassies in the Conduct of Propaganda*, Intelligence Information Cable, 6 September 1968, 2.
18. "China's Aid to Africa,"275. The quote was an unattributed article in the appendix.
19. For example, "The difference between Chinese operations in Latin America and Africa is that in Latin America Chinese efforts are concentrated mainly on the local Communist parties." Ernst Halperin, "Peking and the Latin American Communists," *China Quarterly*, no. 29 (January–March 1967): 115.
20. Chang Ya-chun, *Chinese Communist Activities in Africa*, 1.
21. Director of Central Intelligence, *Communist China's Foreign Policy*, National Intelligence Estimate Number 13–9-65, 5 May 1965, 11.
22. Legum, "Africa and China: Symbolism and Substance," 416.
23. "Communist Chinese Propaganda and Africa," 20.
24. Central Intelligence Agency, *Implications of Growing Communist Influence in URTZ*, 12.
25. Colin S. Gray, "The Coast Guard and Navy: It's Time for a 'National Fleet,'" *Naval War College Review* LIV, no. 3 (Summer 2001): 125.
26. Halperin, "Peking and the Latin American Communists," 111.
27. CIA, *The Current Disarray in Zanzibar*, Intelligence Memorandum, 2 December 1968, 6.
28. Childs, "The New Entry in Africa: China," A14.
29. For contemporary PRC Africa policy, see *China's African Policy* (Beijing: Information Office of the State Council, People's Republic of China, January 2006) and *China-Africa Economic and Trade Cooperation* (Beijing: Information Office of the State Council, People's Republic of China, December 2010).

BIBLIOGRAPHY

BOOKS, MONOGRAPHS, AND EDITED VOLUMES

Addona, A. F. *The Organization of African Unity*. Cleveland, OH: World Publishing, 1969.

Adie, W. A. C. "Chinese Policy towards Africa." In *The Soviet Bloc, China and Africa*, edited by Sven Hamrell and Carl Gösta Widstrand, 43–63. Uppsala: Scandinavian Institute of African Studies, 1964.

Alden, Chris. *China in Africa: Partner, Competitor or Hegemon?* London: Zed Books, 2007.

Alden, Chris, Daniel Large, and Ricardo Soares de Oliveira, eds. *China Returns to Africa: A Rising Power and a Continent Embrace*. New York: Columbia University Press, 2008.

———. "Introduction: China Returns to Africa." In *China Returns to Africa: A Rising Power and a Continent Embrace*, edited by Chris Alden, Daniel Large, and Ricardo Soares de Oliveira, 1–26. New York: Columbia University Press, 2008.

Berry, LaVerle, ed. *Ghana: A Country Study*. Washington, DC: Federal Research Division, Library of Congress, 1995.

Beuchard, Georges. *L'Equivoque algérienne*. Paris: Nourvelles Editions Debresse, 1949.

Bozeman, Adda B. "Knowledge and Method in Comparative Intelligence Studies of Non-Western Societies." In *Strategic Intelligence and Statecraft: Selected Essays*, edited by Adda B. Bozeman, 180–212. Washington, DC: Brassey's, 1992.

Brautigam, Deborah. *The Dragon's Gift: The Real Story of China in Africa*. New York: Oxford University Press, 2011.

Brzezinski, Zbigniew, ed. *Africa and the Communist World*. Stanford, CA: Stanford University Press, 1963.

Chande, Abdin. "Radicalism and Reform in East Africa." In *The History of Islam in Africa*, edited by Nehemia Levtzion and Randall L. Pouwels, 349–370. Athens, OH: Ohio University Press, 2000.

Chang Ya-chun. *Chinese Communist Activities in Africa—Policies and Challenges*. Taipei, Republic of China: World Anti-Communist League and Asian Peoples' Anti-Communist League, 1981.

Chao, Howard H. S. *Story without End: A Chinese Diplomat Escapes*. Hong Kong: Phoenix Press, 1965.

Chau, Donovan C. "The French-Algerian War: Communist China's Support for Independence." In *Military Advising and Assistance, 1815–2007: From Mercenaries to Privatization*, edited by Donald Stoker, 111–26. London: Routledge Press, 2008.

———. *Global Security Watch—Kenya*. Santa Barbara, CA: Praeger, 2010.

"China's Aid to Africa." In *Chinese and Soviet Aid to Africa*, edited by Warren Weinstein, 275–283. New York: Praeger, 1975.

Chou En-lai [Zhou Enlai]. "Political Report, 30 January 1956." In *The People's Republic of China 1949–1979: A Documentary Survey*, edited by Harold C. Hinton, 294–306. Wilmington, DE: Scholarly Resources, 1980.

———. "Report to National People's Congress on the International Situation, 30 July 1955." In *The People's Republic of China 1949–1979: A Documentary Survey*, edited by Harold C. Hinton, 180–184. Wilmington, DE: Scholarly Resources, 1980.

Clausewitz, Carl von, *On War*, trans. Michael Howard and Peter Paret. Princeton: Princeton University Press, 1976.

Clayton, Anthony. *The Zanzibar Revolution and Its Aftermath*. Hamden, CT: Archon Books, 1981.

"Common Program of the Chinese People's Political Consultative Conference, 29 September 1949." In *The People's Republic of China 1949–1979: A Documentary Survey*, edited by Harold C. Hinton, 51–55. Wilmington, DE: Scholarly Resources, 1980.

Communist China in Africa. Taipei, Republic of China: Asian Peoples' Anti-Communist League, 1961.

Cooley, John K. *East Wind over Africa: Red China's African Offensive*. New York: Walker and Company, 1965.

Creel, Herrlee G. *The Origins of Statecraft in China: The Western Chou Empire*, vol. 1. Chicago: University of Chicago Press, 1970.

Crozier, Brian, ed. *"We Will Bury You": Studies in Left-Wing Subversion Today*. London: Tom Stacey, 1970.

Curran, James C. *Communist China in Black Africa: The Tan-Zam Railway, 1965–1970*. Carlisle, PA: U.S. Army War College, 26 April 1971.

Deshpande, G. P., and H. K. Gupta. *United Front against Imperialism: China's Foreign Policy in Africa*. Bombay: Somaiya Publications, 1986.

Dube, Emmannuel M. "Relations between Liberation Movements and the O.A.U." In *Essays on the Liberation of Southern Africa*, edited by N. M. Shamuyarira, 25–68. Dar es Salaam: Tanzania Publishing House, 1971.

Dulles, Allen. *The Craft of Intelligence*. Westport, CT: Greenwood Press, 1977.

Eisenman, Joshua, Eric Heginbotham, and Derek Mitchell, eds. *China and the Developing World: Beijing's Strategy for the Twenty-First Century*. Armonk, NY: M. E. Sharpe, 2007.

Entelis, John P., and Lisa Arone. "Government and Politics." In *Algeria: A Country Study*, edited by Helen Chapin Metz, 173–234. Washington, DC: Federal Research Division, Library of Congress, 1994.

Fage, J. D. *A History of West Africa: An Introductory Survey*. Cambridge, UK: Cambridge University Press, 1969.

Fage, J. D., and Roland Oliver, eds. *The Cambridge History of Africa*, vol. 7. Cambridge, UK: Cambridge University Press, 1986,

Farwell, Byron. *The Great War in Africa, 1914–1918*. New York: W. W. Norton & Company, 1986.

Favrod, Charles-Henri. *Le F.L.N. et l'Algérie*. Paris: Plon, 1962.

Feng Chih-tan. *Glimpses of West Africa*. Beijing: Foreign Languages Press, 1963.

Gibson, Richard. *African Liberation Movements: Contemporary Struggles against White Minority Rule*. New York: Oxford University Press, 1972.

Harris, Gordon. *Organization of African Unity*. Vol. 7. New Brunswick, NJ: Transaction Publishers, 1994.

Heggoy, Alf Andrew. *Insurgency and Counterinsurgency in Algeria*. Bloomington, IN: Indiana University Press, 1972.

Hevi, Emmanuel John. *The Dragon's Embrace: The Chinese Communists and Africa.* London: Pall Mall Press, 1967.
Hinton, Harold C., ed., *The People's Republic of China 1949–1979: A Documentary Survey.* Wilmington, DE: Scholarly Resources, 1980.
Horne, Alistair. *A Savage War of Peace: Algeria 1954–1962.* New York: Viking Press, 1977.
Hutchison, Alan. *China's Africa Revolution.* Boulder, CO: Westview Press, 1976.
Ingham, Kenneth. *A History of East Africa.* New York: Praeger, 1965.
Kahin, George McTurnan. *The Asian-African Conference: Bandung, Indonesia, April 1955.* Ithaca, NY: Cornell University Press, 1956.
Keefe, Eugene K. "National Security." In *Tanzania: A Country Study*, edited by Irving Kaplan, 237–269. Washington, DC: Foreign Area Studies, American University, 1978.
Kelly, George A. "Revolutionary Warfare and Psychological Action." In *Modern Guerrilla Warfare: Fighting Communist Guerilla Movements, 1941–1961*, edited by Franklin Mark Osanka, 425–438. New York: Free Press, 1962.
Kintner, William R. *The Front Is Everywhere: Militant Communism in Action.* Norman, OK: University of Oklahoma Press, 1950.
Larkin, Bruce D. *China and Africa, 1949–1970: The Foreign Policy of the People's Republic of China.* Berkeley: University of California Press, 1971.
———. "Chinese Aid in Political Context: 1971–1973." In *Chinese and Soviet Aid to Africa*, edited by Warren Weinstein, 1–28. New York: Praeger, 1975.
Lefever, Ernest W. *Spear and Scepter: Army, Police, and Politics in Tropical Africa.* Washington, DC: Brookings Institution, 1970.
Legum, Colin. "Africa and China: Symbolism and Substance." In *Policies toward China: Views from Six Continents*, edited by A. M. Halpern, 389–436. New York: Council on Foreign Relations, 1965.
———, ed. *Africa Contemporary Record: Annual Survey and Documents, 1977–78.* New York: African Publishing, 1979.
———. "Socialism in Ghana: A Political Interpretation." In *African Socialism*, edited by William H. Friedland and Carl Rosberg. Stanford, CA: Stanford University Press, 1964.
Listowel, Judith. *The Making of Tanganyika.* New York: London House & Maxwell, 1965.
Liu Shao-chi [Shaoqi]. *Internationalism and Nationalism.* Beijing: Foreign Languages Press, 1954.
———. "Report on the Work of the Central Committee." In *The People's Republic of China 1949–1979: A Documentary Survey*, edited by Harold C. Hinton, 360–388. Wilmington, DE: Scholarly Resources, 1980.
———. "Report to the Trade Union Conference of the Asian and Australasian Countries, 16 November 1949." In *The People's Republic of China 1949–1979: A Documentary Survey*, edited by Harold C. Hinton, 120–123. Wilmington, DE: Scholarly Resources, 1980.
Lowenthal, Richard. "China." In *Africa and the Communist World*, edited by Zbigniew Brzezinski, 142–203. Stanford, CA: Stanford University Press, 1963.
Mao Tse-tung [Zedong]. *Guerrilla Warfare.* Translated by Samuel B. Griffith. London: Cassell & Company, 1962.
———. *On New Democracy.* Beijing: Foreign Languages Press, 1960.
———. *On People's Democratic Dictatorship.* Beijing: Foreign Languages Press, 1950.
———. "On Protracted War." In *Selected Works of Mao Tse-tung*, vol. 1, 113–194. Beijing: Foreign Languages Press, 1975.
———. *On The Ten Major Relationships.* Beijing: Foreign Languages Press, 1977.
———. "Opening Speech to the Eighth Party Congress, 15 September 1956." In *The

People's Republic of China 1949–1979: A Documentary Survey, edited by Harold C. Hinton, 359–360. Wilmington, DE: Scholarly Resources, 1980.

———. "Problems of Strategy in China's Revolutionary War." In *Selected Works of Mao Tse-tung*, vol. 1, 179–254. Beijing: Foreign Languages Press, 1975.

Mathur, Girish. *China in Africa*. New Delhi: Kalamkar Prakashan, 1978.

McLaughlin, James L., and David Owusu-Ansah. "Historical Setting." In *Ghana: A Country Study*, edited by LaVerle Berry, 1–58. Washington, DC: Federal Research Division, Library of Congress, 1995.

Metz, Helen Chapin, ed. *Algeria: A Country Study*. Washington, DC: Federal Research Division, Library of Congress, 1994.

Nelsen, Harvey W. *The Chinese Military System: An Organizational Study of the Chinese People's Liberation Army*. Boulder, CO: Westview Press, 1981.

Neuhauser, Charles. *Third World Politics: China and the Afro-Asia People's Solidarity Organization, 1957–1967*. Cambridge, MA: Harvard University Press, 1968.

Nkrumah, Kwame. *Ghana: The Autobiography of Kwame Nkrumah*. New York: Nelson, 1957.

———. *Handbook on Revolutionary Warfare: A Guide to the Armed Phase of the African Revolution*. New York: International Publishers, 1969.

———. *I Speak of Freedom: A Statement of African Ideology*. New York: Praeger, 1961.

Nyerere, Julius K. *Freedom and Development: A Selection from Writings and Speeches, 1968–73*. London: Oxford University Press, 1974.

———. *Freedom and Socialism: A Selection from Writings and Speeches, 1965–67*. Dar es Salaam, Tanzania: Oxford University Press, 1968.

———. *Freedom and Unity: A Selection from Writings and Speeches, 1952–65*. Dar es Salaam, Tanzania: Oxford University Press, 1966.

Ofcansky, Thomas P. "National Security." In *Ghana: A Country Study*, edited by LaVerle Berry, 255–304. Washington, DC: Federal Research Division, Library of Congress, 1995.

Ogunsanwo, Alaba. *China's Policy in Africa 1958–71*. London: Cambridge University Press, 1974.

Okello, John. *Revolution in Zanzibar*. Nairobi, Kenya: East African Institute Press, 1967.

Othman, Haroub, ed. *Babu: I Saw the Future and It Works*. Dar es Salaam, Tanzania: E & D Limited, 2001.

Owusu, Maxwell. "Government and Politics." In *Ghana: A Country Study*, edited by LaVerle Berry, 101–254. Washington, DC: Federal Research Division, Library of Congress, 1995.

Passin, Herbert. *China's Cultural Diplomacy*. New York: Praeger, 1963.

Pye, Lucian W, *Asian Power and Politics: The Cultural Dimensions of Authority*. Cambridge, MA: Harvard University Press, 1985.

Quandt, William B. *Revolution and Political Leadership: Algeria, 1954–1968*. Cambridge: Massachusetts Institute of Technology Press, 1969.

Richelson, Jeffrey T. *Foreign Intelligence Organizations*. Cambridge, MA: Ballinger, 1988.

Rotberg, Robert I. "China's Quest for Resources, Opportunities, and Influence in Africa." In *China into Africa: Trade, Aide, and Influence*, edited by Robert I. Rotberg, 1–20. Cambridge, MA: World Peace Foundation, 2008.

Rotberg, Robert I., ed. *China into Africa: Trade, Aid, and Influence*. Cambridge, MA: World Peace Foundation, 2008.

Roth, H. Mark. "The Political System." In *Tanzania: A Country Study*, edited by Irving Kaplan, 85–136. Washington, DC: Foreign Area Studies, American University, 1978.

Ruedy, John. *Modern Algeria: The Origins and Development of a Nation*. Bloomington, IN: Indiana University Press, 1992.

Schatten, Fritz. *Afrika—Schwartz oder Rot?* München: R. Piper, 1961.
———. *Communism in Africa*. New York: Praeger, 1966.
Shinn, David H., and Joshua Eisenman. *China and Africa: A Century of Engagement*. Philadelphia: University of Pennsylvania Press, 2012.
Smaldone, Joseph P. "Soviet and Chinese Military Aid and Arms Transfers to Africa: A Contextual Analysis." In *Soviet and Chinese Aid to African Nations*, edited by Warren Weinstein and Thomas H. Henriksen, 76–116. New York: Praeger, 1980.
Snow, Philip. *The Star Raft: China's Encounter with Africa*. Ithaca, NY: Cornell University Press, 1988.
Stark, Christoph. *Die Aussenpolitik der Volksrepublik China in Afrika von 1969 bis 1983, under besonderer Berücksichtigung des südlichen Afrika*. Frankfurt: Peter Stark, 1990.
Talbott, John. *The War without a Name: France in Algeria, 1954–1962*. New York: Alfred A. Knopf, 1980.
Tartter, Jean R. "National Security." In *Algeria: A Country Study*, edited by Helen Chapin Metz, 235–284. Washington, DC: Federal Research Division, Library of Congress, 1994.
Taylor, Ian. *China and Africa: Engagement and Compromise*. London: Routledge, 2006.
———. *China's New Role in Africa*. Boulder, CO: Lynne Rienner, 2010.
Thompson, W. Scott. *Ghana's Foreign Policy 1957–1966*. Princeton, NJ: Princeton University Press, 1969.
Toth, Anthony. "Historical Setting." In *Algeria: A Country Study*, edited by Helen Chapin Metz, 1–66. Washington, DC: Federal Research Division, Library of Congress, 1994.
Van Slyke, Lyman P. *Enemies and Friends: The United Front in Chinese Communist History*. Stanford: Stanford University Press, 1967.
Waldron, Arthur, ed. *China in Africa*. Washington, DC: The Jamestown Foundation, 2008.
Wei Liang-Tsai. *Peking versus Taipei in Africa 1960–1978*. Taipei, ROC: Asia and World Institute, 1982.
Williams, David. "Front Organisations." In *"We Will Bury You": Studies in Left-Wing Subversion Today*, edited by Brian Crozier, 85–100. London: Tom Stacey, 1970.
Wise, David, and Thomas B. Ross. *The Espionage Establishment*. New York: Random House, 1967.
Wright, Richard. *The Color Curtain: A Report on the Bandung Conference*. New York: World Publishing, 1956.

JOURNAL ARTICLES
Adie, W. A. C. "China and the Bandung Genie." *Current Scene* 3, no. 19 (15 May 1965): 1–14.
Bass, Robert H. "Communist Fronts: Their History and Function." *Problems of Communism* 9, no. 5 (September-October 1960): 8–16.
Blake, Alex. "Peking's African Adventures." *Current Scene* 5, no. 15 (15 September 1967): 1–9.
Boorman, Howard L. "The Study of Contemporary Chinese Politics: Some Remarks on Retarded Development." *World Politics* 12, no. 4 (July 1960): 585–599.
Charles, David A. "The Dismissal of Marshal P'eng Teh-huai." *China Quarterly*, no. 8 (October–December 1961): 76.
Chau, Donovan C. "Assistance of a Different Kind: Chinese Political Warfare in Ghana, 1958–1966," *Comparative Strategy* 26, no. 2 (April-June 2007): 141–161.
"Chiang Kwei-lin, Hisn-hua-she Shih-erh nien [Twelve years with the New China News Agency]" (Taipei, ROC: Chen Shen Broadcasting Co., 1962). In "Ideology and Information: Correspondents of the New China News Agency and Chinese Foreign Policy Making," Alan P. L. Liu. *Journal of International Affairs* 26, no. 2 (1972): 134–135.

Coolidge, Archibald Cary. "The European Reconquest of North Africa." *American Historical Review* 17, no. 4 (July 1912): 723–734.

Dalton, John H. "Colony and Metropolis: Some Aspects of British Rule in Gold Coast and Their Implications for an Understanding of Ghana Today." *Journal of Economic History* 21, no. 4 (December 1961): 552–565.

Feit, Edward. "Military Coups and Political Development: Some Lessons from Ghana and Nigeria." *World Politics* 20, no. 2 (January 1968): 179–193.

Good, Robert C. "Changing Patterns of African International Relations." *American Political Science Review* 58, no. 3 (September 1964): 632–641.

Goody, Jack. "Consensus and Dissent in Ghana." *Political Science Quarterly* 83, no. 3 (September 1968): 337–352.

Gray, Colin S. "The Coast Guard and Navy: It's Time for a 'National Fleet.'" *Naval War College Review* LIV, no. 3 (Summer 2001): 112–137.

Grundy, Kenneth W. "Nkrumah's Theory of Underdevelopment: An Analysis of Recurrent Themes." *World Politics* 15, no. 3 (April 1963): 438–454.

Gurtov, Melvin. "Communist China's Foreign Aid Program." *Current History* 49, no. 289 (September 1965): 150–54, 181.

Halperin, Ernst. "Peking and the Latin American Communists." *China Quarterly*, no. 29 (Jan-Mar 1967): 111–154.

Halpern, A. M. "The Foreign Policy Uses of the Chinese Revolutionary Model." *China Quarterly*, no. 7 (July–September 1961): 1–16.

Holbrook, Wendell P. "British Propaganda and the Mobilization of the Gold Coast War Effort, 1939–1945." *Journal of African History* 26, no. 4 (1985): 347–361.

Holzer, Werner. "Die überschätzte 'Gelbe Gefahr': Der sowjetisch-chinesische Konkurrenzkampf um Afrika." *Afrika Heute*, no. 22 (15 November 1966): 325–327.

Ho Wei-Yang. "Die Politik der Chinesen in Afrika." *Aussenpolitik* 12, no. 3 (March 1961): 162–168.

Jackson, Steven F. "China's Third World Foreign Policy: The Case of Angola and Mozambique, 1961–93." *China Quarterly*, no. 142 (June 1995): 388–422.

Klein, Donald W. "Peking's Diplomats in Africa." *Current Scene* 2, no. 36 (1 July 1964): 1–9.

Legum, Colin. "The Soviet Union, China and the West in Southern Africa." *Foreign Affairs* 54, no. 4 (July 1976): 745–762.

Liu, Alan P. L. "Ideology and Information: Correspondents of the New China News Agency and Chinese Foreign Policy Making." *Journal of International Affairs* 26, no. 2 (1972): 131–145.

Markakis, John. "The Organisation of African Unity: A Progress Report." *Journal of Modern African Studies* 4, no. 2 (October 1966): 135–153.

Mazrui, Ali A. "Thoughts on Assassination in Africa." *Political Science Quarterly* 83, no. 1 (March 1968): 40–58.

"The New China News Agency: Mao's Messengers around the World." *Current Scene* 4, no. 7 (1 April 1966): 1–14.

Pipes, Richard. "Why the Soviet Union Thinks It Could Fight and Win a Nuclear War." *Commentary* 64, no. 1 (July 1977): 21–34.

Prybyla, Jan S. "Communist China's Economic Relations with Africa 1960–1964." *Asian Survey* 4, no. 11 (November 1964): 1135–43.

Pye, Lucian W. "Mao Tse-tung's Leadership Style." *Political Science Quarterly* 91, no. 2 (Summer 1976): 219–235.

"Red Onslaught on Southern Africa." *Bulletin of the Africa Institute of South Africa* 10, no. 9 (October 1972): 354–362.

Sacks, Milton. "The Strategy of Communism in Southeast Asia." *Pacific Affairs* 23, no. 3 (September 1950): 227–247.
Segal, Gerald, "China's Strategic Posture and the Great-Power Triangle." *Pacific Affairs* 53, no. 4 (Winter 1980–1981): 682-697.
Tansky, Leo. "China's Foreign Aid: The Record." *Current Scene* 10, no. 9 (September 1972): 1–11.
Taylor, Ian. "China's Foreign Policy towards Africa in the 1990s." *Journal of Modern African Studies* 36, no. 3 (September 1998): 443–460.
Thornton, Thomas Perry. "Peking, Moscow, and the Underdeveloped Areas," *World Politics* 13, no. 4 (July 1961): 491–504.
Tsou, Tang. "Mao Tse-tung and Peaceful Coexistence." *Orbis* 8, no. 1 (Spring 1964): 36–51.
Villiers, C. F. de. "China's Decade in Africa." *Bulletin of the Africa Institute of South Africa* 11, no. 8 (September 1973): 295–303.
Viorst, Milton. "Continental Freedom Struggle: Blackening Africa." *New Republic* 172, no. 15 (14 April 1975): 9–10.
Wang Chia-yu. "Peiping's 'New China News Agency' (NCNA)." *Issues and Studies* 2, no. 3 (December 1965): 7–16.
Yu, George T. "Africa in Chinese Foreign Policy." *Asian Survey* 28, no. 8 (August 1988): 849–862.
———. "China and the Third World." *Asian Survey* 17, no. 11 (November 1977): 1036–1048.
———. "China's Failure in Africa." *Asian Survey* 6, no. 8 (August 1966): 461–468.
———. "Peking versus Taipei in the World Arena: Chinese Competition in Africa." *Asian Survey* 3, no. 9 (September 1963): 439–453.
Zartman, William. "Tiger in the Jungle." *Current Scene* 2, no. 2 (6 August 1962): 1–11.

NEWSPAPERS AND MAGAZINES
"2 African Teams in Peking." *New York Times* 6 July 1970, 4.
"A.A.J.A. Secretariat Meets in Peking." *Peking Review* 9, no. 18 (29 April 1966): 12–15, 24.
"Africa Hears Red Chinese Propaganda." *Washington Post*, 31 May 1960, A7.
"African Assails China's Actions." *Washington Post*, 5 August 1965, A25.
"African Newsletter: Tanzania Develops Its Own Industry." *Peking Review* 16, no. 2 (12 January 1973): 17, 23.
"African Unrest." *New York Times*, 26 January 1964, E1.
"Africa's Revolutionary Tide Cannot Be Stemmed." *Peking Review* 9, no. 11 (11 March 1966): 9–11.
"Albania, Algeria and 16 Other Countries Table Draft Resolution at U.N." *Peking Review* 14, no. 35 (27 August 1971): 6–8.
"Algeria and China Renew Pact." *New York Times*, 4 June 1965, 10.
"Algeria and Peking Sign Cultural Pact." *New York Times*, 12 September 1963, 8.
"Algeria Backing U.N. Entry of the Chinese Communists." *New York Times*, 1 October 1962, 10.
"Algeria Becomes Independent." *Peking Review* 5, no. 28 (13 July 1962): 8–9.
"Algeria Signs Pact for Red China Arms." *New York Times*, 12 February 1965, 13.
"The Algerian People's Great Victory." *Peking Review* 5, no. 12 (23 March 1962): 5–7.
"Algeria's First National Day." *Peking Review* 5, no. 25 (9 November 1962): 22–23.
"Ambassador to U.S. Recalled by Tanzania." *Washington Post*, 15 February 1965, A9.
Anderson, David. "Small Countries Fear Taiwan War." *New York Times*, 25 September 1958, 6.

Anderson, Jack. "Secret Agent Diplomacy." *Washington Post*, 24 March 1974, C7.
"Ankrah Calls Nkrumah Africa's No. 1 Tyrant." *Washington Post*, 1 March 1966, A10.
"Apartheid Must Go." *Peking Review* 7, no. 16 (17 April 1964): 11–12.
"Asian-African Conference Closes." *Survey of China Mainland Press*, no. 1033 (23–25 April 1955): 9–10. Translated by the American consulate general in Hong Kong and originally published in *NCNA*, 24 April 1955.
Astrachan, Anthony. "Proposed Tanzam Railway Becomes an African Issue." *Washington Post*, 16 November 1967.
———. "Tanzania's Socialist 'Revolution' Is Blend of Many Cultures." *Washington Post*, 10 March 1969, A9.
———. "Zambia Threatened at 5 Border Points." *Washington Post*, 5 November 1967, A22.
"At Banquet Welcoming President Boumediene: Premier Chou's Speech." *Peking Review* 17, no. 10 (8 March 1974): 6–7.
"At Banquet Welcoming President Nyerere: Premier Chou's Speech." *Peking Review* 17, no. 13 (29 March 1974): 7–8.
"'The Best Friends of the African People'—Chinese Foreign Aid Personnel in Tanzania." *Peking Review* 11, no. 27 (5 July 1968): 26–28.
Borders, William. "China Quietly Renewing an Active Role in Africa." *New York Times*, 9 April 1971, 1.
Bracker, Milton. "Peiping's Signal Strong in Africa." *New York Times*, 27 June 1959, 2.
Brady, Thomas F. "North Africans Turning to East." *New York Times*, 5 May 1960, 9.
———. "Lag in Peiping Aid to Algeria Likely." *New York Times*, 5 November 1960, 2.
Braestrup, Peter. "Algeria May Ship Oil to Red China." *New York Times*, 26 January 1964, 5.
———. "Algerians Decry Criticism By U.S." *New York Times*, 3 April 1964, 6.
———. "Chou Sees 'Grand Success.'" *New York Times*, 12 January 1964, 21.
———. "Tunis Recognizes Communist China." *New York Times*, 11 January 1964, 7.
Broekhuizen, J. C. van. "Moskau und Peking in Afrika." *Afrika Heute*, no. 21 (1 November 1966): 309–312.
"Burundi Repulse to Peking Noted." *New York Times*, 31 January 1965, 5.
"Cairo Visit Implies Peking Aid to Algeria." *Washington Post*, 25 September 1960, A4.
"Chairman Mao and Vice-Chairman Lin Meet Tanzanian and Zambian Government Delegation." *Peking Review* 13, no. 29 (17 July 1970): 3–4.
"Chairman Mao Receives Delegates and Observers to Afro-Asian Writers' Emergency Meeting." *Peking Review* 9, no. 30 (22 July 1966): 3–4.
"Chairman Mao Tse-tung's Message to President Nkrumah." *Peking Review* 7, no. 3 (17 January 1964): 4.
Chen Kung-chi. "Tanganyika Impressions." *Peking Review* 6, no. 17 (26 April 1963): 20–21.
Childs, Marquis. "The New Entry in Africa: China." *Washington Post*, 10 August 1960, A14.
"China Aid to Tanzania." *Washington Post*, 29 April 1968, A3.
"China-Algeria Joint Communique." *Peking Review* 8, no. 15 (9 April 1965): 10–11.
"China-Algeria Joint Communique." *Peking Review* 8, no. 36 (3 September 1965): 7.
"China and the World: Afro-Asian Youth Conference." *Peking Review* 2, no. 6 (10 February 1959): 18.
"China and the World: 'Algeria Day.'" *Peking Review* 3, no. 14 (5 April 1960): 32.
"China and the World: Algerian Anniversary." *Peking Review* 4, no. 38 (22 September 1961): 22.

"China and the World: Algerian Delegation in China." *Peking Review* 1, no. 42 (16 December 1958): 20.
"China and the World: Algerian Delegation to China." *Peking Review* 1, no. 39 (25 November 1958): 19.
"China and the World: Algerians' Visit Ends." *Peking Review* 2, no. 19 (12 May 1959): 25.
"China and the World: Between China and Ghana." *Peking Review* 4, no. 45 (10 November 1961): 19.
"China and the World: Briefs." *Peking Review,* 1, no. 35 (23 October 1958): 21.
"China and the World: Briefs." *Peking Review,* 2, no. 10 (10 March 1959): 18.
"China and the World: Briefs." *Peking Review,* 2, no. 13 (31 March 1959): 23.
"China and the World: Briefs." *Peking Review,* 5, no. 14 (6 April 1962): 21.
"China and the World: China and Africa." *Peking Review,* 4, no. 38 (22 September 1961): 22.
"China and the World: China–Ghana Diplomatic Ties." *Peking Review,* 3, no. 28 (12 July 1960): 26.
"China and the World: China Recognizes Algeria." *Peking Review* 1, no. 31 (30 September 1958): 25.
"China and the World: China-Morocco Diplomatic Relations." *Peking Review* 1, no. 36 (4 November 1958): 22.
"China and the World: Chinese-African Friendship." *Peking Review* 5, no. 3 (19 January 1962): 23.
"China and the World: Chinese Exhibition in Accra." *Peking Review* 4, no. 33 (18 August 1961): 23.
"China and the World: Chinese Leaders Receive Latin American and African Guests." *Peking Review* 3, no. 31 (2 August 1960): 26.
"China and the World: Chinese Show at Tunis Fair." *Peking Review* 3, no. 43 (25 October 1960): 21.
"China and the World: Cultural News." *Peking Review* 1, no. 3 (18 March 1958): 20.
"China and the World: Cultural News." *Peking Review* 1, no. 8 (22 April 1958): 22.
"China and the World: Donations to Algerians." *Peking Review* 5, no. 25 (22 June 1962): 20.
"China and the World: First Chinese Ambassador to Ghana." *Peking Review* 3, no. 37 (14 September 1960): 41.
"China and the World: Founding of Tanganyikan Republic." *Peking Review* 5, no. 50 (14 December 1962): 27.
"China and the World: Friendly Aid to Algeria." *Peking Review* 1, no. 7 (15 April 1958): 18.
"China and the World: Ghana Likes Chinese Exhibition." *Peking Review* 4, no. 38 (22 September 1961): 22.
"China and the World: Ghanaian Goodwill Delegation." *Peking Review* 6, no. 4 (25 January 1963): 19.
"China and the World: Ghanaian National Day." *Peking Review* 4, no. 28 (14 July 1961): 22.
"China and the World: Ghana's Anniversary Greeted." *Peking Review* 3, no. 11 (15 March 1960): 25.
"China and the World: Greetings to Tanganyika." *Peking Review* 4, no. 50 (15 December 1961): 30.
"China and the World: In Brief." *Peking Review* 1, no. 18 (1 July 1958): 19.
"China and the World: No Carve-up of Algeria." *Peking Review* 4, no. 28 (14 July 1961): 22.

"China and the World: Release Zanzibar Journalist!" *Peking Review* 5, no. 28 (13 July 1962): 20.
"China and the World: Sino-Algerian Friendship." *Peking Review* 3, no. 39 (27 September 1960): 27.
"China and the World: Sino-Algerian Relations." *Peking Review* 5, no. 37 (14 September 1962): 22.
"China and the World: Sino-Ghanaian Co-operation Protocol." *Peking Review* 5, no. 43 (26 October 1962): 23.
"China and the World: Sino-Tanganyikan Ties." *Peking Review* 5, no. 51 (21 December 1962): 22.
"China and the World: Solidarity with Fighting Algeria." *Peking Review* 2, no. 39 (1 October 1959): 28.
"China and the World: Sports." *Peking Review* 5, no. 26 (29 June 1962): 21.
"China and the World: Support for African Peoples." *Peking Review* 3, no. 26 (28 June 1960): 32.
"China and the World: Ties with North Africa." *Peking Review* 2, no. 47 (24 November 1959): 21.
"China and the World: Zanzibar Leader in China." *Peking Review* 3, no. 2 (12 January 1960): 23.
"China Firmly Supports Algerian People's Just Struggle." *Peking Review* 3, no. 45 (8 November 1960): 26–28.
"China Hails African Outlook." *New York Times*, 21 June 1964, 13.
"China Hails Fighting Algeria." *Peking Review* 3, no. 19 (10 May 1960): 13–14.
"China Hails President Nyerere's State Visit." *Peking Review* 8, no. 9 (26 February 1965): 5–7.
"China Lends Ghana Nearly 20 Million." *New York Times*, 22 August 1961, 13.
"China Recognizes the Republic of Algeria." *Peking Review* 5, no. 27 (6 July 1962): 9.
"China Reiterates Support for Algeria." *Peking Review* 4, no. 45 (10 November 1961): 11.
"China Said to Seek Base in Zanzibar for Subversion." *New York Times*, 28 May 1964, 18.
"China Signs Pact with Tanzanians." *New York Times*, 21 February 1965, 21.
"China Strongly Protests against Worsening of Sino-Ghanaian Relations by Ghanaian Authorities." *Peking Review* 9, no. 13 (25 March 1966): 8–10.
"China Supports Africa's Struggle against Imperialism and Colonialism." *Peking Review* 15, no. 6 (11 February 1972): 15–17.
"China to Aid Tanzania." *New York Times*, 6 January 1965, 11.
"China, Tanzania Sign Trade Pact." *Washington Post*, 26 February 1965, A1.
"China-Tanzania Joint Communique." *Peking Review* 8, no. 24 (11 June 1965): 7–8.
"China Welcomes Algerian Delegation." *Peking Review* 1, no. 41 (9 December 1958): 15–16.
"Chinese Arrive in Tanzania." *New York Times*, 18 August 1969, 2.
"Chinese to Help Build Mali-to-Guinea Railroad." *New York Times*, 30 May 1968, 3.
"Chinese Exhibitions Abroad." *Peking Review* 6, no. 41 (11 October 1963): 5.
"Chinese Government Leaders Greet New African States." *Peking Review* 3, no. 27 (5 July 1960): 11.
"Chinese Held Countering the Russians in Algeria." *New York Times*, 1 November 1964, 14.
"Chinese Penetration of Africa." *Afrique Nouvelle (Dakar)*, 10–16 June 1965, 8–9. Found in Joint Publications Research Service (31368), *Translations on Africa*, no. 230, 2 August 1965, 33–39.
"Chinese Reds Set Up 2 Bureaus on Africa." *New York Times*, 27 October 1964, 2.
"Chinese to Build Hall." *Washington Post*, 4 December 1966, A30.

"Chou in Africa." *New York Times*, 10 June 1965, 34.
"Chou in Algiers to See Ben Bella." *New York Times*, 31 March 1965, 2.
"Chou Is Welcomed On Visit to Ghana." *New York Times*, 12 January 1964, 21.
"Communist Chinese Propaganda and Africa." *Afrique Nouvelle* (Dakar), 6–12 November 1969, 1–38. Article found in Joint Publications Research Service (49369), *Translations on Africa*, no. 840, 3 December 1969, 1–29.
"Communique of the Afro-Asian Emergency Writers' Meeting," *Peking Review* 9, no. 29 (15 July 1966): 8–9.
Conley, Robert. "Leftists Strengthen Hold Over Zanzibar." *New York Times*, 20 January 1964, 1, 6.
———. "Nationalism Is Viewed as Camouflage for Reds—Toll 2,000 to 4,000." *New York Times*, 19 January 1964, 1, 3.
———. "Stakes High in Zanzibar." *New York Times*, 28 June 1964, E5.
———. "Tanganyika Vote Complete Union." *New York Times*, 26 April 1964, 17.
———. "Tanzania Recalls Envoy from U.S. in Protest over Expulsion of a Diplomat." *New York Times*, 15 February 1965, 12.
———. "U.S. Fails to Stop Zanzibar's Diplomatic Break." *New York Times*, 21 February 1964, 5.
Cortesi, Arnaldo. "Algerian Implies Reds Offer Arms." *New York Times*, 31 October 1960, 8.
Cotten, Felix. "Purported Peiping Blueprint of Red Conquest Shown Here." *Washington Post*, 31 May 1954, 2.
"Cuban-Type Uniforms Seen." *New York Times*, 15 January 1964, 5.
Dougherty, Carter. "China a Player in African Politics." *Washington Times*, 16 February 2004, A18.
Durdin, Tillman. "Cultural Revolution Led To Diplomatic Isolation." *New York Times*, 14 October 1970, 20.
Eder, Richard. "Peking's Frustration." *New York Times*, 16 August 1965, 8.
Fellows, Lawrence. "Algerians Seek Aid from Peiping." *New York Times*, 1 December 1958, 8.
———. "China Denounced By Kenya Official." *New York Times*, 13 June 1965, 21.
———. "China May Build Africa Railroad." *New York Times*, 22 September 1965, 1.
———. "Chinese Communist Presence in East African Nations Grows." *New York Times*, 25 May 1968, 2.
———. "Chou Visit Perils East Africa Unity." *New York Times*, 8 June 1965, 11.
———. "Chou, in Zanzibar, Attacks U.S. After Welcome by Large Crowd." *New York Times*, 7 June 1965, 2.
———. "Monetary Union in Africa to End." *New York Times*, 11 June 1965, 8.
———. "Nyerere Tempers Welcome to Chou." *New York Times*, 5 June 1965, 7.
———. "Tanzania to Greet Chou Today; Her Capital Is in Festive Array." *New York Times*, 4 June 1965, 4.
Feng Chih-tan. "The Awakening of Africa." *Peking Review* 3, no. 27 (5 July 1960): 13–18.
———. "From Dark Night to Dawn." *Peking Review* 4, no. 34 (25 August 1961): 7–9.
Fleming, Louis B. "China Gets U.N. Ally in Algeria." *Washington Post*, 24 February 1968, A12.
"Foreign Trade New: Sino-Morocco Trade Agreement." *Peking Review* 1, no. 36 (4 November 1958): 22.
Frankel, Max. "U.S. Aides Unconvinced Pro-Reds Run Zanzibar." *New York Times*, 24 January 1964, 11.
"Friendship Fostered in Hard Struggle." *Peking Review* 12, no. 43 (24 October 1969): 32–33, 38.

"Friendship Log: Friendly Co-operation." *Peking Review* 15, no. 50 (15 December 1972): 21.

"Friendship Log: Tanzania-Zambia Railway." *Peking Review* 15, no. 1 (7 January 1972): 21.

"Friendship Log: Teaching and Learning from Each Other." *Peking Review* 15, no. 10 (10 March 1972): 19.

Ganda (pseudonym). "Report on Maoist Subversion in Africa." *ABC (Madrid)*, 22 August 1971, 28–32. Article in Joint Publications Research Service (54615), *Translations on Africa*, no. 1088, 3 December 1971, 1–33.

Garrison, Lloyd. "Chou Greeted Unofficially by Ghana." *New York Times*, 13 January 1964, 4.

———. "Coup in Ghana: Elaborately Organized Upheaval." *New York Times*, 5 March 1966, 2.

———. "Ghana Punishes Security Police." *New York Times*, 18 January 1964, 8.

———. "Nkrumah Praises Chou as a Leader." *New York Times*, 15 January 1964, 7.

———. "Portrait of Nkrumah as Dictator." *New York Times*, 3 May 1964, 15, 108–111.

"Ghana Accuses Chinese of Arming Foes in Guinea." *New York Times*, 7 April 1966, 5.

"Ghana Acts to Revise Accords with Reds." *Washington Post*, 7 September 1966, D5.

"Ghana Adds Backing for Peking." *New York Times*, 11 December 1964, 5.

"Ghana Charges Plot to Return Nkrumah." *New York Times*, 23 February 1967, 28.

"Ghana Joins Chou in Pleas For Talks." *New York Times*, 17 January 1964, 2.

"Ghana Names Peiping Envoy." *New York Times*, 23 October 1960, 24.

"Ghana to Get Red China Loan." *New York Times*, 16 July 1964, 9.

"Ghana, China Exchange Envoys." *Washington Post*, 6 July 1960, A1.

"Ghana, China Sign Economic Accord." *Washington Post*, 20 October 1962, A14.

Grimes, Paul. "Unrest in Africa Is Worrying U.S." *New York Times*, 25 January 1964, 1–2.

Gruson, Sydney. "Tanganyika-Zanzibar Union Is Reported Shaky." *New York Times*, 3 June 1964, 9.

"Guineans Leave China." *Washington Post*, 19 June 1963, A17.

"Heal the Wounded, Rescue the Dying, Practise [sic] Revolutionary Humanitarianism—Chinese Medical Team in Algeria." *Peking Review* 12, no. 31 (1 August 1969): 23–25.

Howe, Marvin. "Zanzibar, Though Heavily Dependent on Chinese Communist Aid, Maintains Independent Policies." *New York Times*, 23 September 1970, 10.

Howe, Russell. "Tanganyika Capital Is Haven For African Revolutionaries." *Washington Post*, 17 February 1963, E4.

Hsiao Ming. "China Hails Independent Algeria." *Peking Review* 6, no. 45 (8 November 1963): 17–18.

Ingalls, Leonard. "Peiping Presses Gains in Africa; Foothold Is Sought in Zanzibar." *New York Times*, 4 September 1960, 2.

"Joint Communique." *Peking Review* 4, no. 34 (25 August 1961): 5–6.

"Joint Communique." *Peking Review* 17, no. 10 (8 March 1974): 10–11.

"Joint Communique of Government Delegation of People's Republic of China and Government Delegation of Democratic People's Republic of Algeria." *Peking Review* 14, no. 32 (6 August 1971): 24–25.

"Joint Communique of China and Tanganyika-Zanzibar." *Peking Review* 7, no. 25 (19 June 1964): 12–13.

"Joint Communique of the People's Republic of China and the Republic of Zambia." *Peking Review* 10, no. 17 (30 June 1967): 12–14.

"Joint Statement of Chinese and Tanganyikan Trade Unions." *Survey of China Mainland Press*, no. 3111 (3 December 1963): 36–37. Translated by the American consulate

general in Hong Kong, and originally published in *New China News Agency*, 28 November 1963.
"Kenyan Backs Red Aid." *New York Times*, 28 June 1961, 6.
Leggett, Karby. "China Flexes Economic Muscle Throughout Burgeoning Africa." *Wall Street Journal*, 29 March 2005, 1.
"Lisbon Confirms Move By Africans." *New York Times*, 11 October 1964, 15.
Liu Ning-i [Ningyi]. "Report on Visit to Five African Countries." *Peking Review* 8, no. 21 (21 May 1965): 20–22.
———. "Unite to Fight against Imperialism." *Peking Review* 6, no. 7 (15 February 1963): 7–9.
"Long Foreign Trip by Chou Expected." *New York Times*, 18 August 1970, 5.
Louchheim, Donald H. "Burundi Gives Peking First Setback in Africa." *Washington Post*, 31 January 1965, A18.
———. "Zambia Wants New Railway as Lifeline." *Washington Post*, 7 September 1965, A14.
"Making More Friends for Better Mutual Understanding." *Beijing Review* 37, no. 8 (21 Feburary 1994): 18–19.
"Mao Sends a Message." *New York Times*, 13 January 1964, 4.
Mao Sun. "A Righteous Cause Will Triumph." *Peking Review* 4, no. 45 (10 November 1961): 10–11.
Matheson, Alastair. "China Steps Up Africa Program." *Washington Post*, 30 August 1963, B6.
Maynes, Seaghan. "Philip Arrives to Raise Flag of Free Tanganyika." *Washington Post*, 9 December 1961, 8.
McDermott, Clare. "China, Ghana Sign Amity, Trade Pacts." *Washington Post*, 19 August 1961, A9.
Meisler, Stanley. "China's Foothold in Tanzania." *Washington Post*, 23 June 1968, H12.
Middleton, Drew. "Ivory Coast Head Calls China Peril." *New York Times*, 10 April 1966, 17.
———. "Tanzanian Denies Peking Influence." *New York Times*, 17 March 1966, 17.
Miniclier, C. C. "Dealings with Peking Defended by Nyerere." *Washington Post*, 19 November 1969, A24.
"Mission Accomplished!" *Peking Review* 1, no. 44 (30 December 1958): 22.
"Mission from China Reaches Tanganyika." *Washington Post*, 27 August 1964, C17.
Mohr, Charles. "Kaunda Leads Tanzam Rail Ceremonies." *New York Times*, 27 October 1970, 2.
"National Support for Algerian Independence." *Peking Review* 2, no. 14 (7 April 1959): 16–17.
"New Zanzibar Chief Vows Ties with All." *New York Times*, 15 January 1964, 1.
"News in Brief." *Peking Review* 6, no. 10–11 (15 March 1963): 79.
"News in Brief." *Peking Review* 6, no. 12 (22 March 1963): 18.
"News in Brief." *Peking Review* 6, no. 20 (17 May 1963): 20.
"New Stage in Sino-Ghanaian Relations." *Peking Review* 4, no. 34 (25 August 1961): 5.
"Nkrumah Arrives in Soviet Capital." *Washington Post*, 13 August 1961, A1.
"Nkrumah Continuing His Drive for a One-Party Socialist State." *New York Times*, 20 January 1964, 64.
"Nkrumah in Peiping." *New York Times*, 15 August 1961, 2.
Nkrumah, Kwame. "The Movement for Colonial Freedom." *Phylon* XVI (4th quarter 1955).
"Nkrumah's Status Explained." *New York Times*, 5 March 1966, 2.
"Nyerere in Shanghai." *Washington Post*, 17 February 1965, A19.

"'Our 600 Million Back Up Algerian People.'" *Peking Review* 1, no. 6 (8 April 1958): 21.
"Peiping and Ghana Set Up Closer Ties." *New York Times*, 19 August 1961, 6.
"Peiping Campaign in Africa Grows." *New York Times*, 10 September 1960, 3.
"Peking Accused in Subversion." *Washington Post*, 14 March 1965, A16.
"Peking Aide Seen in Interim Role." *New York Times*, 15 June 1969, 4.
"Peking Assures Ghana." *Washington Post*, 4 May 1965, C4.
"Peking Buying French Trucks." *New York Times*, 20 November 1965, 14.
"Peking Charges Beating." *New York Times*, 5 March 1966, 2.
"Peking Ending Ghana Ties." *New York Times*, 30 October 1966, 4.
"Peking Starts Withdrawing Embassy Force from Ghana." *Washington Post*, 30 October 1966, A24.
"Police Chief on Tour." *Washington Post*, 12 October 1966, A6.
"Premier Abbas Concludes Visit in China." *Peking Review* 3, no. 41 (11 October 1960): 17–19.
"Premier Abbas Ferhat in Peking." *Peking Review* 3, no. 40 (4 October 1960): 30–40.
"Premier Chou En-lai Greets the Algerian People's Victory." *Peking Review* 5, no. 12 (23 March 1962): 5.
"Premier Chou En-lai's Speech at Banquet in Honor of Premier Abbas Ferhat." *Peking Review* 3, no. 40 (4 October 1960): 40–42.
"Premier Chou Visits Tanzania." *Peking Review* 8, no. 24 (11 June 1965): 5–6.
"President Nyerere Arrives in Peking." *Peking Review* 11, no. 25 (21 June 1968): 3–4.
"President Nyerere's Visit to China." *Peking Review* 11, no. 26 (28 June 1968): 5–10.
"Profound Mourning for Passing of the Chinese People's Great Leader Chairman Mao Tsetung." *Peking Review* 19, no. 40 (30 September 1976): 55–58.
"Protests to Ghanaian Authorities." *Peking Review* 9, no. 11 (11 March 1966): 7–8.
"Red China Envoy in Ghana." *New York Times*, 6 September 1960, 20.
"Red China Offers Algeria a Credit of $50 Million." *New York Times*, 10 October 1963, 13.
"Red China Offers Algeria a Loan." *Washington Post*, 10 October 1963, A26.
"Red China Replaces Ambassador to Cairo." *Washington Post*, 21 January 1966, A17.
"Red China to Aid Rail Project." *New York Times*, 9 April 1968, 5.
"Red China Wants Asian-African Bloc to Fight 'Colonialism,' Premier Says." *Washington Post*, 5 January 1955, 1.
"Reds to Open Embassy." *Washington Post*, 5 August 1960, A11.
"Reds' Use of Zanzibar Feared." *New York Times*, 30 December 1960, 5.
"Resolution on the Ghana Coup." *Peking Review* 9, no. 29 (15 July 1966): 41.
Root, Waverley. "Peking Hits Snags in Africa Trade Promotion." *Washington Post*, 8 November 1962, C18.
"Roots of Zanzibar Upheaval Reach Back Ten Centuries." *Washington Post*, 13 January 1964, A13.
"Round the World: A.A.T.U.F. Congress: U.S. Imperialist Aggression Condemned." *Peking Review* 9, no. 51 (16 December 1966): 38–39.
"Round the World: Africa: Militant Journalism." *Peking Review* 6, no. 47 (22 November 1963): 25.
"Round the World: Africa: Spark of Armed Revolt." *Peking Review* 9, no. 9 (25 February 1966): 28–29.
"Round the World: African Opinion: Origins of Anti-China Slanders." *Peking Review* 9, no. 4 (21 January 1966): 29–30.
"Round the World: Algeria: Bouteflika's Statement on Mediterranean Situation." *Peking Review* 15, no. 41 (13 October 1972): 21–22.
"Round the World: Algeria: F.L.N. Congress." *Peking Review* 7, no. 18 (1 May 1964): 30–31.

"Round the World: East Africa: Operation Return." *Peking Review* 7, no. 6 (7 February 1964): 33–34.
"Round the World: Ghana Hits Back: U.S. Imperialism Exposed." *Peking Review* 7, no. 7 (14 February 1964): 26.
"Round the World: Indian Ocean: 7th Fleet on the Prowl." *Peking Review* 6, no. 51 (20 December 1963): 24.
"Round the World: Tanzam Republic: President Nyerere Protests." *Peking Review* 7, no. 37 (11 September 1964): 30.
"Round the World: Tanzania: Answering Imperialist Provocation." *Peking Review* 9, no. 46 (11 November 1966): 38–39.
"Round the World: Tanzania: U.S. Fleet in Indian Ocean Protested." *Peking Review* 17, no. 7 (15 February 1974): 20.
"Round the World: Tanzania: U.S. Spies Expelled." *Peking Review* 8, no. 6 (5 February 1965): 28.
"Round the World: Youth in Tanzania: A Clean Sweep!" *Peking Review* 9, no. 44 (28 October 1966): 39.
"Round the World: Zanzibar Demands Removal of U.S. Bases." *Peking Review* 7, no. 16 (17 April 1964): 20–21.
"Round the World: Zanzibar: New Government." *Peking Review* 7, no. 4 (24 January 1964): 20.
"Round the World: Zanzibar: On Guard against Intervention." *Peking Review* 7, no. 7 (14 February 1964): 28.
"Rousing Welcoming for President Nkrumah." *Peking Review* 4, no. 3 (18 August 1961): 5–6.
Schmidt, Dana Adams. "Nkrumah Speaks." *New York Times*, 24 September 1960, 1.
Schwartz, Harry. "China's Objective: Expansion of Power." *New York Times*, 2 February 1964, E6.
Shen Su. "Political Map of Africa Changes Fast." *Peking Review* 5, no. 1 (5 January 1962): 14–15.
"Shuffles Mark Year in Peking Diplomacy." *Washington Post*, 9 January 1965, A7.
"Sino-Algerian Communique." *Peking Review* 1, no. 43 (23 December 1958): 24.
"Sino-Algerian Joint Communique." *Peking Review* 3, no. 21 (24 May 1960): 16–17.
"Sino-Algerian Joint Communique." *Peking Review* 3, no. 41 (11 October 1960): 16–17.
"Sino-Tanzanian Joint Communique." *Peking Review* 8, no. 9 (26 February 1965): 8–10.
"Sino-Tanzanian Treaty of Friendship." *Peking Review* 8, no. 9 (26 February 1965): 9.
"South Africa Jails 2 Men For Arms Training in China." *New York Times*, 8 September 1965, 22.
"Soviet Arms Cargo in Zanzibar Denied." *New York Times*, 6 April 1964, 6.
"Speech by Premier Abbas Ferhat at Peking Banquet." *Peking Review* 3, no. 40 (4 October 1960): 42–44.
"Sportsmen Patriots." *Peking Review* 1, no. 4 (30 December 1958): 23.
"Supporting African National-Liberation Movement." *Peking Review* 15, no. 11 (17 March 1972): 11–12.
Szulc, Tad. "Okello, Cuba-Trained Zanzibari, Called Key Man in Power Fight." *New York Times*, 31 January 1964, 2.
———. "Peking Reported in Drive to Play Key Role in Mideast and Africa." *New York Times*, 17 October 1971, 3.
———. "Peking Steps Up Drive for Allies." *New York Times*, 1 April 1965, 3.
———. "Zanzibar Chiefs Tighten Red Ties." *New York Times*, 21 June 1964, 13.
"Tanganyikans to Visit Peking." *New York Times*, 8 June 1964, 32.
"Tanganyikans to Visit Peking." *New York Times*, 26 September 1966, 3.
"Tanganyika-Zanzibar Guests Visit China." *Peking Review* 7, no. 25 (19 June 1964): 5–6.

"Tanzania and China to Start Ship Line." *New York Times*, 8 July 1966, 17.
"Tanzania Expels 2 U.S. Diplomats." *New York Times*, 16 January 1965, 1.
"Tanzania President Back from Red China." *Washington Post*, 25 February 1965, A15.
"Tanzania Radio Station." *Washington Post*, 10 December 1966, A2.
"Tanzanian Ambassador Gives National Day Reception." *Peking Review* 11, no. 18 (3 May 1968): 8, 29–31.
"Tanzanian Defense Chinese Rail Aid." *New York Times*, 23 November 1969, 23.
"Tanzanian Government Delegation and Zambian Government Delegation Visit China." *Peking Review* 13, no. 29 (17 July 1970): 16–17.
"Tanzanian to Visit Red China." *New York Times*, 3 June 1968, 11.
"Tanzanian, Zambian, Chinese Government Representatives Inspect Survey Work on Tanzanian Section of Tanzania-Zambia Railway." *Peking Review* 11, no. 45 (8 November 1968): 27–28.
"Tanzania-Zambia Railway: A Bridge to China?" *New York Times*, 29 January 1971, 65.
"Tanzania-Zambia Railway: Tracklaying Completed and Trial Run Starts." *Peking Review* 18, no. 44 (31 October 1974): 19–20, 30.
Taylor, Sidney. "Ghana Says Nkrumah, Peking Plot." *Washington Post*, 7 April 1966, A22.
"Tenth Anniversary of Algerian Revolution Marked in China." *Peking Review* 7, no. 45 (6 November 1964): 9–10.
"Textile Mill Stone Laid." *Washington Post*, 31 July 1966, A10.
"Text of Joint Statement of Chinese and Ghanaian Trade Unions." *Survey of China Mainland Press*, no. 3091 (30 October 1963): 31–32.
"To the Victory of the Algerian People!" *Peking Review* 1, no. 43 (23 December 1958): 24–25.
Topping, Seymour. "Gains Reported for China." *New York Times*, 9 October 1964, 3.
"Treaty of Friendship." *Peking Review* 4, no. 34 (25 August 1961): 7.
Tung Feng. "The Bandung Spirit Thrives." *Peking Review* 1, no. 9 (29 April 1958): 6–8.
"An Unusual Gift." *Peking Review* 11, no. 11 (15 March 1968): 36.
"U.S. Plot against Tanzania Exposed." *Peking Review* 7, no. 47 (20 November 1964): 15–17.
Vanderwicken, Peter. "Red Threat to Africa Is Eased by Zanzibar's Link with Tanganyika." *Wall Street Journal*, 13 July 1964, 1, 14.
Wald, Richard C. "Tanganyika and Red China Agree on Diplomatic Ties." *Washington Post*, 12 December 1961, A8.
Wang Wei, and Lu Ming-chu. "Algerian Algeria." *Peking Review* 5, no. 25 (22 June 1962): 9–12.
"The Week." *Peking Review* 6, no. 41 (11 October 1963): 3.
"The Week: 5th Anniversary of Zanzibar Revolution Celebrated." *Peking Review* 12, no. 3 (17 January 1969): 3.
"The Week: 6th Anniversary of Sino-Tanzanian Friendship Treaty Celebrated." *Peking Review* 14, no. 9 (26 February 1971): 17.
"The Week: 10th Anniversary of Algeria's Independence Greeted." *Peking Review* 15, no. 28 (14 July 1972): 6.
"The Week: 20th Anniversary of Algerian Armed Revolution." *Peking Review* 17, no. 45 (8 November 1974): 4–5.
"The Week: Agreement on Construction of Tanzania-Zambia Railway Signed in Peking." *Peking Review* 10, no. 38 (15 September 1967): 6, 39.
"The Week: Algeria Delegation Ends Visit." *Peking Review* 16, no. 20 (18 May 1973): 3, 6.
"The Week: Algeria National Day Greeted." *Peking Review* 14, no. 35 (5 November 1971): 4.
"The Week: Algerian Delegation in Peking." *Peking Review* 8, no. 24 (11 June 1965): 4.

"The Week: Algerian Embassy Gives Reception Marking 15th Anniversary of Revolution." *Peking Review* 12, no. 45 (7 November 1969): 3.
"The Week: Algerian Government Delegation Arrives in Peking." *Peking Review* 8, no. 35 (27 August 1965): 5.
"The Week: Algerian Government Delegation Visits China." *Peking Review* 14, no. 31 (30 July 1971): 3, 28.
"The Week: Algerian Guests in Peking." *Peking Review* 7, no. 6 (7 February 1964): 32.
"The Week: Algerian Revolution Anniversary." *Peking Review* 8, no. 45 (5 November 1965): 3, 14.
"The Week: Algerian Special Envoy Visits Peking." *Peking Review* 7, no. 52 (25 December 1964): 3.
"The Week: Algeria's Independence Day Greeted." *Peking Review* 8, no. 28 (9 July 1965): 4.
"The Week: Chairman Liu Receives Zanzibar Guests." *Peking Review* 7, no. 38 (18 September 1964): 4.
"The Week: Chairman Mao Meets President Nyerere." *Peking Review* 17, no. 13 (29 March 1974): 3.
"The Week: Chairman Mao Meets Women's Delegation from Zanzibar." *Peking Review* 8, no. 31 (30 July 1965): 3.
"The Week: Chairman Mao Receives Algerian Guests." *Peking Review* 7, no. 17 (24 April 1964): 3.
"The Week: Chairman Mao Receives Tanganyika Women's Delegation." *Peking Review* 6, no. 22 (31 May 1963): 4.
"The Week: Chairman Mao Receives Tanzania Women's Delegation." *Peking Review* 8, no. 27 (2 July 1965): 3.
"The Week: Chen Yi Visits Algeria and Mali." *Peking Review* 8, no. 38 (17 September 1965): 4–5.
"The Week: China–Algeria." *Peking Review* 15, no. 46 (17 November 1972): 17.
"The Week: China, Tanzania and Zambia Sign Three Protocols For Construction of Tanzania-Zambia Railway." *Peking Review* 11, no. 16 (19 April 1968): 26.
"The Week: Chinese and Zanzibar Youth Stand Together." *Peking Review* 7, no. 27 (3 July 1964): 4.
"The Week: Chinese Government and Military Delegation Leaves For Algeria to Attend National Day Celebrations." *Peking Review* 12, no. 45 (7 November 1969): 3.
"The Week: Chinese Leaders Meet Algerian Delegation." *Peking Review* 8, no. 36 (3 September 1965): 7.
"The Week: Chinese, Tanzanian, Zambian Governments Sign Supplementary Agreement on Tanzanian—Zambian Railway." *Peking Review* 12, no. 48 (28 November 1969): 4.
"The Week: Condolence on Karume's Death." *Peking Review* 15, no. 15 (14 April 1972): 3.
"The Week: Foreign Minister Chi Replies to His Algerian Counterpart." *Peking Review* 17, no. 8 (22 February 1974): 3.
"The Week: Ghanaian Guests Welcomed." *Peking Review* 15, no. 37 (15 September 1972): 22.
"The Week: Ghana's National Day." *Peking Review* 8, no. 11 (12 March 1965): 5.
"The Week: Ghana's National Day." *Peking Review* 7, no. 28 (10 July 1964): 4.
"The Week: Guests from Africa." *Peking Review* 6, no. 36 (6 September 1963): 4.
"The Week: Guests from Tanzania." *Peking Review* 15, no. 22 (2 June 1972): 3–4.
"The Week: Imperialist-Instigated Coups Strengthen African Solidarity." *Peking Review* 9, no. 12 (18 March 1966): 3–4.

"The Week: Madame Karume Leaves Peking." *Peking Review* 8, no. 32 (6 August 1965): 4.
"The Week: Militia Delegation from Algeria." *Peking Review* 8, no. 1 (1 January 1965): 4.
"The Week: News Briefs." *Peking Review* 14, no. 34 (20 August 1971): 23.
"The Week: News Briefs." *Peking Review* 14, no. 52 (24 December 1971): 18.
"The Week: News Briefs." *Peking Review* 15, no. 51 (22 December 1972): 23.
"The Week: News Briefs." *Peking Review* 15, no. 52 (29 December 1972): 4.
"The Week: Premier Chou En-lai in Algiers." *Peking Review* 6, no. 52 (27 December 1963): 3–4.
"The Week: Premier Chou Greets Algeria's National Day." *Peking Review* 13, no. 45 (6 November 1970): 29.
"The Week: President Boumediene Visits China." *Peking Review* 17, no. 10 (8 March 1974): 4–5.
"The Week: President Nyerere Ends Visit to China." *Peking Review* 17, no. 14 (5 April 1974): 7.
"The Week: Protest against Ghanaian Authorities' Anti-Chinese Provocations." *Peking Review* 9, no. 41 (7 October 1966): 38.
"The Week: Protest against Ghanaian Authorities' Unilateral Suspension of Relations Between China and Ghana." *Peking Review* 9, no. 45 (4 November 1966): 5, 38.
"The Week: Resumption of Diplomatic Relations between China and Ghana." *Peking Review* 15, no. 9 (3 March 1972): 3.
"The Week: Sino-Algerian Friendship." *Peking Review* 6, no. 42 (18 October 1963): 3–4.
"The Week: Sino-Algerian Trade Co-operation." *Peking Review* 7, no. 39 (25 September 1964): 3–4.
"The Week: Sino-Ghanaian Anniversary." *Peking Review* 7, no. 35 (28 August 1964): 3-4.
"The Week: Sino-Ghanaian Friendship." *Peking Review* 6, no. 34 (23 August 1963): 4.
"The Week: Talks on Tanzania-Zambia Railway." *Peking Review* 18, no. 39 (26 September 1974): 9.
"The Week: Tanganyika President to Visit China." *Peking Review* 6, no. 49 (6 December 1963): 4.
"The Week: Tanganyika's Independence Anniversary Saluted." *Peking Review* 14, no. 51 (17 December 1971): 3.
"The Week: Tanzania Ambassador Gives National Day Reception." *Peking Review* 12, no. 19 (5 May 1969): 47, 49–50.
"The Week: Tanzania Goodwill Delegation in Peking." *Peking Review* 15, no. 35 (1 September 1972): 4, 22.
"The Week: Tanzanian Ambassador Gives Reception." *Peking Review* 14, no. 18 (30 April 1971): 3, 21.
"The Week: Tanzanian Ambassador to China Gives National Day Reception." *Peking Review* 13, no. 18 (30 April 1970): 30–31.
"The Week: Tanzanian Ambassador to China Gives Reception." *Peking Review* 14, no. 4 (22 January 1971): 3, 17.
"The Week: Tanzanian Economic Delegation Visits Peking." *Peking Review* 9, no. 24 (10 June 1966): 31.
"The Week: Tanzanian Military Delegation Visits China." *Peking Review* 13, no. 45 (6 November 1970): 29–31.
"The Week: Tanzanian Minister Ends Visit." *Peking Review* 9, no. 25 (17 June 1966): 4.
"The Week: Tanzanian Visitors." *Peking Review* 16, no. 5 (2 February 1973): 5, 13.

"The Week: Tanzanian Women's Delegation from Zanzibar." *Peking Review* 8, no. 30 (23 July 1965): 16.
"The Week: Tanzanian Women's Delegation Leaves for Home." *Peking Review* 8, no. 28 (9 July 1965): 4.
"The Week: Tanzania's National Day." *Peking Review* 9, no. 18 (29 April 1966): 4.
"The Week: Vice Premier Sun Chien Returns from Zambia and Tanzania." *Peking Review* 19, no. 32–33 (9 August 1976): 3–4.
"The Week: Vice-Chairman Tung and Premier Chou Congratulate President Nyerere of Tanzania on His Re-election." *Peking Review* 13, no. 46 (13 November 1970): 4.
"The Week: Zanzibar's Independence Day." *Peking Review* 6, no. 50 (13 December 1963): 4.
"Welcome to Algeria's Delegates." *Peking Review* 3, no. 18 (3 May 1960): 5.
"Welcome to Vice President Kawawa." *Peking Review* 8, no. 48 (26 November 1965): 13–14.
"West African Crops Drought-Stricken." *New York Times*, 27 January 1974, 220.
"Wholeheartedly Serving the People of the World—Chinese Aid Personnel Abroad." *Peking Review* 11, no. 11 (15 March 1968): 32–35.
Yu, Maochun. "Ch—y in China." *Wall Street Journal*, 27 April 2004, A18.
"Zambia Seeks More Control of Copper." *New York Times*, 1 September 1973, 29, 33.
"Zanzibar Expels Top British Aide." *Washington Post*, 21 February 1964, A30.
"Zanzibar Promised Big Loan By Peking." *New York Times*, 9 June 1964, 16.

U.S. AND FOREIGN GOVERNMENT DOCUMENTS

Afro-Asian Solidarity against Imperialism: A Collection of Documents, Speeches and Press Interviews from the Visits of Chinese Leaders to Thirteen African and Asian Countries. Beijing: Foreign Languages Press, 1964.
Central Intelligence Agency (CIA). *China Plans to Restore Nkrumah to Power in Ghana*. Intelligence Information Cable, 7 March 1966. Cable found in *CIA Research Reports Africa, 1946–1976* (Frederick, MD: University Publications of America, 1982).
———. *Chinese Communist Activities in Africa*. Memorandum, 30 April 1965. Memorandum found in *CIA Research Reports Africa, 1946–1976* (Frederick, MD: University Publications of America, 1982).
———. *Chinese Communist Ministry of Foreign Affairs Foreign Policy Report*. Information Report, 3 July 1961.
———. *Communist Cultural and Propaganda Activities in the Less Developed Countries*. Intelligence Report, January 1966.
———. "Communist Economic Aid Extensions and Technical Assistance to Selected African Countries." Memorandum for the Defense Intelligence Agency, 20 January 1972.
———. *Communist Economic and Military Aid to Africa*. Memorandum, 18 February 1976.
———. *The Current Disarray in Zanzibar*. Intelligence Memoradum, 2 December 1968.
———. *Drawings on Communist Economic Aid Extended to Less Developed Countries 1954–1967*. 1 May 1968.
———. *Foreign Operations of Chinese Communist News Agency*. Special Report, 7 February 1964.
———. *Growth of Chinese Influence among World Communists*. Special Report, 17 May 1963.
———. *Implications of Growing Communist Influence in URTZ*. Special Memorandum No. 12–64, 29 September 1964. Memorandum found in *CIA Research reports Africa, 1946–1976* (Frederick, MD: University Publications of America, 1982).
———. *Ministry of Foreign Affairs Directive Citing Mistakes Committed By Embassies in the Conduct of Propaganda*. Intelligence Information Cable, 6 September 1968.

———. *The New Look in Chinese Communist Aid to Sub-Saharan Africa*. Intelligence Memorandum, September 1968.

———. *A Reassessment of Julius Nyerere*. Special Memorandum No. 17–65, 10 June 1965. Memorandum found in *CIA Research Reports Africa, 1946–1976* (Frederick, MD: University Publications of America, 1982).

———. "Unclassified Table on Communist Economic Credits and Grants Extended to Less Developed Countries of the Free World, 1954–1970 and Years 1969 and 1970." Memorandum for the Department of State, 4 March 1971.

China-Africa Economic and Trade Cooperation. White paper issued by the Information Office of the State Council, People's Republic of China, December 2010.

China's African Policy. White paper issued by the Information Office of the State Council, People's Republic of China, January 2006.

"China's National Defense." White paper issued by the Information Office of the State Council, the People's Republic of China, 27 July 1998.

Chou En-Lai in Ghana. Accra: Ministry of Information and Broadcasting, 1964.

Director of Central Intelligence. *Chou En-Lai's African Tour*. Washington, DC. Current Intelligence Weekly Review, 17 January 1964.

———. *Communist China*. National Intelligence Estimate Number 13–60, 20 December 1960.

———. *Communist China's Foreign Policy*. National Intelligence Estimate Number 13–9–65, 5 May 1965.

———. *The Outlook for Ghana*. National Intelligence Estimate Number 74–57, 27 December 1957.

———. *Prospects for Communist China*. National Intelligence Estimate Number 13–4–62, 2 May 1962.

———. *Tanzania Taking the Left Turn*. Special Report, 21 May 1965.

Nkrumah, Kwame. *Ghana's Policy at Home and Abroad*. Washington, DC: Information Office, Embassy of Ghana, 1957.

Nkrumah, Kwame. *Speech on Foreign Policy*. Accra: Ghana Information Services, 1959.

Nkrumah's Deception of Africa. Accra: Ghana Ministry of Information, 1967.

Nkrumah's Subversion in Africa: Documentary Evidence of Nkrumah's Interference in the Affairs of Other African States. Accra-Tema: Ghana Ministry of Information, November 1966.

Office of the Secretary of Defense. *Annual Report to Congress on the Military Power of the People's Republic of China*. Washington, DC. Report to Congress Pursuant to Fiscal Year 2000 National Defense Authorization Act, June 2000.

Osagyefo at the United Nations. Accra: Ghana Information Services, 1960.

SPEECHES AND TESTIMONIES

Liu Guijin. "China-Africa Relations: Equality, Cooperation and Mutual Development." Speech to Institute for Security Studies, South Africa, 9 November 2004.

Lyman, Princeton. "China's Rising Role in Africa." Testimony before the U.S. Economic and Security Review Commission. Hearing on "China's Global Influence: Objectives and Strategies," 21 July 2005.

Ranneberger, Michael E. Hearing on "China's Influence in Africa." Testimony before the Subcommittee on Africa, Global Human Rights and International Operations, Committee on International Relations, U.S. House of Representatives, 28 July 2005.

Shinn, David H. "China's Approach to East, North and the Horn Africa." Testimony before the U.S. Economic and Security Review Commission. Hearing on "China's Global Influence: Objectives and Strategies," 21 July 2005.

INDEX

Africa: anti-imperialist objectives in, 19; beachhead in, establishment of, 16; bond of shared historical past with China, 2, 21, 148; Chinese approach to expansion of influence in, 2, 145–48, 184n19; coup outcomes and bilateral relations in, 99; current influence of China in, 2–3, 5, 143, 148; democracy in, Chinese efforts to subvert, 90–91; entry point for Chinese influence in, 38–41, 143; exploitation of by China, 1–2; independence and liberation movements in, support for, 16–17, 18, 31–32, 63, 108–9, 153n38; influence of China in, 183–84n8; influence of China in, methods of expansion of, 96–97; international unity and, 18; leadership role of China, 20–21; military training operations, 58; NCNA locations, 23; NCNA role, 24–25; nonwhite states, 31; opinions and perceptions about Chinese presence in, 3–4; organizations to gain influence in, 22–32, 154nn1–2, 156n44; strategic value of, 3, 50, 145, 147; UN vote for China, 66–67; Western influence in, elimination of, 18. *See also* Algeria; Chinese aid to and activities in Africa; Ghana; Tanzania
African Association for Immigrant Workers (African Association), 104
African Liberation Committee (ALC), 31–32, 157n65, 157n71, 157n75
Afro-Asian People's Solidarity Conference, 43, 46–47, 159n13
Afro-Asian People's Solidarity Organization (AAPSO), 29–30, 39, 156n53, 156n55
Afro-Asian Youth Conference, 46–47
Afro-Shirazi Party (ASP), 105, 108, 131, 140

agriculture: Algeria-China relations and aid, 55, 61, 67; economic construction exhibition, 84; Feed Yourself program, 99–100; Four Modernizations and, 16; Ghana-China relations and aid, 85, 87, 96, 100; science and technology to support, 13; Tanzania-China relations and aid, 118, 129, 131
Albania, 59, 62, 139, 163n35, 165n92, 168n16
Albanian Union of Working Youth, 28, 59
Algeria: access to by China, 38; aircraft for, 62, 164n50; ALC role, 31; bank delegation visit, 67–68, 165n92; bond of shared historical past with China, 49–50; context of Chinese operations in, 4–5, 147; coup d'état, 62–63, 164n50; cultural agreement with China, 56, 60, 61; diplomatic visits to and relations with China, 44–46, 47–49, 50–51, 160nn23–24, 161n55; French army service of Algerians, 36, 38, 157n6; front organizations working in, 28; independence of, 4–5, 38, 53–54, 143; independence of, Chinese support after, 54–69; independence of, Chinese support for, 4–5, 38, 40–53, 69, 143; influence of China in, 40–41, 43–44, 52, 55–69, 88, 113, 143; international economic relations, proposal for development of system for, 68; liberation movements and military training base, 58, 63, 64, 68–69, 90, 143; map of, 34; military regions, 42; militia formation, 61; national day of solidarity with the Algerian people, 43, 158–59n39; nationalism and independence movement in, 35–38, 157n6, 157nn1–4; natural resources in, 60; NCNA locations, 23; negotiations with France, 43; partnerships and relationships between China and, 44–46,

205

47–49, 50–51, 55–61, 62–63, 65–66, 67–69, 143, 160nn23–24, 161n55, 165nn92–93; political and military leadership for independence movement, 42–43, 159n6; political environment after independence, 162n5; provisional government, recognition of and aid for, 44–45, 47, 49, 53, 160n21, 160–61n48, 161n55; refugees from, support for, 47, 48; size of, 143, 183n2; strategic value of, 59, 68–69, 143; supply route to, 45; Support Algeria demonstration in China, 43–44; support for Chinese interests, 49, 55, 64–67; trade relations with China, 56, 60, 63, 67; UN vote for China, 55, 64–65, 66–67, 90
Algerian People's Party (Parti du Peuple Algérien, PPA), 35, 36–37, 157n3, 158n17
All-African People's Conference, 78
All-African Trade Union Federation (AATUF), 109, 179n138
All-China Federation of Trade Unions (ACFTU), 44, 48, 52–53, 105, 109
All-China Journalists' Association (ACJA), 107–8
Angola, 58, 88, 90, 113, 117
anti-revisionism, 19–20
Armée de Libération Nationale (ALN, National Liberation Army), 42, 46, 143
Asia: anti-imperialist objectives in, 19; Communist activities in, combating of, 153n39; independence and liberation movements in, support for, 16–17, 18, 63, 153n38; international unity and, 18; political culture of, 151n4

Babu (Abdul Rahman Mohamed), 105, 107, 111–12, 113, 115, 118, 138, 174n6, 175n30, 175–76n43
Bandung Conference, 17, 29, 38, 46–47, 53, 69, 153n37, 153n39
Burma, 153nn38–39
Burundi, 24, 68–69, 90, 119, 120

Cameroon, 76–77, 78, 89–90, 91
censorship, 23
Central African Republic, 23, 91–92
China: approach to expansion of influence, 2, 145–48, 184n19; authoritarian government creation, 11; bond of shared historical past with Africa, 2, 21, 49–50, 107, 148; Cultural Revolution, 134, 180n19; current Africa policy, 2–3, 5, 143, 148; Four Modernizations, 16; inauguration of PRC, 151n3; International Fair participant, 51–52; national interest and influence expansion, 1–2, 145–46; opinions and perceptions about, 2, 3–4, 77, 85, 106, 146, 147; political culture of, 10, 151n4; recognition and support of, 19, 20; Soviet threat to, 19–20, 154nn55–56; understanding of through analysis of historical actions, 5; world power and superior civilization identity of, 10, 145; world status and global power of, 2, 4, 9–18, 20–21, 144–45, 151–52n18. *See also* foreign policy of China
China Democratic League, 28–29
China-Africa People's Friendship Association (CAPFA), 28, 52–53, 81–82
Chinese aid to and activities in Africa: African perspective on, 3–4; announcements of, 146; context and strategic flexibility of operations, 4–5, 32, 146–47, 184n19; Cultural Revolution and, 134, 180n19; objectives of, 1–2, 4–5, 9–21, 124, 144–45, 147–48, 183–84n8; organizations for, 22–32, 154nn1–2, 156n44; resources for, 147, 148; targeting of, 146–47; timing and targeting of, 146; Western assessments of, 2, 49–50, 88, 113, 149n4, 149–50n6. *See also* commerce and trade
Chinese Committee for Afro-Asian Solidarity, 48, 52–53, 57–58, 88, 160n24
Chinese People's Association for Cultural Relations with Foreign Countries (CPACRFC), 27–28, 156n42
Chinese People's Political Consultive Conference (CPPCC), 11–13, 151n10
The Circle (secret society), 73–74
Clausewitz, Carl von, 152n21
colonial and semicolonial countries, independence, 14, 16, 75
commerce and trade: Africa-China trade relations, 1, 145, 149n1; Algeria-China trade relations, 56, 60, 63, 67–68; Egypt-China trade relations, 39; Ethiopia-China trade relations, 39; Ghana-China trade relations, 39, 40, 83, 84, 98, 100; international united front objective, 11–15, 151n10; Libya-China trade relations, 39; Morocco-China trade relations, 40; Nigeria-China trade relations, 39; Tanganyika-China trade relations, 39; Tanzania-China shipping company, 125–26, 139, 182n76; Tanzania-China trade relations, 120; trade relations, terms for establishment of, 12; truck purchases by China, 63; Tunisia-China trade relations, 39
Commission for Cultural Relations with Foreign Countries (CCRFC), 27–28, 77, 108, 155n30, 155n36
Common Program, 11–13, 16, 19, 151nn10–11
Communism: foreign policy of China and, 11; front organizations, 28–29, 39, 121, 154n1,

156n48; history of in China, 150n11; importance of youth to movement, 146; spread of ideology in Africa, 97, 183–84n8
Communist Party of China (CPC): benefit of Africa activities for, 1–2; influence and power of, 10; International Liaison Department (ILD), 25–27, 28; Mao's statement at National Conference, 16–17
Conference of Independent African States, 77
Congo-Brazzaville, 23, 90, 92, 127, 170n85, 177n78
Congo-Kinshasa (Zaire), 31, 64, 90, 91, 118–19, 177n78
Convention People's Party (CPP), 74, 75–76
Cuba, 90, 112, 174n3
cultural and friendship associations, 25, 26, 27–28, 155n30
currencies, 159n18

defense and national defense, 13, 16, 17
Deng Xiaoping, 16
developing world (Third World): Algeria as part of, 68; China as part of, 2, 68, 141; influence of China in, 2, 149n4; leadership role of China, 20–21; Tanzania as part of, 141; united front with China and, 14, 16–18, 21, 74, 151n10, 153nn40–41

East Africa: army mutinies in, 112–13; British control of territories in, 103; front organizations working in, 28; nationalism and independence movements in, 103–4; radio communications with, 105–6; strategic value of, 3, 127. *See also* Tanzania
economics and economic aid: Algeria-China relations, 56, 57, 63, 64, 69, 164n62; economic construction exhibition in Ghana, 84; Ghana-China relations, 83, 84, 85, 88, 98–99, 100; Guinea-China relations, 64; international economic relations, proposal for development of system for, 68; international unity and, 17; learning and applying lessons from other countries, 15; national defense and, 16; priority for development of, 16; Tanzania-China relations, 115, 116, 117–19, 121–22, 123–24, 125–26, 128, 129–31, 133, 135–36, 138, 140–41, 175–76nn41–43, 178nn128–129, 179n131, 179n149; Zambia-China relations, 128; Zanzibar-China relations, 113, 115–16, 117–19, 132–33, 136, 140, 144, 176n49, 180n17, 181–82n48
Egypt: AAPSO headquarters in, 29–30; Algerian independence, call for, 38; entry point for Chinese influence in, 38–41, 143;
military mission to, 50; military training operations in, 68; NCNA locations, 23, 39; relations between China and, 38–40; strategic value of, 39–40; trade relations with China, 39
Equatorial Guinea, 93, 170n96
Ethiopia: ALC role, 31; Chinese cultural mission to, 38; Conference of Independent African States, 77; NCNA locations, 23; trade relations with China, 39
European nations: Algerian support for guerrilla war against, 58; interests in Africa, 4; NCNA locations, 23; opinions and perceptions about Chinese presence in Africa, 4; trade relations with Ghana, 98

Feed Yourself program, 99–100
FLN. *See* National Liberation Front (Front de Libération Nationale, FLN)
foreign policy of China: active foreign policy under Mao, 3; central objectives of, 9–18, 20–21, 124, 151–52n18; diplomatic relations, terms for establishment of, 12; educated skepticism to determine objectives of, 9, 151n1; independence and liberation movements, support for, 14, 16–17, 18, 146, 153n38; international united front objective, 11–15, 16–18, 21, 74, 151n10, 153nn40–41; pragmatic and realistic foreign policies, 15–16, 19–20; secondary objectives, 9, 18–21; Third World policy, 14. *See also* Chinese aid to and activities in Africa
France: Algerian independence from, 4–5, 38, 53–54; Algerian nationalism and independence movement and, 35–38; bank delegation visit, 165n92; Ivory Coast relationship with, 97; Morocco and French colonial Africa, 40; negotiations with Algeria, 43; World War II losses of, 36
front organizations, 28–29, 39, 121, 154n1, 156n48

Ghana: agriculture policy, 96, 99–100; anti-imperialist objectives, 19; British relationship with, 97; CAPFA visit, 81–82, 168n17; Chinese targeting West Africa through, 90–91; colonial occupation of, 73; Conference of Independent African States, 77; context of Chinese operations in, 5, 147; counterrevolution in, 97, 98; coup d'état, 92, 94–96, 97, 99, 144; creation of Republic of Ghana, 76; cultural agreement with China, 83; divisions between Nkrumah regime and people in, 144; economic aid, 83, 84, 85, 88, 98–99, 100; economic construction exhibition in,

84; embassy of China in, 81, 89, 168n11; embassy of U.S. in, 87–88; expulsion of China from, 95–96, 97–98, 141, 144; Feed Yourself program, 99–100; friendship agreements between China and, 83, 84–86, 88–89, 91; Ghana-Guinea-Mali Union, 77–78, 85, 167n34; independence of, 73, 75, 76, 80; influence of China in, 74, 77–79, 83–93, 94–95, 113, 143–44; influence of in West Africa, 75–76; lessons learned by China in, 99; liberation movements and military training base, 81, 82, 89–93, 98–99, 100; map of, 72; military training operations, 58, 95; natural resources in, 82; NCNA locations, 23; partnerships and relationships between China and, 39–40, 76–79, 80–89, 91–92, 97–100, 168nn16–17; people's militia establishment in, 93, 144; regional and tribal loyalties, 75–76; restoration of relations between China and, 99–100, 144; social and economic conditions in, 73, 75–76; strategic value of, 73; trade relations with China, 39, 40, 98, 100; UN vote for China, 78, 90

Gold Coast, 73. *See also* Ghana

Great Britain: army mutinies, role in, 112–13; colonial occupation of Ghana, 73; control of East Africa territories, 103; Ghana relationship with, 97; Zanzibar revolt, China involvement in, 112

Guinea: ALC role, 31; Algeria operations, role in, 49; Algerian support for liberation movement in, 58; arms from China for, 97; Ghana-Guinea-Mali Union, 77–78, 85, 167n34; independence of, 77, 78; military and intelligence training operations, 90, 91, 141; NCNA locations, 23; Nkrumah role in, 96; partnerships and relationships between China and, 77–78, 80, 91–92, 127; strategic value of, 77; UN vote for China, 90

Hanga, Abdullah Kassim, 112, 174n14
Ho Ying, 49, 66, 68, 100, 108, 110, 112, 114, 138
Houphouet-Boigny, Felix, 96–97, 124, 144
Huang Hua, 80, 85, 87, 99, 106, 180n19

imperialist powers and anti-imperialist allies, 11, 14–15, 19, 21, 46, 83–84, 92, 154n61
independence and liberation movements: African national liberation movements, Nkrumah support for, 76–77, 79; African national liberation movements, resources for, 79; African national liberation movements, successes of, 99; Algeria as base for, 58, 63, 64, 68–69, 90; colonial and semicolonial countries, independence, 14, 16, 75; funding for, 31–32; Ghana as base for, 81, 89–93, 98–99, 100; journalist support for, 86; military assistance for, 31; priority of support for, 41; revolutionary warfare strategy, 74–75; support for, 14, 16–17, 18, 38, 63, 88, 146, 153n38, 157n75; Tanganyika as base for, 108–9; Tanzania as base for, 31, 89, 90, 91, 117, 118–19, 121, 122, 124, 129, 139, 141; Zanzibar support for, 112

Indian Ocean, 3, 5, 110, 126, 131
Indonesia, 90, 153n39
industry: Algeria-China relations and aid, 61, 67; control of by China, 96–97; economic construction exhibition, 84; Four Modernizations and, 16; Ghana-China relations and aid, 83, 85, 87, 100; science and technology to support, 13; Tanzania-China relations, 118, 121, 134; Zanzibar-China relations and aid, 105
intelligence operations: CAPFA role, 81–82; CCRFC role, 27, 155n36
International Liaison Department (ILD), 25–27, 28
Islamic Association of People's China, 28, 44
Ivory Coast, 78, 89, 90, 91, 96–97, 124

Karume, Abeid, 112, 113–14, 119, 122, 138–39, 140, 174n11
Karume, Fatuma, 123, 178n113
Kawawa, Rashidi, 108, 115, 116, 123, 130, 134, 142, 176n49
Kawawa, Sophi, 122–23
Kenya, 23, 90, 112, 121
Kidunda water conservancy project, 179n149
Korea and Korean War, 4, 160n23, 160–61n48, 180n14
Kuomintang Revolutionary Committee, 29

Latin America: anti-imperialist objectives in, 19; independence and liberation movements in, support for, 16–17, 18, 63; international unity and, 18; NCNA role, 24–25
liberation movements. *See* independence and liberation movements
Libya, 28, 39, 50, 77
literature about China-Africa relations, 2–3
Liu Shaoqi: Algeria-China relations and visits, 50, 51, 53, 57, 61, 63; Algerian independence, congratulations following, 54; Chinese diplomatic visit, invitation for, 40; colonial and semicolonial countries, independence, 14, 16; Ghana-China relations and visits, 79, 80, 82, 85–86, 88, 91; influence and power of, 13; international unity objective, 17;

policy speeches by, 13–14; Tanzania-China relations and visits, 120; Zanzibar-China relations and visits, 105

Mali: Ghana-Guinea-Mali Union, 77–78, 85, 167n34; influence of China in, 88, 113; military training operations, 58; NCNA locations, 23; relations between China and, 85, 91–92, 127; UN vote for China, 66–67, 90

Mao Zedong: Algeria-China relations and visits, 49, 51, 56, 57, 60, 63; authoritarian government creation, 11; death of, 69, 100, 142; foreign policy during rule of, 3; guerrilla warfare propaganda, 58, 127; influence and power of, 3, 10; Nkrumah assassination attempts, messages about, 86–87; Nkrumah ideology and ideas of, 74–75; pragmatic and realistic foreign policies, 15–16, 19–20; revolutionary warfare strategy, 74–75; rule of, 3, 150n11; Tanganyika-China relations and visits, 109; Tanzania-China relations and visits, 123, 135, 139, 141; Zanzibar-China relations and visits, 105

Mao Zedong writings: *On New Democracy*, 14–15; *On People's Democratic Dictatorship*, 10–11, 14, 17; *On the Ten Major Relationships*, 15–16, 152n31; *Problems of Strategy in China's Revolutionary War*, 58; *Selected Works*, 58

Mediterranean Sea, 3, 59

Middle East, 23, 24–25

military and military power: Algerian militia formation, 61; containment of Chinese military power, 153n39; Ghana militia formation, 93; learning and applying lessons from other countries, 15–16, 152n31; training operations, 31, 40, 46, 47, 58, 68, 81, 82, 89, 90, 91, 95, 117, 118–19, 121, 122, 124, 129, 139, 141, 143, 154n1, 160–61n48

Ministry of Foreign Affairs (MFA), 24, 27, 155n15

Morocco: Algeria operations, role in, 45, 47, 49; Algerian refugees in, support for, 47; Chinese cultural mission to, 38, 49; Chinese technicians and specialists in, 50; Conference of Independent African States, 77; diplomatic visit to China, invitation for, 41; French colonial power in Africa and, 40; front organizations working in, 28; independence of, Chinese support for, 38; military training operations in, 47, 58; NCNA locations, 23; relations between China and, 38, 40–41, 92, 127; strategic value of, 40; trade relations with China, 40

Movement for the Triumph of Democratic Liberties (Mouvement pour le Triomphe des Libertés Démocratiques, MTLD), 36–37

Mozambique, 58, 90, 109, 117, 118–19, 121, 129, 137, 141, 176n69

names, format of, 150n11

National Association of Socialist Students Organizations (NASSO), 74

National Council of the Algerian Revolution (Conseil National de la Révolution Algérienne, CNRA), 159n6

national defense, 13, 16, 17

National Liberation Army (Armée de Libération Nationale, ALN), 42, 46, 143

National Liberation Council (NLC), 94, 95, 96, 97–99

National Liberation Front (Front de Libération Nationale, FLN): aid for, 40, 44, 46, 47–48, 49, 50, 51, 52, 55, 160–61n48, 161n74; Bandung Conference attendance, 38; establishment of, 38, 42; exiled forces in Morocco, 41; organization of, 42; partnerships and relationships between China and, 40, 42, 43, 143; propaganda operations, 58; responsibilities of, 42; training operations, 40, 46, 47, 160–61n48

National People's Congress (NPC), 40, 57, 69, 91–92, 95, 108, 120, 125, 130, 170n85

natural resources: access to by China, 2, 145; Algerian oil and resources, 60; Ghanaian gold, diamonds, and bauxite, 82; interest in, 3; Tanzanian mineral resources, 129, 140–41; Zambian copper, 129, 137, 182n61

New China News Agency (NCNA), 22–25, 26–27, 39, 107, 111, 155n15, 155n28

Niger, 81, 84, 89, 90, 91, 92

Nigeria, 31, 39, 84, 90, 91

Nkrumah, Kwame: African national liberation movements, support for, 76–77, 79; African unity objectives, 74, 77–78, 79, 167n34, 167n37; assassination attempts, 86–87; counterrevolution in Ghana, 97, 98; coup d'état and removal from power, 92, 94–96, 97, 144; death of, 100; education of, 73; Guinea, role in, 96; ideology of, 74–75; influence and power of, 73, 75–76, 92–93; nonviolence beliefs, 75, 166n17; people's militia establishment under, 93, 144; regime and power of, 143–44; relations between China and, 5, 39–40, 80–81, 82–84, 86–87, 88, 89, 90, 91, 92–93, 94–95, 144, 168nn16–17; relations between China and, establishment of, 76–79; revolutionary warfare strategy, book about, 95, 171n6; secret society creation by, 73–74

North Africa: Chinese technicians and specialists in, 50; entry point for Chinese influence in, 38–41; independence movements in, Chinese support for, 38; Mediterranean port for operations in, 59; strategic value of, 3, 59; unity of, 46. *See also* Algeria
North African Star (Étoile Nord Africaine, ENA), 35, 157n1, 157n3
Nyerere, Julius: ASP party support, 108; assassinations in Tanzania, 138–39; economic, ethnic, and social divisions, 104; expulsion of U.S. diplomats, 119–20; inauguration of, 108; military mission and military training and arms, 116–17; PAFMECA role, 105; relations between China and, 106–7, 108, 110, 119–20, 131, 136, 137, 139, 140–41, 142, 180n14; Tanganyika presidency, 104; Tan-Zam railway, 123, 140; union between Zanzibar and Tanganyika, 114; Westerners, distrust of, 113

Okello, John, 111–12, 174n8
On New Democracy (Mao), 14–15
On People's Democratic Dictatorship (Mao), 10–11, 14, 17
On the Ten Major Relationships (Mao), 15–16, 152n31
Organization of African Unity (OAU), 30–32, 157n64, 157n71
Oussedik, Omar, 47, 66

Pakistan, 153n39, 165n92
Pan-African Freedom Movement for East, Central and Southern Africa (PAFMECSA), 109, 157n65
Pan-African Freedom Movement for East and Central Africa (PAFMECA), 105
pan-African movement, 74, 77–78, 79, 167n34, 167n37
pan-Arabism, 74
People's Daily, 24
People's Republic of China (PRC). *See* China
Political and Administrative Organization (Organization Politique et Administrative, OPA), 43
Problems of Strategy in China's Revolutionary War (Mao), 58
propaganda operations: activities in Algeria, 57; activities in Ghana, 87; activities in Zanzibar and Tanganyika, 105–6, 107–8; CCRFC role, 27; context of Chinese operations, 146–47; Cultural Revolution and, 180n19; guerrilla warfare propaganda, 58, 127; journalist role in, 107–8; organizations for, 28–29, 156n44, 156n48; radio role in, 25, 105–6, 155n21

Provisional Government of the Algerian Republic (Gouvernement Provisionel de la République Algérienne, GPRA), 44–45, 47, 49, 53, 160n21, 160–61n48, 161n55
public statements: Algerian people, support for, 43–45, 47, 48, 49–50, 51, 52–53, 57–58, 59; expansion of influence through, 2, 143, 146; Ghanaian people, support for, 78–79, 82, 85–86, 88–89, 91; Liu policy speeches, 13–14; Tanganyika people, support for, 106–7

radio and propaganda operations, 24, 25, 105–6, 155n21
Red China News Agency, 22, 154n3
Republic of China (ROC, Taiwan), 4, 12, 19, 20, 38, 49, 66
Revolutionary Committee of Unity and Action (Comité Révolutionnaire d'Unité et d'Action, CRUA), 37–38, 42

science and technology: Algeria-China relations, 57, 63, 164n62; Four Modernizations and, 16; international unity and, 17; learning and applying lessons from other countries, 15, 152n31; national power and, 13, 15–16, 152n31
Selected Works (Mao), 58
Senegal, 23, 31
Socialism and Socialist states: aid for Chinese independence, 14–15; foreign policy of China and, 11; Nkrumah ideology and Ghana, 86–87
Somalia, 23, 127
South Africa: Algerian support for liberation movement in, 58; influence of China in, 88; military training operations, 58, 90; Tanganyika support for political parties from, 109
South Sudan, 183n2
Soviet Union: aid for FLN from, 161n74; Albania-China relations and, 163n35; alliance between China and, 11; military training operations, 183n89; threat to China from, 19–20, 154nn55–56; trade relations with Ghana, 98
Special Organization (Organisation Spéciale, OS), 37, 158n17
Sudan, 23, 38, 77, 85, 183n2
Syria, 23, 39

Taiwan. *See* Republic of China (ROC, Taiwan)
Tanganyika: ALC role, 31; bond of shared historical past with China, 107; economic, ethnic, and social divisions in, 103–4, 144; embassy of China in, 107, 173n24; indepen-

dence of, 106, 108; influence of China in, 110, 111, 113, 114; mutiny of soldiers in, 112–13, 175n20; nationalism and independence movement in, 103–4, 108–9; nationalism in, protection of from Communist subversion, 114; political organizations in, 103–4, 108–9; propaganda operations, 107–8; relations between China and, 106–7, 108–9, 110; trade relations with China, 39; union between Zanzibar and, 114, 144; uprisings in, 174n12; Zanzibar revolt, China involvement in, 112
Tanganyika African Association (TAA), 104
Tanganyika African National Union (TANU), 104, 109, 118, 144
Tanganyika Territory African Civil Service Association (TTACSA), 103–4
Tanzania: ALC headquarters in, 31; assassinations in, 138–39; bank delegation visit, 165n92; closeness of relationship between China and, 5; colonial histories in, 144; context of Chinese operations in, 5, 147; creation of, 114, 144; economic aid for and development projects in, 115, 116, 117–19, 121–22, 123–24, 125–26, 128, 129–31, 133, 135–36, 138, 140–41, 144, 175–76nn41–43, 178nn128–129, 179n131, 179n149; exploitation of by China, 144; expulsion of U.S. diplomats from, 120; friendship agreements between China and, 120, 123, 136, 139; influence of China in, 109, 114, 127, 142, 144; liberation movements and military training base, 31, 89, 90, 91, 117, 118–19, 121, 122, 124, 129, 139, 141; map of, 102; military mission and military training and arms, 116–17, 121, 126, 134–35, 139, 141; natural resources in, 129, 140–41; NCNA locations, 23; relations between China and, 114–15, 116, 119–28, 129–32, 133–42, 180n14, 182n68; shipping company, 125–26, 139, 182n76; social, economic, and ethnic divisions in, 144; strategic value of, 130–31, 139–40; UN vote for China, 55, 120, 137. See also Tanzania-Zambia (Tan-Zam) railway
Tanzanian People's Defence Force (TPDF), 121, 144
Tanzania-Zambia (Tan-Zam) railway, 115, 123, 127–28, 129–32, 133–34, 135–36, 137, 140, 141–42, 144, 178n114, 180n9, 182n61
Third World. See developing world (Third World)
Togoland, 76, 81, 84, 91
trade. See commerce and trade

Tunisia: Algerian refugees in, support for, 47; Chinese cultural mission to, 38; Chinese technicians and specialists in, 50; Conference of Independent African States, 77; front organizations working in, 28; independence of, Chinese support for, 38; International Fair, 51–52; military training operations in, 47, 160–61n48; NCNA locations, 23; partnerships and relationships between China and, 127, 163n31; supply route to Algeria through, 45; trade relations with China, 39

Uganda, 23, 31, 112, 121, 174n12
Umma Party, 111
Union of the Peoples of Cameroon (Union des Populations du Cameroun, UPC), 76–77, 78, 89–90
United Arab Republic (UAR), 23, 31, 77, 85, 106, 173n18. See also Egypt; Syria
united front objective, 11–15, 16–18, 21, 74, 151n10, 153nn40–41
United Nations (UN): international economic relations, proposal for development of system for, 68; representation in, 9, 19; Security Council meeting in Africa, 99; Security Council seat, 19, 64–65; support for admission of China, 55, 64–65, 66–67, 78, 81, 90, 120, 137
United States (U.S.): Africa policy development, 148; analysis of Chinese interest in Africa, 49–50, 88, 113; embassy in Ghana, 87–88; expulsion of diplomats from Zanzibar, 119–20; Indian Ocean region, expansion into, 110; influence of, elimination of, 18; satellite tracking station (rocket base) in Zanzibar, 105, 106, 113–14, 132, 175n30

Vietnam and Viet-Minh movement, 43, 64, 94, 97, 153n39, 160n23
Villiers, C. F. de, 144–45, 183n4
visits/exchange visits: acrobatic troupe visits, 77; Albania-China relations, 59, 163n35; Algeria-China relations, 44–46, 47–49, 50–51, 55–61, 62–63, 65–66, 67–69, 160nn23–24, 161n55, 165nn92–93; Algeria-China relations after independence, 55; bank delegation visit, 67–68, 165n92; Cairo military mission, 50; communication of messages in person, 146; CPACRFC role in, 27–28; expansion of influence through, 2, 41, 143; Ghana-China relations, 39–40, 78–79, 80–89, 91–92, 100, 168nn16–17; Guinea-China relations, 91–92; Mali-China relations, 91–92; Morocco-China relations, 41, 92; table tennis team visits, 85;

Tanganyika-China relations, 106–7, 108, 109, 110; Tanzania-China relations, 114–15, 116, 120, 121–23, 126, 127–28; Zambia-China relations, 127; Zanzibar-China relations, 105, 106, 117

war, character of, 152n21
West Africa: CAPFA visit, 81–82; entry point for Chinese influence in, 76–79, 90–91; influence of China in, 84; influence of Ghana in, 75–76; strategic value of, 3, 73, 77. *See also* Ghana
Western countries and societies: analysis of Chinese interest in Africa, 2, 49–50, 88, 113, 149n4, 149–50n6; influence of, elimination of, 18; NCNA locations, 23
white populations and governments, turning people of color against, 148
World Federation of Trade Unions (WFTU), 13–14, 39
World War II, 36, 155n21

youth and young Africans: African youth activities, 91; Algerian youth activities, 46–47, 50, 161n65; Ghanaian youth activities, 82, 90; Tanzanian youth activities, 126–27, 140; targeting of operations toward, 146; Zanzibar youth activities, 116

Zaire (Congo-Kinshasa), 31, 64, 90, 91, 118–19, 177n78
Zambia: bank delegation visit, 165n92; economic aid for and development projects in, 128; military training operations, 31, 90, 91, 141; natural resources in, 129, 137, 182n61; NCNA locations, 23; relations between China and, 127. *See also* Tanzania-Zambia (Tan-Zam) railway
Zanzibar: anti-U.S. demonstrations in, 113–14; economic, ethnic, and social divisions in, 103–4, 106, 108, 144, 173n30; economic aid for and development projects in, 113, 115–16, 117–19, 132–33, 136, 140, 144, 176n49, 180n17, 181–82n48; embassy of China in, 113, 116; entry point for Chinese influence in Tanzania, 105–6, 144; expulsion of U.S. diplomats from, 119–20; Ghanaian aid to, 113; independence of, 109–10, 111; influence of China in, 88, 105–6, 110, 111, 112, 119–20, 127; military training and arms, 58, 90, 116; nationalism and independence movement in, 103–4, 112; nationalism in, protection of from Communist subversion, 114; political organizations in, 103–4; prohibition of foreign states to enter, 174n11; propaganda operations, 105–6, 107–8; relations between China and, 105–6, 107–8, 109–10, 115–16, 117, 132–33, 180n17; revolution in, 87, 110, 111–12, 174n3, 174n8, 174n12; union between Tanganyika and, 114, 144; U.S. satellite tracking station (rocket base) in, 105, 106, 113–14, 132, 175n30
Zanzibar Nationalist Party (ZNP), 104, 105, 106, 107–8, 111, 112, 113, 144
Zanzibar Revolutionary Council, 112
Zhou Enlai: advice to Nkrumah, 96; Albania-China relations and visits, 59, 62; Algeria-China relations and visits, 44, 48, 50, 51, 53, 56, 57, 59, 61, 62, 63, 65–66, 67, 68, 163n31; Algerian independence, congratulations following, 54; Algerian youth, targeting of, 46; anti-imperialist objectives, 19; French-Algerian negotiations, call for, 43; Ghana agriculture policy, 87, 96; Ghana-China relations and visits, 78–79, 82, 83, 84, 85–86, 87, 88, 89, 91, 92; influence and power of, 10, 17, 153n37; international unity objective, 17–18, 153n38, 153nn40–41; Tanganyika-China relations and visits, 106–7, 108; Tanzania-China relations and visits, 120, 121–22, 123, 135, 136, 137, 138; Zanzibar-China relations and visits, 105

ABOUT THE AUTHOR

Donovan C. Chau is an associate professor of political science at California State University, San Bernardino. Educated at Claremont McKenna College, Missouri State University, and the University of Reading, his teaching and research focus on international politics, particularly in Asia and Africa. Prior to entering academia, Dr. Chau worked as a subject-matter expert on U.S. government contracts and as a professional staff member in the U.S. House of Representatives.

The Naval Institute Press is the book-publishing arm of the U.S. Naval Institute, a private, nonprofit, membership society for sea service professionals and others who share an interest in naval and maritime affairs. Established in 1873 at the U.S. Naval Academy in Annapolis, Maryland, where its offices remain today, the Naval Institute has members worldwide.

Members of the Naval Institute support the education programs of the society and receive the influential monthly magazine *Proceedings* or the colorful bimonthly magazine *Naval History* and discounts on fine nautical prints and on ship and aircraft photos. They also have access to the transcripts of the Institute's Oral History Program and get discounted admission to any of the Institute-sponsored seminars offered around the country.

The Naval Institute's book-publishing program, begun in 1898 with basic guides to naval practices, has broadened its scope to include books of more general interest. Now the Naval Institute Press publishes about seventy titles each year, ranging from how-to books on boating and navigation to battle histories, biographies, ship and aircraft guides, and novels. Institute members receive significant discounts on the Press's more than eight hundred books in print.

Full-time students are eligible for special half-price membership rates. Life memberships are also available.

For a free catalog describing Naval Institute Press books currently available, and for further information about joining the U.S. Naval Institute, please write to:

Member Services
U.S. NAVAL INSTITUTE
291 Wood Road
Annapolis, MD 21402-5034
Telephone: (800) 233-8764
Fax: (410) 571-1703
Web address: www.usni.org